7

THE SERAPION BROTHERS

SLAVISTIC PRINTINGS AND REPRINTINGS

edited by

C. H. VAN SCHOONEVELD

Indiana University

XLIV

1966

MOUTON & CO.

THE HAGUE · PARIS

THE
SERAPION BROTHERS

THEORY AND PRACTICE

by

HONGOR OULANOFF

Ohio State University

1966
MOUTON & CO.
THE HAGUE · PARIS

Printed in The Netherlands by Mouton & Co., Printers, The Hague.

FOREWORD

The present study derives from my doctoral dissertation which I wrote under the direction of Professor Vsevolod M. Setschkareff and Professor Roman O. Jakobson.

I thankfully remember Professor Setschkareff's expert advice and unceasing encouragement.

I express my respectful gratitude to Professor Jakobson, a gratitude that goes beyond what mere bibliographical references might convey.

I extend my cordial thanks to Professor Francis W. Cleaves of Harvard for his thoughtful editorial observations.

While writing the final manuscript for publication I had the benefit of the help of Professor Leon I. Twarog, Chairman of the Slavic Department, The Ohio State University, which I thankfully acknowledge.

University Hall   H.O.
The Ohio State University
Columbus, Ohio
December 1963

NOTE ON TRANSLITERATION

The transliteration system used in this study is the following: a, b, v, g, d, e, ë, ž, z, i, j, k, l, m, n, o, p, r, s, t, u, f, x, c, č, š, šč, ", y, ', ě, è, ju, ja. It is the transliteration system used in *The Slavic and East European Journal* (*vid. The Slavic and East European Journal*, Spring 1962, vol. VI, Number 1, p. 98).

CONTENTS

INTRODUCTION

The challenge confronting the investigator in this study is twofold: on the one hand, he should adopt toward the topic an attitude sufficiently general to view the Serapion Brotherhood as a literary group sharing a common belief and observing a common practice; on the other hand, he should preserve an attitude sufficiently particular in order to understand the literary idiosyncrasies characterizing the Serapion Brothers individually.

To make the study exhaustive would be the ideal aim. However, it appears unlikely that such a broad subject can be exhaustively treated within the framework of this inquiry. Under the given circumstances, I think it more convenient to attempt to find out significant features and patterns.

I have chosen to circumscribe the topic insofar as the *genre* is concerned: I concern myself with the Serapion Brothers' works of *prose fiction* primarily, i.e., *short stories*, *tales* and *novels*. Therefore I have eliminated from my study the Serapion Brothers' verse works – namely those of Nikolaj Tixonov, Elizaveta Polonskaja, Vladimir Pozner – and the drama, i.e., Lev Lunc's plays. Even in discussing the Serapion Brothers' works of prose fiction, I find it necessary to be selective and to focus my attention on those works that seem particularly significant.

A similar effort rigorously to circumscribe the topic in time seems less necessary. The young writers who joined the Serapion Brotherhood had met for the first time on the 1st of February 1921.[1] The year 1929, when the RAPP headed by the notorious Leopol'd Averbax assumed dictatorship over writers, marked the debasement of the intrinsic value of literary creation. It was the time of the advent of the "literature of fact", when writers, penned up in "artistic brigades", had to contribute their mite of

---

[1] Mix. Slonimskij, "Serapionovy Brat'ja o sebe", *Literaturnye Zapiski*, 3 (Aug. 1, 1922), p. 25. (On the front page of section 2 of the same issue there is a photograph of the Serapion Brothers.)

ink to the furtherance of the Five-Year Plan.[2] So, these two years – 1921 and 1929 – form landmarks significant for my purpose. However, within these relative limits, it would be hardly practicable to procede in a strict chronological sequence.

No effort has been made to engage in any biographical research. Unfortunately, under the present circumstances, personal interviews with the former Serapion Brothers have turned out to be impracticable. It is my conviction that literary scholarship is the study of the *literary text* primarily. Therefore less interest has been taken in purely biographical research. We must see to the most urgent things first.

In order to furnish the essential biographical data, let me merely cite three passages dealing with the history of the Serapion Brotherhood. These passages come from V. Šklovskij's *Sentimental'noe putešestvie*, K. Fedin's *Gor'kij sredi nas* and V. Pozner's *Littérature russe*.

At mid-winter the "Serapion Brothers" made their appearance on the ground floor. Their origin is as follows: Ev. Zamjatin was lecturing in the studio of the "House of Arts". He lectured simply, but about craftsmanship; he taught how to write prose.

Of students he had rather many, among them Nikolaj Nikitin and Mixail Zoščenko. Nikitin was of small stature, he was blond, we called him a "man of counselor-at-law's enthusiasm". This with reference to his domestic affairs. He is under the influence of Zamjatin. He leans on his [i.e., Zamjatin's, H.O.] right shoulder. But he writes not in imitation of him but in a more complicated manner. Zoščenko is black-haired and quiet. He is handsome in person. In war he had been poisoned by gases; he has a heart disease. That's what makes him quiet. He is a man who is not self-confident; he never knows how he will write next? He began to write well already after the studio at the "Serapions". His *Stories by Nazar Il'ič, Mr. Sinebrjuxov* are very good.

In them there are unexpected sentences turning the whole meaning of the story. With Leskov he is connected not so closely as it seems. He can write outside of [the literary tradition of] Leskov, for example, he wrote "A Fish Female". When his book had been turned into the printing-house to be set in long primer, type-setters composed it, without authorization, in pica.

"It's a very good book", – they say, – "let folks read it."

In the middle of the "Serapions" lies Mixail Slonimskij. Formerly everyone respected him, he served as a secretary in the publishing house Gržebina and was writing "Literary salons". Then he wrote a bad story "Nevskij Avenue";[3] then he began to write sketches and mastered the technique of the absurd. He

---

[2] Gleb Struve, *Soviet Russian Literature 1917-1950* (Norman, Okla., 1951), p. 209.
[3] In the Russian text: "Nevskij prospekt". I have not been able to find this title among Mix. Slonimskij's works. Most likely Šklovskij is misquoting here: Mix. Slonimskij wrote a story entitled *Srednij Prospekt*.

writes well. Now no-one respects him, because he is a good writer. He has rejuvenated to the time when he was his twenty-three years. He lies on the bed, sometimes he works twelve hours a day. In the smoke. Before he obtained a scholar's food ration, just as Nikitin and Zoščenko – he had suffered from hunger fabulously. The pathos of his writing is a complex plot without psychological motivation. One floor lower, in the monkey's cage,[4] lives Lev Lunc. He is about twenty. He has just graduated from the university in the Romance and Germanic department. He is the Benjamin of the "Serapions". However, they have three Benjamins. Lev Lunc, Volodja Pozner who is now in Paris, and the real Benjamin – Venjamin Kaverin.

Lunc is writing all the time and every time differently; often well. He possesses some wild boyish joy of living.

When he had graduated from the university, the "Serapions" in the house of Sazonov tossed him into the air. All of them. And then the glum Vsevolod Ivanov threw himself forward with the war-cry of a Kirghiz. They nearly killed him [i.e., Lunc, H.O.], having dropped him onto the floor. Then professor Grekov came to their place at night, passed his finger over Lunc's vertebral column and said:

"It's nothing, his legs need not be amputated."

They nearly made him legless. After two weeks Lunc danced with a cane. He has two dramas, many comedies. And he is solidly stuffed, there is something to extract from him. Lunc, Slonimskij, Zil'berg, Elizaveta Polonskaja are my students. But I don't teach writing; I told them what literature is. Zil'berg Kaverin is a boy of about twenty or less, broad-chested, rosy-cheeked, although at home together with Tynjanov he remains often times without bread. Then they chew the emergency store of dry roots. He is a tough fellow.

He began to write with me around. He is a very distinct writer. He operates with plot. He has a story "Candles and Shields", in which people are playing cards, and the cards have their own action. Kaverin is a mechanician, a constructor of plot. Of all the "Serapions" he alone is not sentimental. As for Zoščenko – I don't know, he speaks quietly.

Elizaveta Polonskaja together with A. Veksler used to wear black gloves on the hands, it was the sign of their order.

She writes poetry. In the world she is a doctor, a person quiet and vigorous. A Jewish woman, not an imitatrix. Of real thick blood. She writes little. She has good verses about to-day's Russia, the type-setters liked them. Elizaveta Polonskaja is the only female "Serapion Brother". The name of the society is accidental. The "Serapions" do not take a great interest in Hoffmann, even Kaverin is rather interested in Stevenson, Sterne and Conan Doyle.

There was still wandering about Petersburg Vsevolod Ivanov. He wandered alone, in a worn sheepskin coat, with shoe soles tied up with strings.

---

[4]   In the Russian text: "v obez'jannike". In his *Literaturnye Stat'i i Vospominanija*, Izdatel'stvo imeni Čexova (New York, 1954), Vladislav Xodasevič included an article "Dom Iskusstv" (pp. 397-412). In this interesting article Xodasevič gives an account of what this "House of Arts" looked like; he also explains and describes this "monkey's cage": it was a humid hall and four uncomfortable, ever dark rooms in the basement of the "House of Arts" (p. 406). The basement bore this name because it reminded one of the actual places in which monkeys were lodged in winter in zoological gardens.

He had come from Siberia to see Gor'kij. Gor'kij was not in Petersburg. Proletarian writers gave shelter to Ivanov. They are themselves folks in rags. They are not court writers. They gave to Ivanov what they could – a room. There was nothing to eat. Close by was a depot for mackle-paper. Ivanov heated his room with the paper, at [minus] some 18 degrees. He would warm himself and would not want to eat.

Gor'kij arrived, had him registered at the "House of Scholars" – and not for a ration but for distributions.[5] They would not give him a ration: the man had not written any books. And Gor'kij introduced Ivanov to me, I consigned him to the care of the "Serapions".

Vsevolod himself is a man of large stature, with a beard behind his cheek-bones and his chin, slant-eyed like a Kirghiz but with a pince-nez. Formerly he was a type-setter.[6] The "Serapions" received him very affectionately. I remember, we had gathered in the room of Slonimskij, we are heating the stove with the back side of a desk. Ivanov is sitting on the bed and begins to read:

"In Siberia palm-trees don't grow."

Everyone had brightened up with joy.

Ivanov is now writing much, not always evenly. I do not like his *Colored Winds*. Not on the ground of ideology, of course. What do I care for ideology? I do not like the fact that "The Lacy Herbs", as Zoščenko said,[7] is written too much in earnest. The thing has been made by dint of affectation. But the writer should not, presenting things, give prominence to himself. What is needed is not irony but free hands. The story "The Baby" is very good. It develops first as if in the manner of Bret Harte: crude people find a child and nurse it. But next the thing unfolds unexpectedly. The child needs milk. For it they steal a Kirghiz woman with an infant, but in order to have enough for their own child, they kill the yellow, little competitor.

Ivanov is married, recently he had a daughter.

There is among the "Serapions" the theoretician Il'ja Gruzdev, a student of Boris Eixenbaum and Ju. Tynjanov.

Toward the end of the winter there came still another poet Nikolaj Tixonov. He is one of the Red Army cavalrymen.

He is 25 years old; it seems that he has ash-colored hair, but he is in fact a grey-haired blond. His eyes are frank, grey or light blue. He writes good verses. He lives downstairs, in the monkey's cage with Vsevolod Roždestvenskij.

---

[5] In the Russian text: "na vydači". I have not had an opportunity to ascertain what technical difference there was between "na paëk" and "na vydači". The first was a special privilege accorded to scholars which permitted them to obtain provisions during the difficult post-revolutionary time.

[6] One of his very first collections of stories, *Rogul'ki*, Vsevolod Ivanov wrote, set and published all by himself (*vid.* I. V. Vladislavlev, *Literatura velikogo desjatiletija 1917-1927*, p. 117).

[7] Mix. Zoščenko, "Družeskie parodii", II. Vsevolod Ivanov, "Kruževnye travy", *Literaturnye Zapiski*, 2, p. 9. This "Kruževnye travy" is a parody of Vsev. Ivanov's ornate style. Here is an excerpt from this parody by Zoščenko: "Ах, травы, травы! Горючий песок! Нерадостны прохожему голубые пески, цветные ветра, кружевные травы."

Tixonov narrates well about horses. How, for example, captured German horses engaged in sabotage and betrayal.

There is still Konstantin Fedin. That one came, delivered from captivity in Germany. He missed the Revolution. He dwelt in captivity. A good chap, only somewhat traditionalist.

Here I have let the "Serapions" into my little book. I lived with them in one house. And I think that the main governmental political department will not get angry at them for the fact that I drank tea with them. The "Serapions" grew amidst hardships; were it not for Gor'kij, they would have perished. Aleksej Maksimovič treated them at once very seriously. They became more confident in themselves, Gor'kij almost always understands another's manuscript; he has good luck in recognizing new writers.

Russia has not yet been trampled down and knocked out. People are growing in her as oats through a bast shoe.

They will live, the great Russian literature and the great Russian science.

For the time being the "Serapions" on their evenings every Friday eat bread, smoke cigarettes and play afterward at blind-man's-buff. Lord, how strong people are! And no-one can see with what man is laden, from his footprints, only the footprint is now shallower, now deeper.[8]

The retrospective view of K. Fedin appears less spontaneous but it does not basically contradict V. Šklovskij's words:

The circle of literary youth, into which Gor'kij had introduced me, acquired fame under the name of the "Serapion Brothers" or simply – "Serapions". Its membership was established quickly and subsequently continued unchanged. They were the prose writers: Vsevolod Ivanov, Mixail Zoščenko, Veniamin Kaverin, Lev Lunc, Nikolaj Nikitin, Mixail Slonimskij, Konstantin Fedin; the poets: Elizaveta Polonskaja, Nikolaj Tixonov and the critic Il'ja Gruzdev.

The life of the circle was connected with the House of Arts. In Slonimskij's room, resembling a room of an actor's lodgings,[9] every Saturday we assembled in full strength and stayed into the deep night, listening to the recitation of some new story or verses and then debating about the merits and flaws of the recited matter. Of course, an outstanding discipline and angelic characters would be needed, in order to endure over the extent of many years these sittings in a can of preserved tobacco fume, were it not for our passion for literature which substituted for us both discipline and generally speaking all conceivable virtues. This passion united in friendship men, extraordinarily different as for their artistic tastes, and this passion was not transient, – it from the very beginning excluded the possibility of amateurish attitude toward art and strengthened in us the feeling of vocation.

One might ask: who of the Serapions was the "main" one? No-one.

We lived in the nearest neighborhood with prerevolutionary writers; veritable

---

[8] Viktor Šklovskij, *Sentimental'noe putešestvie*, *Vospominanija 1917-1922* (Moskva-Berlin, 1923), pp. 377-381.
[9] In the Russian text: "V komnate Slonimskogo, poxožej na nomer aktërskix 'meblirašek', [...]"·

whirlwinds of heterogeneous aesthetics were spinning next to us; a multitude
of influences flowed round us: and one might also ask: who of the senior
writers was the "main" one in the eyes of the Serapions. No-one.

Gor'kij's admonition that he gave in a conversation with me about criticism
was the ineffable motto of the Serapions: "Listen, but don't obey."

And, as a matter of fact, the "main" one was Gor'kij, who prompted everyone to try to solve his problem independently, separately. For there could not
have been an average, common solution in literature, Gor'kij did not prompt
anyone as to what should be done and how, and the young literature by his
side, by the side of his overpowering individuality, was perfectly free.

Each of us came with his own taste, more or less marked and subsequently
molded under the influence of contradictions. We were different. Our work
was an uninterrupted struggle under the conditions of friendship. We did not
think of any school or any "group", and therefore Gor'kij, far from implanting
schools, easily found us to be a vital phenomenon.

My coming to the Serapions was accompanied with a quarrel. I met in the
gloomy room with an abundance of irony, laughter, gaiety, fun, and all that
in appearance was directed at the foundation-stones of its holiness – of literature.
Art is the fruit of the quest, the throes and the meditations of the artist, it is
serious, it is responsible before the highest judge – man –, this was the strongest
of my convictions and the most precious of all my feelings. But here they were
jesting with literature, they were playing with it. I understood that it was a
manner. That here they loved Puškin and revered Tolstoj not less than I. But
this manner seemed to me strange. Here it was spoken about literary works
as about "things". Things were "made". They could have been made well or
made badly. "Xadži-Murat" was made excellently. "Don-Quixote" was made
unsurpassedly. Uspenskij Gleb did not know how to make things. Uspenskij
Nikolaj made them rather well. For the making of things there existed
"devices". For devices there was a multitude of names. But it was possible to
make oneself understood without names too, by using general concepts and
saying that the thing is made with the devices proper to Gogol', with the devices
proper to Leskov. From here, it goes without saying, it was rather near to
Gogol' and within the reach of the arm to Leskov, to those jests and gay gibes,
in which Gogol' and Leskov turned out to be – o, horror – in one lump with
all of us. How could I have endured the like of it?

At the third meeting I gave vent to my settled protest against "play" in
defense of "seriousness". Lev Lunc accepted the blow.

The encounter was severe. Truth was sitting somewhere in the corner of the
room, chuckling, behind the backs of the Serapions, who maintained neutrality.

The argument was pursued thus.

Lunc said: Russian prose has ceased "to move", it "lies", in it nothing
happens, nothing is going on, in it they either reason or experience feelings,
but do not act, do not perform deeds; it must die from an absence of circulation
of the blood, of bedsores, of dropsy; it has become a simple reflection of
ideologies, programs, a mirror of the journalism of publicists and has ceased
existing as art; only plot can save it, plot – a mechanism that will stir it up,
will force it to move, to perform volitional acts; the tradition of plot is in the
West; we must bring this tradition from there and impregnate with it our

recumbent prose, overcoming in ourselves the trivial fear, inspired by literary uncles, of the novel of adventures, learning from the writer, who possesses the secret of action, be it Sterne or Dumas, Stevenson or Conan Doyle; and there is no reason to bestow protection upon Russian literature, it is so great that it does not stand in need of protection, to fence it off from the Western neighbor – means to doom [it] to the repetition of the past, but the great, being repeated, ceases to be great. Therefore our motto is – "to the West!"

I spoke thus: the dream of literature consists not in multiplying the models found in books, it does not matter which – Western or Russian; what is important is to what the mechanism of such and such tradition will be applied, for nothing will result, if we, for the sake of giving mobility to Russian prose, make Oblomov ride in a streetcar; the material of literature itself will determine, what mechanism is needed for its life; the material of literature is feeling, and the whole fact is whether you possess the feeling that you want to express; by what means you achieve it does not matter, – with the help of the celebrated plot or with the help of the despised rhetoric, – all means are good, and they, in any case, are good in *The Queen of Spades* and in *The Portrait*, although these tales are in direct relationship with the allegedly plotless Russian prose; and since feeling always keeps in step with time, is always contemporaneous, one cannot conceive in our time of a writer without passion for all that is being created by the revolution. Therefore at first it must be understood by us in all depth what we want to say, then we will find out, how it must be said...

Lunc was twenty years old. I have never met debators similar to him, – the heat of debate would reduce him to ashes, one could have suffocated being next to him.

– Confess, confess! Are you intending to study the laws of literature? – he shouted, shaking his trembling hands, lifted over his head in a biblical fashion.

After all everyone in this room intended to study the laws of literature, and the question about the fact whether they exist as such, – whether it is possible to consider, how a work of literature is made independently of what content it is devoted to, – this question in different ways had been raised for many years in succession.

We were different. Jesting and parodying one another, we divided the Serapions into gay "leftists", with Lunc at their head, and serious "rightists" – under the smiling leadership of Vsevolod Ivanov. In constant skirmishes there was being groped for the aim of our joint voyage, and after all inwardly everyone admitted, that we had one and the same: the creation of a new literature of the epoch of the war and the revolution. This understanding of the historicity of our task, which was dawning slowly, made us identical, in spite of all differences between us.

The Serapions were the fruit of their time not only in the conventional sense. Among us there were perfect youngsters with an experience furnished by parents' home, university and motion pictures. But the majority of us went through unusual trials, and never at other times could seven or eight young men have tried out so many professions, experienced so many situations in life, as it fell to our lot. Eight men embodied in their persons a medical orderly, a type-setter, an officer, a shoe-maker, a medical doctor, a fakir, a clerk, a soldier, an actor, a teacher, a cavalryman, a singer, they had to fill tens of most

variegated positions, they had fought on the fronts of the world war, participated in the civil war, it was impossible to astonish them with either hunger or disease, they had too long and too often looked death in the face.

So what could they have written about, what was their imagination filled with, what did they want to say?

Yes, they liked, they kept in their pockets "Nicholas Nickleby". But their hands by themselves wrote "In the Fire".[10]

The first who succeeded in introducing into literature the new material of the war and the revolution were Vsevolod Ivanov with his *Partisans*, Nikolaj Tixonov – in his ballads about the war, Mixail Zoščenko – in his stories about the funny hero whose intonation the reader has already been perceiving for twenty years in succession.

And it is noteworthy: just the new material introduced by them into literature outlined the features of the new literary form.[11]

Fedin evaluates the attitudes that the Serapion Brothers adopted toward literature, and, in a sense, tries retrospectively to adapt these attitudes to the Soviet official philosophy in this field.

Pozner's view quite differs from that of Fedin. It is simply a pleasant and vivid recollection of youth:

Un an environ après la publication du premier livre de Pilniak, plus exactement le 1er février 1921, se formait à Petrograd le groupe de Frères Sérapion. Les jeunes gens qui le composaient et dont presque aucun n'avait atteint la trentaine s'étaient connus à la Maison des Arts, établissement unique au monde, espèce de musée où, au lieu d'œuvres d'art, seraient rassemblés les artistes eux-mêmes. Fondée, comme presque tous les centres de la vie intellectuelle en Russie révolutionnaire, sous l'instigation de Gorki, la Maison des Arts, occupait l'hôtel particulier d'un marchand richissime. Les écrivains et les artistes y étaient logés et nourris. Des soirées littéraires y avaient lieu où l'on put entendre Blok, Bély, Maïakovski, Goumiliov, Mandelstam, et beaucoup d'autres. La salle de conférences, ornée aux quatre coins d'arbres en verre de Bohême, était toujours bondée de monde. En plus, on avait organisé à la Maison des Arts des cours où des jeunes gens apprenaient l'art de la prose, de la poésie, de la critique et de la traduction. Goumiliov y dirigeait un séminaire poétique, Zamiatine s'occupait des prosateurs, Tchoukovski parlait de la critique, Chklovski, Evréinov, Volynski professaient chacun selon sa spécialité. L'auditoire se composait d'éléments les plus hétéroclites. Il y avait des demoiselles en mal de poésie, des vieillards qui tenaient à un endroit chauffé et éclairé, et aussi quelques écrivains professionnels qui tout en suivant les cours lièrent connaissance et amitié et formèrent le groupe de Frères Sérapion.

On était en vingt-et-un. La vie de tous et chacun était réglée à une minute près. On avait l'impression d'habiter une énorme caserne noyée dans de la

---

[10] Dickens' novel is opposed undoubtedly to the novel by Henri Barbusse, *Le Feu: journal d'une escouade* (1916), a novel about 1914-1918 war.
[11] Konst. Fedin, *Gor'kij sredi nas*. Dvadcatye gody OGIZ, [1943?], pp. 103-110.

paperasserie. [...] Tous ces écrivains prirent le nom de Frères Sérapion non pas parce qu'ils étaient des admirateurs ou des disciples de Hoffmann. Je doute même qu'ils eussent tous lu le grand romantique allemand. On se rappelle que les héros du roman de Hoffmann proclament la liberté absolue d'opinions et de goûts, à l'exemple de leur maître Sérapion qui, loin de l'humanité intelligente, croit en la réalité de ses visions de fou. [...]

Les réunions, strictement privées (seuls Mandelstam, Akhmatova et Zamiatine ont pu y assister) se tenaient une fois par semaine à la Maison des Arts, dans la petite pièce de Slonimski, ancienne chambre de domestiques.

Une fenêtre donnant sur la cour. Des murs peints à la chaux. Dans l'air flotte une épaisse fumée de cigarette. Lorsque l'œil s'y habitue, on distingue un lit où est étendu, les pieds en l'air, un jeune homme brun en veston d'uniforme auquel manque un bouton. C'est Slonimski. Il a fait toute la révolution sans ce bouton, le troisième en comptant du haut. Autour de lui, par terre, sur la table, sur le lit même, sont installés les autres Sérapions, Zochtchenko, bien coiffé, bien rasé, poudré et mélancolique; Grouzdev, frais, rose et mou comme de la pâte dentifrice, Fédine au regard d'un bleu à faire rêver les jeunes filles.

L'un des Frères lit sa nouvelle œuvre. On la discute sans ménagements. Un autre récite des vers. On cause. Il y a des invitées, deux ou trois jeunes filles, toujours les mêmes, et dont les Sérapions tombent amoureux à tour de rôle. On joue à colin-maillard dans la grande salle, on représente un film. Nikitine esquisse les pas d'un tango-fantaisie et se brûle le coude contre un poêle. Slonimski imite Max Linder (Chaplin est encore inconnu). Les demoiselles essaient – mais en vain – d'apprendre la valse à Luntz. Bénédiction suprême! personne, sauf Chklovski, n'a publié ne fût-ce qu'une ligne.[12]

For the sake of efficiency of analysis I have divided the study into three parts. First, I attempt to survey the *theoretical* positions proper to the Serapion Brothers, i.e., the opinions that they formulated in their works about what literature is or should be. Then I inquire into the *verbal medium* by which I mean peculiarities of verbal expression (stratum of "the units of meaning").[13] Finally I deal with *representation*, that is to say, with the questions of over-all construction, such as plot (stratum of the "world" of the novelist).[14] These three subdivisions – *theory, verbal medium* and *representation* – are not separated from one another rigidly. I sometimes find it indispensable to cite concrete, literary examples when a matter of theory is under discussion. Conversely, the analysis of concrete literary texts may result in more general considerations. Cross-references are provided whenever they appear useful.

I do not hesitate to quote extensive passages from the original works. Experience teaches that the understanding of literary problems comes from the persistent and assiduous scrutiny of the literary text.

[12]   Vladimir Pozner, *Littérature russe* (Paris, 1929), pp. 324-326.
[13]   *Vid.* p. 47 of this study.
[14]   *Vid.* p. 47 of this study.

PART ONE

I. THE THEORY

Russian literature has never adequately overcome the opposition between aspiration toward aestheticism and its adverse pressure. The antagonism opposing these two trends reached in the twenties of this century a particularly high degree of poignancy and fascination.

The trend of criticism unresponsive or even intolerant toward aestheticism in Russian literature has frequently wielded too corrosive an influence upon literary creation.

One attitude consisted – and consists – in focusing attention on the philosophic ideas which literary works have conveyed. The rich philosophic commentary interpreting Dostoevskij's works offers an instance of this attitude.

Another attitude dwelt upon the social significance of the literary creation. This tradition, of which Belinskij appears to be a particularly striking example, viewed literature as "the expression and the mirror of Russian society".[1] What is more, it wanted this "mirror" to be a tool of social action. The present-day Soviet conception of socialist realism derives from this thinking.

The trend of criticism responsive toward aestheticism assumes the shape of Formalist thinking in Russian literature during the period under study. In this thinking the literary fact as such – and not as a vehicle of ideology or as a "mirror" of society – became the primary concern of inquiry.

The Serapion Brotherhood was intimately connected in its thinking with Formalist criticism. The literary awareness of the former responded to the fundamental tenets of the latter, so much so that to draw a distinct line between Formalist thinking and the specific opinions of the Serapion Brothers presents a real difficulty.

---

[1] Belinskij, quoted from V. V. Vinogradov, *O jazyke xudožestvennoj literatury* (Moskva, 1959), p. 475.

The literature throughout the twenties developed under the ever increasing pressure of a monistic dogma. The basic issue that pitted the
Formalists and the Serapion Brothers against the Marxist critics involved
the problem of "self-value"[2] of art and literature. This problem of "self-
value" of art and literature leads ultimately to that of freedom in artistic
creation. Does art possess its own dynamics?

Marxist critics denied any intrinsic dynamics in art. Trockij explained
the movement in art by changes in psychology which in its turn results
from changes in the social environment. In his argument with Formalists
Trockij expounded his view in these terms:

The poet can find material for his art only in his social environment and trans-
mits the new impulses of life through his own artistic consciousness. Language,
changed and complicated by urban conditions, gives the poet a new verbal
material, and suggests or facilitates new word combinations for the poetic
formulation of new thoughts or of new feelings, which strive to break through
the dark shell of the subconscious. If there were no changes in psychology
produced by changes in the social environment, there would be no movement
in art; people would continue from generation to generation to be content
with the poetry of the Bible, or of the old Greeks.[3]

So the movement of art and literature is explained in terms of Marxist
socio-economic thinking. For instance, the emergence of the Impressionist way of perceiving colored surfaces partakes of urban civilization:

[...] Impressionism with its vivid contrasts, as well as with its anaemia of color,
would be inconceivable outside the culture of big cities.[4]

Other Marxist critics also undertake attempts at the sociological explanation of literary facts. For instance, one of them, G. Gorbačëv, says:

[...] the very form of short tales and stories was prompted to Čexov, Garšin,
Korolenko both by the growing power of the business-minded, nervous, busy
city which distracts attention and by lyrical and romantic themes assigned as a
task [to the authors].[5]

The Marxist critics affirmed the basically utilitarian nature of art and
literature. Trockij said in this respect:

[2]   Gleb Struve, *Soviet Russian Literature 1917-1950* (Norman, Okla., 1951), p. 195.
[3]   Leon Trotsky, *Literature and Revolution* (New York, 1957), p. 167.
[4]   B. Èixenbaum, "V ožidanii literatury", *Literatura. Teorija, kritika, polemika*
(Leningrad, 1927), p. 286.
[5]   *Ibid.*, p. 287.

The quarrels about "pure art" and about art with a tendency took place between the liberals and the "populists". They do not become us. Materialistic dialectics are above this; from the point of view of an objective historical process, art is always a social servant and historically utilitarian.[6]

This utilitarian outlook accounted for the fact that the post-revolutionary Marxist critics narrowed down their literary consciousness to the political contemporaneity. They strove for a politically educational, a normative literature. The nature of their critique flowed quite logically from this utilitarian and politically conditioned outlook. G. Gorbačëv's critique furnishes an arresting instance of this outlook. In his book *Sovremennaja russkaja literatura* of 1928 he passes certain judgments pertaining to literary form. He approaches the over-all problem with a thoroughly sociological mind. The plan of the work betrays the basic subordination of his aesthetic judgment to a socio-political ideology. Actually the plan displays a frankly socio-political spectrum of writers nicely arrayed from the "right" to the "left": neobourgeois literature; petty-bourgeois literature; the left wing of petty-bourgeois literature; proletarian literature. In Part II he lumps together B. Pil'njak and K. Fedin because he brings them both into the category of "petty-bourgeois literature". Now this is a classification motivated by a purely socio-political consideration. From a strictly literary point of view the two authors in question are very dissimilar. B. Pil'njak belongs to the "dynamic", "ornamental" prose tradition breaking the patterns of articulated over-all construction. On the contrary, K. Fedin preserves much of the older novelistic tradition with its care for over-all construction and articulation of plot elements.

The same political conditioning of Gorbačëv's mind reveals itself when he blames the two Serapion Brothers, Zoščenko and Nikitin, for using the anecdote genre – speaking more exactly over-use of whimsical anecdotes – in depicting the Revolution.[7]

In this perspective literature develops into a psychological tool in the service of a monistic dogma. It is not the purpose of this study to enter into a detailed and extensive discussion of how Marxist thinking conceives of literature. The disagreement which opposed the Marxist critics to the Formalists and the Serapion Brothers was irreconcilable because their criteria of evaluation stood in a fundamental opposition.

The Formalists and the Serapion Brothers affirmed that art and literature do possess their own dynamics.

[6]   Leon Trotsky, *op. cit.*, p. 168.
[7]   Georgij Gorbačëv, *Sovremennaja russkaja literatura* ("Priboj", 1928), p. 114.

In Trockij's thinking art and literature owe their evolution to social changes, to mutations in society, specifically to class struggle.

Quite naturally the question arises then whether art and literature will possibly evolve and change in the hypothetical socialist society. Marxist theoreticians predict the disappearance of class contradictions, class differentiation and class struggle in this hypothetical socialist society. The logical conclusion of the preceding assumptions is that the evolution of art and literature will cease in the hypothetical socialist society. Now, to ratiocinate about what will befall art and literature in the hypothetical socialist society is, for my purpose, an entirely idle occupation. The significance of this question lies in the *method* resorted to when Trockij tries to evade this difficulty. Speaking about "pre-socialist" society, Trockij attributed the evolution of art and literature to "changes in the social environment".[8] Since no social change would occur in the hypothetical socialist society, Trockij ascribed the cause of the evolution of art to such phenomena – vague as these terms may sound – as "collective, nervous energy", or "collective psychic impulses" or even "the human personality with its invaluable basic trait of continual discontent".[9] This argument proves misleading: one and the same phenomenon is attributed to two different sets of causes, and Trockij arbitrarily excluded one set of causes for the sake of bolstering his argument. In this connection B. Eixenbaum pointedly observed:

It turns out that art has some function of its own, that is connected with human psyche as such and therefore acting not only under the influence of social stimuli from outside. But surely then Trockij will have to agree with the fact that art, because of its very nature, is really not so firmly tied in its progress to the "regrouping of social classes" and that from ever-lasting refrains it is saved by its own dynamism.[10]

B. Eixenbaum put forward a thoughtful and convincing objection to Trockij's assertion.[11] The gist of Eixenbaum's thinking is this: a positive scientific explanation must operate on the same level and within the same category as the phenomenon to be explained. Or else the researcher does not discover the *efficient cause*. Then he either assumes metaphysical premises or resorts to specious, pseudo-scientific phraseology. In either case he does not explain anything at all. By connecting a literary fact

---

[8]   Leon Trotsky, *op. cit.*, p. 167.
[9]   *Ibid.*, p. 231.
[10] B. Èixenbaum, *op. cit.*, p. 284.
[11] *Ibid., pass.*

with a socio-economic fact one deprives the former of its *specificity* and explains it by a link which need not be causal.

As a matter of fact, the same problem of *specificity* and *efficient cause* beset sociological methodology at its beginning. E. Durkheim, one of the founders of the French sociological school, warned against all pre-conceptions in the observation of social phenomena,[12] i.e., against the introduction of any explicatory factors that are not themselves *specifically* social phenomena. Moreover, it is no small merit of Durkheim's to have opposed to H. Spencer's explanation of social phenomena by finality the fundamental concept of *efficient cause* in sociological methodology.[13]

Now, the Marxist explanation of literature does lack specificity: word masses and representations resulting therefrom are interpreted in terms of socio-economic causation. Moreover, the Marxist interpretation of literature tends to explain it by finality, i.e., by function that literature performs in society, and not by the efficient cause that lies at the root of literary performance.

To Trockij's attempt to attribute the Impressionist way of perceiving to urban civilization – I quoted this excerpt above – Eixenbaum objected convincingly:

Let it even be so, but is it really an explanation? From "being inconceivable" to existing there is too great a distance, isn't there? The culture of big cities leaves room for the possibility of other forms of painting too.[14]

Gorbačëv's linking short stories with the civilization of the big cities turns out to be still less convincing and Eixenbaum rejected that argument saying:

Why then that same "power of the city" had not prevented the great novels of Dickens, Hugo and Zola from appearing in the world in their time? The Paris of the middle of the XIXth century was, perhaps, more nervous than the Moscow of the eighties.[15]

The Serapion Brothers defended the "self-value" of art even more force-fully. Lev Lunc – one of the prominent theoreticians of the Serapion Brotherhood – formulated the basic tenets of the Serapion Brotherhood in his article "Počemu my Serapionovy Brat'ja".[16] This "manifesto" does not bring forth a scholarly treated conceptual argument as Eixenbaum

[12] Emile Durkheim, *The Rules of Sociological Method* (Glencoe, Ill., 1950), p. 31.
[13] *Ibid.*, p. 89.
[14] B. Èixenbaum, *op. cit.*, p. 286.
[15] *Ibid.*, p. 287.
[16] Lev Lunc, "Počemu my Serapionovy Brat'ja", *Literaturnye Zapiski*, 3 (Aug. 1, 1922), pp. 30-31.

does in his debate with Trockij. It is rather a straightforward, emotionally colored, plea for the writer's freedom of creation. Here is the text of this article:

The Serapion Brothers is a novel by Hoffmann. Well then, we write in imitation of Hoffmann, so we are a school of Hoffmann.

This conclusion is drawn by any person who has heard of us. And he too, having read through our collection or separate stories by the brothers, is at a loss: "What do they have from Hoffmann? Surely, generally speaking, they do not have a single school, a single trend. Everyone writes in his own way."

Yes, it is so. We are not a school, not a trend, not a studio in imitation of Hoffmann.

And that is why we named ourselves "Serapion Brothers."

Lothar is scoffing at Ottmar: "Shouldn't we decree what it will be permissible and what it will not be permissible to speak about? Should we not make everyone tell three pointed anecdotes or determine the invariable sardine salad for dinner? By doing this we will sink into such a sea of philistinism as can flourish only in clubs. Don't you really understand that any definite condition entails compulsion and boredom, in which pleasure drowns? ..."

We have named ourselves Serapion Brothers, because we do not want compulsion or boredom, we do not want everyone to write identically, even if it were in imitation of Hoffmann.

Each of us has his own personality and his own literary tastes. In each of us it is possible to find the most diverse literary influences. "Everyone has his own drum" said Nikitin at our first meeting.

But surely Hoffmann's six brothers are not twins either, they are not a rank of soldiers marshalled according to their height. Sylvester is quiet and modest, taciturn, whereas Vinzenz is frantic, ungovernable, inconstant, effervescent. Lothar is a stubborn growler, a grumbler, a wrangler, whereas Cyprian is a pensive mystic. Ottmar is a wicked mocker, and, at last Theodor, the host, a tender father and a friend of his brothers, who is inaudibly directing this wild circle, stirring up and putting an end to debates.

And there are so many debates. The six Serapion Brothers are not a school or a trend either. They attack one another, eternally disagree with one another, and therefore we have named ourselves Serapion Brothers.

In February of the year 1921, in the period of the greatest regulations, registrations and barrack-like ordering, when everyone was given one iron-clad and boring set of rules, – we decided to gather without any rules or chairmen, without elections or voting. Together with Theodor, Ottmar and Cyprian we believed that "the character of the future meetings would take shape by itself, and we undertook the vow of being faithful to the end to the rules of hermit Serapion".

2

As for these rules, here they are.

Count P* declared himself to be hermit Serapion, the very same that had

lived under emperor Decius. He retired into a forest, there he built a hut far
from the amazed world. But he was not lonely. Yesterday Ariosto visited him,
today he has had a talk with Dante. Thus the *senseless* poet lived to a ripe
old age, laughing at the *sensible* people, who tried to persuade him that he was
count P*. He believed his vision. No, I don't say so: for him they were not
visions but truth.

We believe in the reality of our fictional heroes and fictional events. There
lived Hoffmann, a man, there also lived Nutcracker, a doll, it lived its special,
but also real life.

This is not new. What shabbiest, most lowbrowed publicist has not written
about living literature, about the reality of works of art?

Well, we are not advancing new slogans, we are not publishing manifestoes
or programs. But for us the old truth has a great practical meaning, mis-
understood or forgotten, especially in our country, in Russia.

We consider, that the Russian literature of our days is astonishingly sedate,
stiff and monotonous. We are permitted to write stories, novels and tedious
dramas, either in the old orthography or in the new one, – but without fail on
everyday life and without fail on contemporary themes. Novel of adventure is
a harmful phenomenon; classical and romantic tragedy is archaism or
stylization; a tale of the boulevard is immoral. Therefore: Alexander Dumas
père is pulpe literature; Hoffmann and Stevenson are writers for children.

But we think that our patron of genius, creator of the incredible and of the
improbable, is equal to Tolstoj and Balzac; that Stevenson, an author of novels
about robbers, is a great writer; and that Dumas is a classic like Dostoevskij.

This does not mean that we recognize only Hoffmann, only Stevenson.
Almost all our brothers are precisely writers of everyday life. But they know
that another thing is possible. A work of literature can reflect an epoch but
need not reflect it, it will not become the worse for it. And so Vsev. Ivanov, a
steadfast writer of everyday life, who describes the revolutionary, oppressive
and bloody countryside, recognizes Kaverin, an author of confused romantic
short stories. And my ultra-romantic tragedy gets on with the noble, old-
fashioned lyricism of Fedin.

Because we demand only one thing: a work of literature must be organic,
real, live its own special life.

[A work of literature must live] its own special life. [It must] not be a
copy from nature, but live on a par with nature. We say: Hoffmann's Nutcracker is closer to Gor'kij's Čelkaš than this literary vagabond is to a living
vagabond. Because both Nutcracker and Čelkaš are fictional, are created by
an artist, only different pens have drawn them.

3

And still another great practical meaning the rules of hermit Serapion have
disclosed for us.

We gathered in the days of revolutionary, in the days of powerful political
strain. "Who is not with us, is against us – they said to us on the right and

on the left. – So with whom are you, Serapion Brothers? With the Communists or against the Communists? For the revolution or against the revolution?"

So with whom are we, Serapion Brothers?

We are with hermit Serapion.

So, with no-one? Slough? An intelligentsia idly indulging in beauteousness? Without ideology, without conviction, the devil may care?

No.

Each of us has an ideology, political convictions; everyone paints his hut in his own color. So it is in life. And so it is in stories, tales, dramas. But we together, we – a brotherhood – demand one thing: that the voice should not be false. That we should believe in the reality of literary work whatever its color may be.

Too long and poignantly public affairs have directed Russian literature. It is time to say that non-communist story can be inane but it can be a work of genius. And it makes no difference to us with whom Blok – the poet, author of *The Twelve*, Bunin – the writer, author of *The Gentleman from San Francisco*, side.

These are commonplace truths, but each day convinces us that this must be said over and over again.

So with whom are we, Serapion Brothers?

We are with hermit Serapion. We believe that literary chimeras are a special reality, and we do not want any utilitarianism. We are writing not for propaganda. Art is real as life itself. And, as life itself, it is without aim and without meaning: it exists because it cannot help existing.

Brothers!

To you my last word.

There is still something that unites us, what cannot be proved or explained, – our brotherly love.

We are not fellow members of a club, not colleagues, not comrades, but

Brothers!

Each of us is dear to another, as a writer and as a man. At a great time, in a great city we have found one another, – adventurers, intellectuals and simply people, – just as brothers find one another. My blood said to me: "Here is your brother!" And there is no such force in the world but will destroy the unity of blood, will disrupt the union of brothers.

And now, when fanatical cheap politicians and weak-sighted critics on the right and on the left instigate dissension among us, hit at our ideological divergences and shout: "Disperse and go to your respective parties!" – we will not answer them. Because one brother can pray to God, and the other to the Devil, but brothers they remain. And no-one in the world shall rend the unity of blood of brothers.

We are not comrades, but –

Brothers!

Lev Lunc[17]

Lunc advocated the individual freedom of artistic creation. He welcomed

[17]   See footnote 16.

creative diversity at the time of a stifling spiritual uniformity. He professed that literary creation draws *from itself* its *raison d'être*. Therefore it does not need any utilitarian motivation. He repudiated the idea that the sole purpose of literature consists in reflecting the epoch or – still worse – reflecting an exclusive ideology.[18] Tedium weighs upon literature when literature suffers under the domination of such an exclusive ideology. Lunc emphasizes – although he did not elaborate much on this point – that a literary work occupies its own ontological status. He affirmed the *purposeless* nature of art, which precipitated the virulent attack of the Marxist critics such as Poljanskij and Arvatov.[19]

As a matter of fact, the above-mentioned article by Lunc, as well as his other polemical articles, sometimes fail to reach an adequate cogency. When he says:

Art is real as life itself. And, as life itself, it is without aim and without meaning: it exists because it cannot help existing.[20]

he does not quite compel the reader's mental assent.

Still, this represents one of the essential elements in his aesthetic outlook. The implied meaning of this statement can easily be connected with the Formalist definition of aesthetic significance.[21]

One kind of activity in which man is engaged pursues a "practical" purpose: man focuses his mind on devising the means that will enable him to affect the world around him. Man participating in such an activity tries to accomplish changes – perhaps improvements – in his material or social environment, in politics, education, religion or any other field pertaining to mankind's life.

Another type of activity proper to man does *not* pursue any of the preceding purposes. In this respect, it serves no "practical" purpose. To this type of activity belongs *aesthetic* experience. Absence of "practical" purpose – "practical" being understood as defined in the foregoing lines – in art and literature spells the *neutralization*[22] of the material to be aesthetically molded. Trockij accused the Serapion Brothers of "lack of principles":

---

[18] L. Lunc, "Ob ideologii i publicistike", *Sovremennaja russkaja kritika 1918-1924*. Ed. by Innokentij Oksenov (Leningrad, 1925), p. 241.
[19] William Edgerton, "The Serapion Brothers: an Early Soviet Controversy", *The American Slavic and East European Review*, vol. VIII, 1 (February 1949), pp. 47-64.
[20] *Vid.* p. 28 of this study.
[21] Gleb Struve, *Soviet Russian Literature 1917-1950* (Norman, Okla., 1951), p. 192 *et seq.*
[22] *Ibid.*, p. 195.

The most dangerous trait of the Serapions is that they glory in their *lack of principles*.[23]

Now, what stood for "lack of principles" in the mind of Trockij – who conceived of "principles" within the context of a socio-political revolution – represented the necessary process of *aesthetic neutralization*[24] in the creative effort of the Serapion Brothers. And it was not in vain that Lunc insisted with such vehemence on the irrelevancy of "practical" purpose in art since the essential nature of art consists in the lack of "practical" purpose.

This tenet appears basic in Lunc's thinking. And if so, he – consciously or unconsciously – arrives at the Aristotelian view on art. If art claims to be an activity maintaining a status ontologically independent, then art must possess its *specific* medium. This medium is provided by "a world of images and appearances"[25] in which art creates "after a pattern existing in the mind".[26] Now, this medium requires objects free from the accident to which they are subjected in the empirical world. For that effect the artist must develop a sense of detachment and disengagement from the function that the above-mentioned objects perform in the empirical world. As soon as the artist loses this sense of detachment and disengagement, aesthetic activity loses its independence and leaps into another type of activity, e.g., cognitive. Let me illustrate this affirmation. In Fedin's novel *Goroda i gody* one chapter begins in the following manner:

Мостовые моют так.
Коротконогие люди в брезентовых штанах и брезентовых куртках широкой струей воды, искристым веером бьющей с рассеивателя брандспойта, обильно поливают гладкие кубики-камни. Потом щетками из стальной проволоки долго и крепко протирают каждый кубик. Стёртую щетками грязь смывают новым вееровидным, веселым дождем. Железными крюками, насаженными на палки, выковыривают навоз из щелей между камней. Сильной и тонкой струей воды – без рассеивателя – промывают щели. Потом возят по мостовой частый и бойкий душ, от тротуара к тротуару, как в бороньбе – по одной полосе против другой, – дальше, дальше по пятам за людьми в брезентовых штанах и куртках, волочащими

---

[23] Leon Trotsky, *Literature and Revolution* (New York, 1957), p. 70. (The italics are mine.)
[24] Gleb Struve, *op. cit.*, p. 195.
[25] *Aristotle's Theory of Poetry and Fine Art*. Translated and with critical notes by S. H. Butcher (New York, 1951), p. 128.
[26] *Ibid.*

толстую, набухшую, как сытый удав, кишку. И потом, когда мато-
вая, чуть влажная в скважинах и щелях, вымытой протянется
мостовая на два-три квартала, – на толстозадых, мохнатокопытых
лошадях везут по ней тяжелый щетинистый вал, и он прилизывает
и сандалит кубики – камни, как круглая щетка парикмахера – корот-
ко подстриженный затылок.[27]

Did Fedin intend to give instructions on how to clean roads, thereby
rendering a service to the Roads Department or any other Department in
charge of the maintenance of the roads? Of course not. In such an
aesthetic context, the communication is diverted from its *cognitive* –
"practical" – function. The author does not concern himself with road
cleaning as such. This matter does not preoccupy his mind – and still
less does it preoccupy the reader's – under its empirical aspect. Words
and phrases cease to act as conventional signs, i.e., as logical or algebraic
symbols, literally transcribing the empirical world, just as "[...] spoken
words are symbols of mental states, written words are symbols of spoken
words [...].[28] Words and phrases convey mental impressions bearing
likeness to the objects that, as such, belong to the empirical world but
are removed from their empirical – "practical" – function through the
artist's attitude of detachment and disengagement from the empirical –
"practical" – function attached to these objects.

In the passage cited above, the switch from cognitive information
toward something else comes out almost at first sight. When the author
begins saying "Mostovye mojut tak", this *tak* foreshows a cognitive
information which will ensue. The expectation fails right away, because
the immediately following sequence "korotkonogie ljudi v brezentovyx
štanax i brezentovyx kurtkax [...]" does not absolutely pertain to a
context of cognitive information. In a cognitive information concerning
maintenance of roads it is quite superfluous to say, or to know whether
public-work employees in charge of street cleaning and street washing
are *short-legged*. All these terms, apparently related to the "objective
reality" of street cleaning, come estranged (ostraneny) from their
"logical", or "technical" or "empirical" or "cognitive" function. Using
these terms, the author endeavors to arouse with the reader an emotion
independent on all previously mentioned factors, i.e., the aesthetic
emotion. An accumulation of seemingly minute technical details appears
to serve the "practical" purpose of providing directions for the cleaning
of pavements. However, the infusion of descriptive details incongruous

---

[27] Konstantin Fedin, *Goroda i gody* (Moskva, GIXL, 1959), p. 151.
[28] *Aristotle's Theory* ... (*vid.* footnote 25), p. 125.

with this simulated "practical" purpose discloses the real purpose, disengaged from the "practical" purpose: to achieve the effect of the ludicrous and to provoke a feeling of estrangement.

So, when expanded, Lunc's thinking revolves about a few themes which are obviously Aristotelian. Namely, they are these. Aesthetic activity draws its distinctive quality from the fact that the given medium – namely words and phrases –, instead of reproducing the original as this original is in itself, reproduces it as this original appears to *senses*. This seems to explain Lunc's statement:

[...] Because both Nutcracker and Čelkaš are fictional, are created by an artist, only different pens have drawn them [...][29]

Instead of symbolically representing empirical reality by means of conventional, logical signs, this medium bears *likeness* to empirical reality; instead of providing a literal transcript of empirical reality, this medium imitates things as they "*ought to be*"[30] (the italicized expression does not convey any ethical significance; it implies only an aesthetic meaning).[31] Lunc speaks quite in the same key:

[...] Because we demand only one thing: a work of literature must be organic, real, live its own special life.
   [A work of literature must live] its own special life. [It must] not be a copy from nature, but live on a par with nature. We say: Hoffmann's Nutcracker is closer to Gorkij's Čelkaš than this literary vagabond is to a living vagabond.[32]

The "*ought to be*" we find in Lunc's article "Na Zapad":

Art transforms the world, but does not draw a copy of it,[33]

Therefore words and phrases, as an independent – aesthetic – medium of activity, do not have final cause ("[...] Art [...] is without aim and without meaning [...]"),[34] they have only *formal* cause. They repudiate any instrumental value which would respond to extrinsic control. They preserve intrinsic value. Lunc must have had this in mind when he said:

---

[29]   *Vid.* p. 27 of this study.
[30]   *Aristotle's Theory* ... (*vid.* footnote 25), p. 97.
[31]   *Ibid.*, pp. 122, 151.
[32]   *Vid.* p. 27 of this study.
[33]   Lev Lunc, "Na Zapad", *Beseda*, Berlin, 3, Sept.-Oct. 1923 (ed. by Gor'kij), p. 267 *et seq.*
[34]   *Vid.* p. 28 of this study.

Art [...] exists because it cannot help existing.[35]

The Serapion Brothers borrowed from the Formalist thinking their insistence on conceiving of a literary work as a *construction* integrating diverse components reciprocally motivated and subordinated to one, common aesthetic purpose. Il'ja Gruzdev, another Serapion theoretician, expounded these views in his article "Utilitarnost' i samocel' "[36] and "Lico i maska".[37] Ideology – whatever it may be – represents only one component in this construction. Now, the Marxist critics such as Poljanskij and Arvatov in fact demanded from the Serapion Brothers that they subordinate their creative effort to Marxist ideology. Lev Lunc promptly detected this point wrapped in the specious phraseology of the Marxist critics:

But the official critique affirms – no, it is afraid of affirming [it] openly, but it is clear from its [i.e., the official critique's, H.O.] every article, – that *ideology in art is all*. With this I will never agree. Ideology is one of the elements of a work of art. The more elements there are, the better. And if in a novel integral and original convictions, political, philosophic or – *horribile dictu!* – religious, are developed, I welcome such a novel. But it should not be forgotten that a novel without an accurate and clear "Weltanschauung" can be beautiful, whereas a novel only of ideology alone can be unbearable.[38]

Subordinating creative effort to an exclusive ideology and shaping the whole construction in compliance with what this exclusive ideology requires the author impoverishes his work at best and spoils it altogether at worst. What in a work of art represents a common aesthetic purpose to which reciprocally motivated components are subordinated is the author's will to construct. The emphasis should be laid upon the *process* of integrating multiple elements. This constructing appears, in E. Husserl's terminology, as "a duty which I have to realize".[39] When one component – e.g., political ideology – dominates all the others, then the will to construct, to integrate *all* components – which it is the artist's "duty" to do – yields to the will, perhaps rather to the compulsion, to disintegrate the construction by undertaking attempts at subordinating to one partic-

---

[35]   *Ibid.*
[36]   Il'ja Gruzdev, "Utilitarnost' i samocel', *Sovremennaja russkaja kritika (1918-1924)*. Ed. by Innokentij Oksenov (Leningrad, 1925), pp. 245-250.
[37]   Il'ja Gruzdev, "Lico i maska", *Serapionovy Brat'ja, Zagraničnyj Al'manax* (Berlin, 1922), pp. 205-237.
[38]   L. Lunc, "Ob ideologii i publicistike", *Sovremennaja russkaja kritika* (*vid.* footnote 36), pp. 204-244.
[39]   René Wellek and Austin Warren, *Theory of Literature* (New York, 1956), p. 141.

ular component all other components. In this case the aesthetic purpose tends to fade out. Now, aesthetic neutralization means that the artist, the writer in our case, does not favor one component in preference to another for the sake of preserving the aesthetic integrity of the whole construction.

At the time when the Serapion Brotherhood came into existence – it met for the first time on the 1st of February 1921 – the problem of "aesthetic neutralization" narrowed down to the writer's political attitude toward the Bolshevik Revolution.

Lev Lunc's article "Počemu my Serapionovy Brat'ja" and the Serapion Brothers' lively autobiographical sketches published in *Literaturnye Zapiski* date from 1922. It appears from these writings that at that time the Serapion Brothers evinced sympathy for the Revolution. Yet they were no more than "artistic fellow-travelers"[40] of proletarian revolution. Measured by the Marxist critique of the time, the significance of such "artistic fellow travelers" consisted in their furthering a "transitional art".[41] Bourgeois art was quitting the stage of history, whereas the new art, the art of the Revolution, had not yet emerged. Some provisional forms of art had to patch the gap separating the prospective socialist art from the fading bourgeois art. Pil'njak, the Serapion Brothers, Esenin and others produced this transitional art. These young writers "accepted" the Revolution, but, to quote Trockij,

[...] in these individual acceptances, there is one common trait which sharply divides them from Communism, and always threatens to put them in opposition to it. They do not grasp the Revolution as a whole and the Communist ideal is foreign to them.[42]

How did a writer or a poet at that time earn the label of "proletarian"? He would display a certain revolutionary enthusiasm, depict romantic and heroic aspects of the Revolution, glorify factory labor and eulogize collectivism. Proletkul't poets operated in this way: for instance A. Gastev, author of *Shockwork Poetry* (1918), extolling industrialization and the "iron state".[43] Likewise, writers such as D. Furmanov, author of *Čapaev* (1923), promoted this "proletarian" fashion in prose fiction.

Now, the Serapion Brothers' works also belonged to the Revolution. But they did so only thematically, only in so far as choice of topic was

---

[40]   Gleb Struve, *op. cit.*, p. 72.
[41]   Leon Trotsky, *Literature and Revolution* (New York, 1957), p. 56.
[42]   *Ibid.*, p. 57.
[43]   Vyacheslav Zavalishin, *Early Soviet Writers* (New York, 1958), p. 146.

concerned. Thematically these works may have coincided with "proletarian" works. But a fundamental difference set the Serapion Brothers'
approach apart from that of "proletarian" writers.

The difference lay in what Il'ja Gruzdev maintained in his paradoxical
contention: a "simple", "sincere", "spontaneous expression of thoughts
and feelings" is impossible *within the limits of art*.[44] Between the addresser
and the addressee the message – if intended to be an aesthetic construction
– erects a wall of "forged armor" which does not let a single idea of the
addresser pass through without refracting it artistically.

The artistic refraction neutralizes the initial emotional or ideological
impulses of the addresser and confers on the message a special ontological
status, that of poetic function. This situation justifies Lunc in maintaining that Hoffmann's Nutcracker stands closer to Gor'kij's Čelkaš
than the latter stands to a living vagrant. If the artistic refraction does
not occur by way of the message, then the message loses its aesthetic
significance.

Il'ja Gruzdev readily and somewhat paradoxically uses the term of
"mask" for artistic creation. The "dynamic integration" of devices[45] or,
to use Gruzdev's words, "sorazmernost' postroenija"[46] forms this mask.
In Formalist thinking the notion of *device* pertains to the construction
of a given plot. The notion of *motivation* refers to the fable: it means that
certain motives (episodes) enter into the fable in order to "justify"[47] the
construction of the plot in terms of circumstantial verisimilitude. For
instance, in Kaverin's *Konec Xazy*[48] the motive (episode) of the abduction
of Molotova constitutes a device of plot construction that enables the
requirement of the theme to be fulfilled at the *dénouement*. Its motivation,
i.e., the motivation of this device, consists in the fact that the gang needed
her for secretarial work and the leader of the gang fell for her. Thus
motivated, the device – functional piece of the plot – gains "lifelikeness"
sufficiently persuasive for the reader.

Russian Formalism was primarily a movement of criticism and of re-
evaluation of literary standards. This theoretical concern may explain
the Russian Formalists' laying so special a stress upon the *device*: it is
the *device* which poses the problems of structure in the message and those
of creative process involving the agent-producer, the process of making

---

[44] Il'ja Gruzdev, "Lico i maska", *Serapionovy Brat'ja, Zagraničnyj Al'manax* (Berlin, 1922), p. 208.
[45] Victor Erlich, *Russian Formalism. History – Doctrine* (The Hague, 1955), p. 70.
[46] Il'ja Gruzdev, *op. cit.*, p. 213.
[47] Victor Erlich, *op. cit.*, p. 166.
[48] *Vid.* p. 132 *et seq.* of this study.

and the product. Still, the device as such – the "bare" one – is but "mexanika iskusstva".[49]

The Serapion Brothers, essentially writers, viewed the message from the angle of receptive process, in terms of – to use P. Valéry's expression – aesthetic "consumption";[50] which places emphasis on the receptor's attitude. The receptive process by its very nature must entertain and prolong the illusion of a certain reality with the receptor. Otherwise, it seems, the two-fold process "creation-reception" forfeits its meaning and its ontological status.

It is the *motivation* or, using the Formalist term, the motivation of device, that relates to this receptive side of aesthetic communication.

With good right Gruzdev amplifies in this sense the Formalist thinking. The spirit of Pygmalion hides in each receptor's – i.e., in each reader's – mind: the latter expects a "living art"[51] rather than a skeleton of devices "laid bare". What endues a literary work with life is the "masking"[52] of its always conventional devices by motivating them with those "beskonečno-malye momenty"[53] to which L. Tolstoj referred and in the creating of which he himself so matchlessly excelled. In the second volume of *War and Peace* L. Tolstoj mentions the inauguration of the Council of State (Gosudarstvennyj Sovet). The event occurred on the day following the ball where prince Andrej met Nataša. To this in-auguration prince Andrej attached an anticipatory importance. The author, agreeable to his own over-all purpose, wanted his character to feel disappointed with the inauguration of the Council of State. In order to indicate this circumstance Tolstoj could simply have stated, as an omniscient author, that the inauguration had occurred and prince Andrej had been disappointed with it, indeed. Such a procedure would smack of a journalistic commonplace account. Actually it would have been a cognitive communication, and not an aesthetic one. Tolstoj shuns such an unartistic way. He shapes a special human figure for the specific purpose of ushering in the event in question. The motive of the in-auguration of the Council of State blends into the story through the mind of a man and acquires a certain quality imparted to this motive by the disposition of this man's mind. The man – Bickij – "služivšij v različnyx komissijax",[54] turns up only once in the whole novel. His role

---

[49] Il'ja Gruzdev, *op. cit.*, p. 215.
[50] Paul Valéry, *Introduction à la Poétique* (Paris, 1938), p. 7.
[51] Il'ja Gruzdev, *op. cit.*, p. 215.
[52] *Ibid.*
[53] *Ibid.*
[54] L. N. Tolstoj, *Vojna i mir* ("Pravda", 1948), II, p. 181.

consists but in introducing the motive of the inauguration of the Council of State seen from a specific point of view.[55] This motivation – one of L. Tolstoj's "beskonečno-malye momenty" – creates a living scene convincing for the reader in its "lifelikeness" and therefore perfectly "masks" the device whereby the author promotes the spiritual development of his character in the intended direction.

The problem consists, as Gruzdev affirms, in subordinating all these "beskonečno-malye momenty" – whether they result from the author's experience or originate from his sole imagination – to the general aesthetic purpose of the work. The more credibly the author succeeds in motivating his devices – "maskirovka sxem"[56] – by integrating the multifarious material of life into his work, the more perfect is his creation. And, an inevitable conclusion, the greater artistic value the author achieves in his work, the more delusory becomes the "mask". The latter creates in the receptor's mind an illusion of a world more real than a circumstantial reality, one which possesses "truth to reality".[57]

This illusion elicits divers responses from the spell-bound receptor. An unsophisticated one would take it seriously. He would take the aesthetic message at face value. In an extreme case he would "beat up the actor who played Judas".[58]

The philosopher's attitude toward the receptive process is a critical one. The literary scholar, going beyond the receptive process, focuses his critical mind on the creative process hidden behind the message. In Gruzdev's words:

The study of *belles-lettres* takes not the course of creating the "complexion" of the writer, but the course of setting apart and differentiating those artistic means that the given author has at his disposal.

I mean certain *devices*, the general schemes of which are similar with a number of authors. The change and the struggle of these devices form the object of the history of art as science. All reproaches of false abstraction and harmful schematism here are baseless, – science *has* to abstract and to classify phenomena according to their group signs.[59]

The sophisticated receptor also participates in the play but, of course, he does so on a level higher than the one who "beats up the actor who

---

[55] Viktor Šklovskij, *Mater'jal i stil' v romane L'va Tolstogo "Vojna i Mir"* (Moskva, [1928]), pp. 114-115.
[56] Il'ja Gruzdev, *op. cit.*, p. 215.
[57] René Wellek and Austin Warren, *Theory of Literature* (New York, 1956), p. 25.
[58] Jakobson, quoted from Victor Erlich, *op. cit.*, p. 57.
[59] Il'ja Gruzdev, *op. cit.*, 215.

played Judas". The sophisticated reader partakes of a culture in which
the *play* constitutes a significant element.[60]

Both the sophisticated reader and an unsophisticated one may apprehend literary work as a *myth*.

The Serapion Brothers wanted, with varying degrees of awareness, to
provoke these responses.

When Nik. Tixonov describes a lady practising the art of theatrical
reciting in these words:

[...] Дежурная – Рахиль Нейман неистово выкрикивала из Гомера.
Она готовилась в студию, и длинный гекзаметр кусками летел из
её треугольного рта, как будто она выплёвывала жёсткие макароны.[61]

Or when he exhibits a landscape such as this:

[...] Он прошёл мимо разваленной мельницы, точно взятой на прокат
из оперы. Огромное колесо висело разломанное, только не хватало
каркающего ворона.[62]

he fosters an aesthetic tendency common for all the Serapions. In varying
degrees they adhere to the purpose of *shocking* the reader rather than
pleasing him. The theoretical motivation breeding this attitude consists
in maximizing the contrast growing from the fact that a certain notion is
extracted out of its habitual, "neutral" semantic context and placed into
another context, very disparate from the first. It is a matter of attitude.
It is not a property specific to one aesthetic device. In the foregoing
example from Nik. Tixonov, the author draws an extravagant and
elaborate comparison: a verse of hexameters is compared to undercooked
macaroni. What connects the object of comparison (verse of hexameter)
with the image of comparison (macaroni) is the sign on the basis of which
the author institutes the comparison: namely, the similarity of respective
actions: "kuskami letel" and "vyplěvyvala".

To this aesthetic attitude V. Šklovskij gave a brilliant and provocative
formulation in his theory of *ostranenie*. What constitutes the inner
mechanism of this device is a "semantic shift",[63] or a "deviation from the

[60] *Vid.* p. 145 *et seq.* of this study.
[61] Nikolaj Tixonov, *Riskovannyj člověk. Rasskazy* (Leningrad, 1932), p. 163.
[62] Nikolaj Tixonov, *Riskovannyj člověk. Rasskazy* (Leningrad, 1932), p. 176.
[63] Viktor Šklovskij, "Paralleli u Tolstogo", *Xod Konja* (Moskva-Berlin, 1923),
pp. 115-125, and Victor Erlich, *Russian Formalism. History — Doctrine* (The Hague,
1955), p. 151.

norm".[64] A certain experience is removed from its habitual semantic context and placed into another, an unusual one.

Since Šklovskij introduced this happy term into the practice of literary critique, we have traditionally referred – by way of an example of *ostranenie* – to Šklovskij's analysis of the well-known description of an opera performance in *War and Peace*. The narrator looks upon the event *from the point of view of his hero* and the hero *does not understand* or *recognize* the event. The hero interprets the event not in terms of those norms or conventions that are meaningful for the event in question but in terms of others which remove all motivations giving the meaning to the event described. The author places his hero in a situation in which the hero, semantically speaking, does not – or cannot – follow the "rules of the game". So one of the sequences that Nataša sees in the well-known opera performance represents the actor who "stal pet' i *razvodit' rukami*" (the italics are mine, H.O.). In this last case the narrator strips the gesture of its motivation and thereby annihilates its socially conventional meaning. Only a naked mechanical gesture remains. Thus the event becomes meaningless.

This device – or at least the literary application of it – viewed by Šklovskij does not disclose anything fundamentally new in the literary field. Professor D. Čiževskij is able to trace this device back to Xenophanes, the Eleatic philosopher of the 6th century B.C.[65] Professor Čiževskij discovers the features common both to this device and to allegory: in both cases "real things are represented by certain 'substitutes'".[66] They work in diametrically opposite directions. Allegory describes one thing under the image of another, conventionalizes this correspondence and thereby contributes to our grasping of the meaning of the thing. The device of *ostranenie* – Čiževskij calls it "negative allegory" – operates in quite an opposite direction: it deprives the thing of its meaning. It does so either by substituting one thing by another thing, the latter having semantic associations quite distinct from those of the former (i.e., "boxes and chests" with "a separate inscription and a title" substitutes "books"),[67] or by using an inappropriate "scale of perception" when the thing is described (e.g., "glittering pieces of metal" substitutes "money").[68]

[64] Victor Erlich, *op. cit.*, p. 151.
[65] Dmitry Čiževsky, "Comenius' *Labyrinth of the World*: its themes and their sources", *Harvard Slavic Studies*, Vol. I (Cambridge, Mass., 1953), p. 121.
[66] *Ibid.*, p. 120.
[67] *Ibid.*, p. 119.
[68] *Ibid.*, p. 121.

Because of its property to remove the meaning of the thing to which this artistic device is applied, it turned out to be a powerful tool in the hand of a social – or any other – critic. As Professor Čiževskij points out,[69] the device worked its way during the period of Enlightenment.[70] Authors – primarily social and political critics – developed its most efficient form: things perceived from the point of view of an uninitiated foreigner or even a non-human or unearthly being. Let me refer to one example among many of the kind – *Les Lettres Persanes* (1721) in which Montesquieu, adopting the point of view of a Persian traveler, mocks French mores.

The device brings about a "sense of novelty".[71] The literary onlooker enters a "sphere of new perception".[72] In *Xolstomer* – after Šklovskij this story of Tolstoj is also traditionally referred to as an example of the device of *ostranenie* – the literary onlooker does so through the eyes of a horse who does not understand the meaning of the conventional norms that rule the life of human society. Thus deprived of its meaning, human life with its facts and gestures assumes the aspect of a weird "ballet mécanique".

This "sense of novelty" – if it is to elicit a full aesthetic effect – coexists with another phenomenon: I mean a "sense of recognition".[73] Reverting to our last example we realize that behind the grotesque and estranged description of human life by the hypothetical horse of Tolstoj, we still come to recognize actual human life with its conventional norms. The aesthetic effect results from the fact that the second phenomenon – the "sense of recognition" – tends to offset the first one – the "sense of novelty". The tension between these two phenomena is responsible for aesthetic experience in a literary work.

In one of his articles Nik. Nikitin says the following:

But an artist starts from material. He senses the world as material, hence his understanding of it, he takes the world as portrayal and from it he proceeds. Often one sound, or a complex of sounds, interlaced into a casual idea suffices for a work of art to be born [...]

From the sentence of the author Utočkin – "at sunset our prison is extraordinarily beautiful" were born *My Notes* by L. Andreev [...]

Thus borrowing – art *transforms* [the italics are mine, H.O.]. Often listening to a serious speech, political or economic, *you apprehend it in a certain trans-*

---

[69]   *Ibid.*, p. 121 *et seq.*
[70]   *Ibid.*, p. 121 *et seq.*
[71]   René Wellek and Austin Warren, *Theory of Literature* (New York, 1956), p. 225.
[72]   Victor Erlich, *op. cit.*, p. 150.
[73]   René Wellek and Austin Warren, *op. cit.*, p. 225.

position of words, sentences and instead of seriousness you get a joke [the italics are mine, H.O.]. Everyone sees and hears in his own way, because the eye and the ear are not instruments from the observatory of Pulkovo. Only a seismograph reflects oscillations in a curve, but one should not demand of an artist to be a public seismograph, this is not the main aim of art, he has his *own* ear, his *own* play proper only to him. If the world presented itself as though through an objective (so it should be for a politician), art would not be needed, because this art would not fascinate, over it there would be only one thing left for us to do – to be bored. Just the fact that *the artist always suffers from a kind of Daltonism* [the italics are mine] – is attractive, for the world is handed as if on a platter, and everyone has a different world.[74]

This excerpt contains many significant points common for the literary views that the Serapion Brothers professed. The following idea:

Often listening to a serious speech, political or economic, you apprehend it in a certain transposition of words, sentences and instead of seriousness you get a joke.

suggests a variant application of the same mechanism of the *ostranenie*: while passing from "reality" to literary representation one changes one's "scale of perception", so that the initial "real" association of meanings yields place to another one.

The device of *ostranenie* points to a broader significance. It does not matter whether the new context became "meaningless" – as Comenius' description of the library and the books – or not. What matters is "not the direction of the 'semantic shift', but the very fact that a shift had occurred, that a deviation from the norm had been made. It was this deviation, insisted Šklovskij, this 'quality of divergence' that lay at the core of aesthetic perception."[75]

The view of Nik. Nikitin on art and literature almost literally reproduces Šklovskij's point of view ('creative distortion of nature by means of a set of devices').[76]

The Serapion Brothers may have used *ostranenie* as a means to establish their own artistic identity: by opposing their own "manner" to the vague and mythical notion of the "norm" they may have expected to develop their literary personality.

Ostranenie works in all strata of literary creation. "Shifts" and "deviations" produce a perpetual renewal of the artistic material in the

[74] Nik. Nikitin, "Vrednye mysli", *Pisateli ob iskusstve i o sebe. Sbornik statej*, 1 (Moskva-Leningrad, 1924), pp. 117-118.
[75] Victor Erlich, *op. cit.*, p. 151.
[76] *Ibid.*, p. 57.

stratum of the units of meaning.[77] These "shifts" and "deviations" brought about freshness, strangeness and originality in the *imagery* prevailing in the Serapion works. At the same time, this need for accentuated and striking contrast from the "norm" did not spare the Brothers certain extravagance and stylistic mannerism. Stylistic mannerism is frequently manifest in Nik. Nikitin's works. Describing a ride on a winter's night he says:

... И по накатам *орут* бешенно санки, и *хрякает* от скачки лошадиное горло... – хорошо. ...

Рядом, чуть ли в голову, цепляются столбы, проволоки – *намерзшие бахромой, бородами, зимою* – и летит все быстро, *хрякая*, как это горло. Хорошо![78]

Such an imagery expresses nothing else than a tasteless and obtrusive mannerism.

Ostranenie also operates in the stratum of the novelist's "world".[79] It suffices to read the *titles* of the stories published in the first – and the only *Almanac* of the Serapion Brothers (both Petersburg edition of 1922 and Berlin edition of the same year)[80] in order to feel their taste for *thematic exoticism* which is another aspect of psychological *ostranenie*: Zoščenko's "Viktorija Kazimirovna" – a view of the world disfigured through the use of a peculiar type of language, *skaz*;[81] Lunc's "V pustyne" – a biblical stylization of the Exodus; Ivanov's "Sinij zverjuška" – an attempt artistically to reproduce Siberian folklore and dialect; Slonimskij's "Dikij" – a story about a dignified and traditionalist Jewish tailor in revolutionary Petrograd, story in which biblical stylization alternates with the *presto* style of a war account; Fedin's "Pes'i duši" – world seen through the eyes of dogs; Kaverin's "Xronika goroda Leipciga za 18.. god" – a rampant experimentation *à la* E. T. A. Hoffmann and L. Sterne; Nikitin's "Pes" – story about savage episodes of the Civil War; also Nikitin's "Dezi" – a story about a tiger's cub trying to understand men and learning how to live with them; Gruzdev's article "Lico i maska" the very title of which is sufficiently revealing.

This need for contrasting self-expression – which represents an extension of the same principle of *ostranenie* – leads, on the one hand, to

---

[77]   *Vid.* p. 47 of this study.
[78]   Nik. Nikitin, *Polët. Povest'* (Berlin, 1924), p. 17.
[79]   *Vid.* p. 47 of this study.
[80]   *Serapionovy Brat'ja. Al'manax pervyj* (Peterburg, 1922), and *Serapionovy Brat'ja. Zagraničnyj Al'manax* (Berlin, 1922).
[81]   *Vid.* Chapter III of this study (p. 72 ff.).

emotional "over-representation", and, on the other hand, to emotional "under-representation".

In the first case, the real phenomenon and its mental representation are expressed through a verbal medium marked with emotionally keyed and high-pitched diction. This holds particularly true for writers such as Nik. Nikitin and Vsevolod Ivanov. Here things happen as if the emotional significance assigned to the verbal medium were excessively disproportionate to the corresponding emotional significance proper to the real phenomenon mentally represented. Then, communication may be reduced to a gibberish of this kind:

Густая потная тысячная толпа топтала его визг:
– Верна-а...
– Не да-а-ай!...
– На-а!...
– О-о-о-у-у-у!!
– О-о!!! (Vsevolod Ivanov. *Bronepoezd 14-69*)[82]

In the second case, there occurs just the contrary. The mechanism of *ostranenie* is based on the contrast between the real phenomenon charged with highly emotional significance and its mental representation conveyed in a verbal medium emptied of corresponding emotional significance. This attitude brings about a sort of weird *detachment* in descriptions of the bloodiest episodes of the Revolution. Slonimskij's novel *Lavrovy* is written in this key. Descriptions picturing grisly horrors fill Šklovskij's *Sentimental'noe putešestvie*. Still, on no occasion does Šklovskij abandon his calm and free and easy attitude. Here are two examples of this estranging attitude:

Кстати о жалости. Мне описали следующую картину. Стоит казак. Перед ним лежит голый брошенный курденок. Казак хочет его убить, ударит раз и задумается, ударит второй и задумается.
    Ему говорят: "Убей сразу", а он: "Не могу – жалко".[83]

and:

Недели три тому назад я встретил в вагоне поезда, идущего из Петрограда в Москву, одного солдата персидской армии.
    Он рассказал мне еще подробность про взрыв.
    После взрыва, солдаты, окруженные врагами, ждущие подвиж-

---

[82] Vsevolod Ivanov, *Bronepoezd 14-69* in the collection *Partizanskie povesti* (Leningrad, 1932), p. 36.
[83] Viktor Šklovskij, *Sentimental'noe putešestvie. Vospominanija 1917-1922* (Moskva-Berlin, 1923), p. 140.

ного состава, занялись тем, что собирали и составляли из кусков
разорванные тела товарищей.

Собирали долго.

Конечно, части тела у многих перемешали.

Один офицер подошел к длинному ряду положенных трупов.

Крайний покойник был собран из оставшихся частей.

Это было туловище крупного человека. К нему была приставлена
маленькая голова, и на груди лежали маленькие, неровные руки,
обе левые.

Офицер смотрел довольно долго, потом сел на землю и стал
хохотать ... хохотать ... хохотать ...[84]

And, surely, the officer did not laugh under the influence of a nervous
break-down at the sight of such a horror. He must have laughed because
the picture was actually grotesque. The aesthetic effect of such emotional
"under-representation" consists in magnifying and aggravating the given
feeling (horror).

Lunc found it regrettable that Russian prose fiction developed only a
one-sided tradition – although a brilliant one – that he called "realističeskoe".[85] This one-sided development down-graded other genres such
as historical novels, or novels of adventure or even detective stories, all
of which in Western literatures at their best became classical.

We can easily understand why Lunc specifically mentioned these
"lesser" and "Romantic" literary genres. The problems of plot are more
compelling for, say, an author of an adventure novel than they are, for
example, for an author of a novel of mores (*bytovoj roman*). Things are
happening as if in the latter case the author were taking a photograph of
"reality", that is to say, "reality" integrally fills the pages of a novel – or
chronicle – of mores. In the former case the author starts, so to speak,
with his wheels clogged insofar as credibility is concerned. Here things
are happening as if the author had made up his story from end to end.
A reader is vaguely aware of the fact that it simply did not "happen",
whereas the story of mores did "happen" or may have "happened".
Therefore if a writer of an adventure novel wants his work to be convincing and "life-like", he has to achieve a greater efficiency in its plot
construction than the writer of a novel of mores may care for. The
author has to offset this "handicap" by a skilful construction of his novel.
In this connection the terms such as "uvlekat'" and "zanimatel'nost'" –

---

[84] *Ibid.*, p. 178.
[85] Lev Lunc, "Na Zapad", *Beseda*, Berlin, 3, Sept.-Oct. 1923, p. 263 *et seq.*

attributes of good art in Lunc's thinking – emerge frequently in the Serapion Brothers' writing. In Lunc's own words:

That which in the West is considered classical we called vulgar rubbish and child's play. The plot! The skill of handling a complex intrigue, of tying and untying knots, of weaving and unweaving, – this has been earned by dint of a laborious work of many years, created by a continuous and beautiful culture.[86]

So Lunc defines literary performance in terms of the contrast between that which has a "fabula" and that which has not. And this is the leitmotiv of the Serapion Brothers' "experiment". Lunc defined the Serapion Brotherhood as a "bratstvo jarko fabul'noe":

When two years ago our fraternity was organized, we – the two or three founders – conceived it as a *pronouncedly plot-minded fraternity, even as an anti-realist one*...[87]

Affirming this, Lunc showed maturity in his evaluation of literary phenomena; he evidenced a keener insight into their nature than had certain other literary schools. A newly emerging school or trend in literature often claims that it stands nearer to "real life" than the preceding school or trend. No-one has, probably, betrayed greater innocence in his literary "*profession de foi*" than E. Zola with his dubious naturalism and his *roman expérimental*.[88] Claude Bernard's *Introduction à l'étude de la médecine expérimentale* was for Zola like the proverbial Russian bell: he has heard it but does not know where it is. Zola's ambition to attain the scientific knowledge of man through fiction writing was as absurd as Claude Bernard's experimenting on the pancreas was thoughtful. The wish of Zola to draw nearer in his fiction to "real life" points to a definite phenomenon recurring in literature, namely, that a fresh literary convention supersedes an overused one. The Formalist critics, e.g., Tomaševskij,[89] have argued very convincingly in this respect.

The sagacity of the Serapion Brothers' thinking – namely that of Lunc, Kaverin and Gruzdev – manifested itself in the fact that they denied the "transcript" character of fiction prose. They worked on the level of an avowed convention. (Here we can find again the Aristotelian distinction between "symbolic representation" – "transcript of reality" – and

---

[86] *Ibid.*, p. 260.
[87] *Ibid.*, p. 268 *et seq.* (The italics are mine.) The italicized words read as follows in Russian: "[...] bratstvo jarko fabul'noe, daže anti-realističeskoe...".
[88] Miriam Allott, *Novelists on the Novel* (New York, 1959), pp. 68-70.
[89] B. Tomaševskij, *Teorija literatury* (Leningrad, 1925).

"likeness".[90]) The better the plot technique and the plot construction, the greater the value of the given work. Actually, the "western"[91] wing of the Brotherhood primarily shared this concern for plot construction.

The writing of the Serapion Brothers does not offer any elaborate and systematic literary terminology. At least, I have not been able to discover any so far.

Lunc himself provides terms which are not entirely clear. He operates with general concepts such as "realističeskie" or "anti-realističeskie" which can easily create confusion. These two approaches – "realističeskoe" contrasted with "anti-realističeskoe" – correspond to two different emphases in the sphere of the techniques of representation and we should have liked Lunc to be more explicit on these techniques. He defines "fabula" as "the skill of handling a complex intrigue, of tying and untying knots, of weaving and unweaving...".[92]

When he says "[...] my zabyli pro *fabulu*, pro kompoziciju",[93] we do not make out the difference between the two terms. It is not clear either what discrimination Lunc makes between "iskusstvennaja fabula"[94] and "iskustvennyj sjužet".[95] He appears to use the terms "'sjužetnye' pisateli" and "fabul'nye prozaiki"[96] indiscriminately. What does he mean specifically by these two terms: "čistaja intriga"[97] and "golaja fabula"?[98] When he says "Russkij teatr gonitsja ran'še vsego za *social'nymi motivami*"[99] he definitely bestows upon the term "social'nye motivy" a meaning different from that which he does upon the word "motivy" in "Dvux *motivov* svjazat' uže ne umeem ..."[100] He does not specify it.

Literary terminology suffers considerable inaccuracy. Different authors ascribe different meanings to the same term. "Fabula" is one of those controversial terms. What really matters in this connection is the awareness of the specific meaning that we attach to each term. In order to avoid confusion I find it appropriate consistently to use, insofar as

[90]   *Aristotle's Theory of Poetry and Fine Art*. Translated and with critical notes by S. H. Butcher (New York, 1951), p. 124.
[91]   Gleb Struve, *Soviet Russian Literature 1917-1950* (Norman, Okla., 1951), p. 61.
[92]   Lev Lunc, *op. cit.*, p. 260.
[93]   *Ibid.*, p. 264.
[94]   *Ibid.*, p. 268.
[95]   *Ibid.*
[96]   *Ibid.*, p. 269.
[97]   *Ibid.*, p. 270.
[98]   *Ibid.*, p. 271.
[99]   *Ibid.*, p. 262. (The italics are mine.)
[100] *Ibid.*, p. 265. (The italics are mine.)

possible, one set of terms, interpreting the fiction prose material under discussion from this unified terminological point of view.

A literary work may be conceived of as a structure which different strata more or less tightly hold together. Each stratum in itself represents a system binding subordinate elements into harmony.[101] Here I need not draw up an exhaustive inventory of all strata at play. To find out how and at which moment different strata shade off into one another constitutes a special problem which I will not try to attack. The *sound stratum* includes problems concerning euphony, rhythm and meter.[102] From this stratum there arises the *stratum of the units of meaning*: it involves syntactic structuration. There is another stratum which René Wellek terms the "world" of a novelist[103] ("die Schicht des dargestellten Gegenständlichkeiten", Ingarden).[104] It is on this level that notions such as theme, fable, narrative structure, plot and motive emerge.[105] In other words this is the stratum pertaining to the *techniques of representation*.

Judging from the whole context of Lunc's article "Na Zapad" I may assume that by the term "fabula" he meant the totality of the techniques of representation. Those entities that belong to the stratum of the units of meaning – such as imagery or stylistic devices – and, *a fortiori*, those questions that pertain to the sound stratum – such as eupony, rhythm and meter –, find themselves relegated to an inferior and less important position.

Indulging too much in "ornamental prose" interlarded with dialectalisms and lyrical comments *à la* Vsevolod Ivanov constitutes a ballast which may prevent the writer from rising higher in the craft of prose fiction. This would mean that the stratum of the units of meaning prevails over the stratum of the techniques of representation. Once given to the painting of genre pictures, the author forgets – or is unable – to devote sufficient creative attention to what constitutes the backbone of a prose fiction work: the dramatic unfolding and progression of the action. He then writes "stojačie"[106] works of fiction. Lunc proves drastic when he criticizes this addiction to ornamental prose:

[...] When two years ago our fraternity was organized, we – the two or three

---

[101] René Wellek and Austin Warren, *Theory of Literature* (New York, 1956), pp. 129-145, and Roman Ingarden, *Das Literarische Kunstwerk. Eine Untersuchung aus dem Grenzgebiet der Ontologie, Logik und Literaturwissenschaft* (Halle, 1931), p. 24 *et seq*.
[102] René Wellek and Austin Warren, *op. cit.*, p. 145.
[103] *Ibid.*, p. 140.
[104] Roman Ingarden, *op. cit.*, p. 218.
[105] *Vid.* p. 122 *et seq.* of this study.
[106] Lev Lunc, "Na Zapad", *Beseda*, Berlin, 3, Sept.-Oct. 1923, p. 265.

founders – conceived it as a *pronouncedly plot-minded fraternity, even as an anti-realist one* [the italics are mine, H.O.]. So what has come of it? None of us then, in the January of 1921, hoped that we would achieve such a brotherly solidarity, but, on the other hand, it had never crossed anyone's mind what physiognomy this plot-oriented trend would assume.

It has turned out that there is no trend at all. That does not matter. What does matter is that the majority of our prose writers have returned whence we departed. To populism! You are populists, the typical Russian provincial and *boring, boring* writers!

We said: plot is needed. We said: let us learn from the West. We said – and that was all.

To us still is attributed the title of "plot-minded" writers. I feel it now as a taunt. Vsevolod Ivanov, Nikitin, Fedin – if these good populists are called plot-minded prose writers, where then, o Just Reason, is plotless literature.

[...] We have turned out to be weak, we gave up and threw ourselves along the easy, beaten track. Nikitin, you, who have written "Angel Abaddon" and "Daisy", – believe in these weak attempts there are more possibilities than in the finished "Dogs" and "Stakes". And you, Slonimskij, you betrayed plot and after "Dikij" and "Warsaw" are writing commonly respected "Lancer Regiments".

[...] We all know how to do more or less well: to weave ponderous words, to knit greasy imagery similar to overlarded pies, to write solid "succulent" lyrics. But this *everyone* knows how to do in Russia, more or less well. But to bind at least only two motives we do not know how and we don't want to learn.[107]

The modern Russian prose fiction – Lunc speaks specifically of the novel – is "boring" because it lacks a solid tradition of firmly molded "fabula". In other words, the techniques of representation maintaining the plot construction in Russian fiction works have not reached a sufficiently high degree of elaboration.

It is these techniques of representation that Lunc urged the Brotherhood to master first of all:

[...] We wield everything, except plot. So, let us introduce plot into the ready-made crude figure of lyrical, psychological, everyday life stories.

Never mind that we have a tempting and fallacious thesis. And that we at once want a synthesis. We will fail. And even now we are failing. Surely you all agree with me – harmony! And you all try to give it. But a word, an image, details, which you skilfully wield, engulf you, seduce you with their easiness – and plot crumbles. The thesis wins, – and so there is no synthesis.

We must create a naked antithesis just as now is reigning a bare thesis. Learn the intrigue and do not turn your attention toward anything: either toward language or toward psychology.

Mere intrigue.

[107]   *Ibid.*, p. 269 *et seq.*

[...] You will write badly – you know, bare plot is one-sided. Yes, badly – much worse than you write now. But you will learn. Kaverin is doing so, and so I am trying to do. And Kaverin writes stories far from perfect, and I am scribbling without end, I don't even read it to you – so poorly it is turning out. Look, Kaverin has learnt how to tie an intrigue but he is not in any way able to untie it: he cuts it or abandons it half way along, getting off with an eccentric twist of the plot. As for me, mastering the plot in a play I am not in any way able to cope with it in a tale. Well – we will learn it, and then we will turn to good account our arsenal of images and telling expressions.

[...] The Russian plot tradition has disappeared – we must build it up anew.[108]

It is quite significant that Lunc voiced his challenging appeal to his fellow Serapions in the terms of dialectic process of thought. He discerned ever-present disruptive contradictions in literary creation. He also felt the necessity of having these contradictions merged in a higher form of synthesis.

The trend toward ornamental prose – Lunc's "golyj tezis" – and the trend toward plot construction – Lunc's "golyj antitezis" – seem to act in opposite directions. When the author focuses his creative effort on elaborating the sound stratum or the stratum of the units of meaning, he tends to lose sight of the "world". Conversely, when he concentrates his creative efforts on shaping the "world", he reduces his attention to the sound stratum and the stratum of the units of meaning.

The causes producing that effect reside in divers circumstances. Man can focus his attention on only a single object at a time. Ideally in a literary work the author integrates *all* the strata into aesthetic organization. In actualization, however, this integrating process may encounter serious obstacles arising from the "scale of perception". Each stratum requires its own "scale of perception", so that once the aesthetic consciousness is keyed to a specific "scale of perception", it cannot perceive other strata requiring different "scale of perception".

Most frequently the author himself chooses, under the influence of a literary tradition or because of his own temperament, a specific "scale of perception" to the exclusion of any other. Among the Serapion Brothers Zoščenko appears particularly typical in this respect. More consistently than any other of his fellow Serapions he uses one specific device in reflecting reality through his literary works: that of *skaz*. In his literary output this "scale of perception" – which in the terminology that I am using would pertain to the stratum of the units of meaning – prevails

[108] *Ibid.*, p. 270 *et seq.*

over all others. One can speak of a stylistic "dominanta",[109] that imposes its rule upon all the strata of the given literary work and twists them into a shape agreeable to this "dominanta".

Finally the essential agent at play – the artistic medium itself – sustains the assumption that the two trends in question stand in a conflict. Ornamental, that is to say, "word-conscious" prose which we find in Vsevolod Ivanov's and Nik. Nikitin's works and its subgenus, the *skaz* technique as practised in Zoščenko necessarily require for their own actualization a narrator linguistically and psychologically singularized. The more the narrator is so, the more the prose becomes "word-conscious". Now, communicating events through a linguistically and psychologically singularized narrator means slowing down action and narrowing perspective. On the contrary, plot construction means action – even an accelerated one – and a broad perspective.

---

[109] B. Èixenbaum, "Teorija 'formal'nogo metoda", *Literatura. Teorija, kritika, polemika* (Leningrad, 1927), p. 136.

PART TWO

THE VERBAL MEDIUM

II. THE IMPACT OF THE "ORNAMENTAL" AND "DYNAMIC" PROSE

The generation of the young post-revolutionary writers, in their quest for their own style and language, attempted to absorb the most disparate elements belonging to different stylistic cultures. Among these young writers the Serapion Brothers held a prominent place. Vladimir Pozner, one of the Serapion Brothers, went so far as to attribute to them the initiative of renewing Russian literature.[1] Their writings pertinently illustrate the extreme amplitude of stylistic variations in which resulted their endeavor to develop their own style and language.

One of the features incorporated with varying degrees of success into their works may be designated by the somewhat vague term of "ornamentalism", of "ornamental" prose. The style that this term implies offers different facets.

In the narrow technical sense "ornamental" – or, "dynamic" – prose designated all those stylistic techniques conspicuously practiced in Russian prose during the period of the "revolutionary romanticism" following the Revolution, and prevailing approximately until 1924 (the year when the stories of Babel' appeared). The young authors who emerged on the morrow of the Revolution virtually all indulged in this "ornamental" or "dynamic" prose.

In order to evaluate the place of this "ornamental" prose, one should view it against the background of the novelistic tradition of the XIXth century. The novel in that tradition appeared as a syncretic construct in which there blended divers components. Description of mores and nature, digressions lyrical and philosophic, representation of character, convincing motivation of full individual destinies, conveying of various forms of dialogue, all these components, integrated, brought to the foreground a consistent and aesthetically coherent story of people's lives. This "realistic" and psychological novel reached its peak in L. Tolstoj's monumental form and *Anna Karenina* (1877) served as a landmark in

[1]   Vladimir Pozner, *Littérature russe* (Paris, 1929), p. 327.

literary history. A certain limit of the genre was attained. It is a sympto-
matic circumstance that L. Tolstoj himself, after completing *Anna
Karenina*, adopted a simpler narrative style proper to his popular tales;
moreover he turned to composing plays. Without necessarily attaching
any derogatory connotation to the term, one may speak about the "dis-
integration" of the great syncretic form. The latter shrank, in Čexov,
to short stories, psychologically incisive and aimed at the "'differential'
of mind".[2] The prose issuing from Gor'kij-Andreev school lacked
intellectual and cultural vigor.

The Symbolists brought about the actual renewal of the verbal medium.
Their attempts revitalized the style of the prose. They created their own
solid tradition of prose fiction.

The post-revolutionary generation – among them B. Pil'njak and the
Serapion Brothers – in the quest for their own style had willy-nilly to
reckon with those changes that the Symbolists had worked in prose.
Whereas Kaverin, Slonimskij and Zoščenko remained less pervious to
the Symbolist impact, Nikitin and – in his own way – Ivanov profited
copiously by this inheritance. In this respect the "poetical prose"
("poètičeskaja proza") of A. Belyj exerted prevailing influence.

L. Tolstoj's prose elicited an effect of crystal transparency: people's
emotional and mental experiences flow through words and sentences so
that the reader apprehends those experiences rather than words and
sentences; verbal medium accurately conveys representation; it signifies
less for its own sake.

The Symbolists aspired to render more intense the reader's awareness
of style and of the language of prose. Syntactical peculiarities in A. Belyj's
prose let it present a "disintegrated" appearance. Composition, shifting
abruptly from one level to another, rendered impossible a consistent and
deliberate development of the narrative. Instead, there predominated a
disjointed and broken narrative, with planes now running parallel and
now interlocking. A. Belyj imitated the pattern of a musical theme,
setting off his rhythmical prose with recurring leitmotifs, refrains and
variations. Distortions of syntax; emphasis on the rhythmical effect of a
prose reflecting declamatory character; frequently solemn and highly
expressive (èkspressivnyj) tone; all these features, and certain others,
formed this "ornamental" prose. The "ornamentalist" writers tried to
adjust prose to a pre-arranged rhythmical pattern, i.e., they applied the
principles of versification to prose.

The impact of A. Belyj's prose to a high degree impresses the style of

D. S. Mirsky, *A History of Russian Literature* (New York, 1955), p. 361.

[2]

such post-revolutionary writers as Pil'njak and Nikitin. For example, it is significant how compositional "confusion" affects the style of these three writers. A. Belyj initiated the style in which several levels of representation run parallel ("mnogoplannost'") and interlock. In order to achieve this effect he uses a network of semanticly complex words, i.e., simultaneously offering several levels of interpretation. Metaphoric expression, words semanticly unrelated and phonetically close to one another, assonantal constructions (specifically, puns), intertwining, form a "spiral"[3] of unfolding semantic series. Anthroposophic digressions, thoughts on philosophy of history, delirium and dream motivate the multi-storied narrative structure. In *Peterburg* characters act and live on different levels; likewise, things and places are simultaneously situated on different levels.

A comparison with L. Tolstoj sheds light on the problem. L. Tolstoj subordinates the description of mental processes and verbal medium to reality. Thus, the novelist, while relegating to the background both mental processes and verbal medium, projects reality to the foreground. In *Peterburg* A. Belyj undertakes to project to the foreground *all the three* factors – reality, mental processes, verbal medium (sounds) – simultaneously. Speaking more accurately, each of these three factors stands in its own aesthetic right; it does not serve as an artistic "background" to others. (This reminds us of the dramatic technique that Lunc devised in his play *Vne zakona*: the stage was divided into three parts; less important scenes went on on the two smaller side stages in order to do away with entr'actes and thereby to accelerate the rhythm of the play.[4] Of course, the two techniques, Belyj's in novel and Lunc's in drama, offer only a relative analogy.)

In Chapter V of *Peterburg* Nikolaj Apollonovič Ableuxov meets a certain "gospodinčik s borodavkoj u nosa" who appears to be simultaneously a secret agent of the Government and an undercover member of an anti-governmental terroristic organization. This "gospodinčik", in view of Nikolaj Apollonovič's previous commitments and connections, bade him commit a political assassination, namely that of his own father, Senator Apollon Apollonovič Ableuxov. Brought to bay, Nikolaj Apollonovič seems to take upon himself this villainy. Apollon Apollonovič, who feels that something is going wrong with his son, wants to clear up the matter. Their talk, however, does not allay the suspense:

[3] Vikt. Gofman, "Mesto Pil'njaka", Collection *Mastera sovremennoj literatury. Bor. Pil'njak* (Leningrad, 1928), p. 15.
[4] Vladimir Pozner, *op. cit.*, p. 331.

the news of the unexpected return of Apollon Apollonovič's wife, who left him, going off with another man, causes Apollon Apollonovič to change the topic of this talk with his son. When Nikolaj Apollonovič returns to his room after the unsuccessful talk, he winds up the clockwork of the delayed-action bomb destined for his father.

All this is the *reality* which occurs in this chapter. Now, the author bestows as much attention upon the *mental processes* related to the reality depicted in the chapter. The Flying Dutchman with all sails set approaches Petersburg as Nikolaj Apollonovič and the "gospodinčik" are conversing in the wretched dive. The Bronze Horseman also is present at the conversation and then pushes Nikolaj Apollonovič to the villainous act. While musing over the delayed-action bomb in his room, Nikolaj Apollonovič sinks into a delirious and ghastly dream: a dream is an astral journey; he sees someone who in turns happens to be "prepodobnyj mongol", Cronus, "staryj turanec", his father Apollon Apollonovič, and Saturn. Then Nikolaj Apollonovič realizes that he himself is a bomb, blows up and wakes up.

The Flying Dutchman, the Bronze Horseman and "staryj turanec" do not, of course, act on the same footing as Nikolaj Apollonovič or the "gospodinčik". Nikolaj Apollonovič or the "gospodinčik" act on the level of reality; the Flying Dutchman, the Bronze Horseman and "staryj turanec" float on the level of mental processes. All those ill-defined, uncontrollable processes evolving through the subconscious motivate such inconsistencies of the narrative structure as the Flying Dutchman, or the Bronze Horseman or Nikolaj Apollonovič's delirium entitled "Strašnyj sud". Nikolaj Apollonovič's – or perhaps the author's – words speak to this effect:

Петербург, Петербург!
Осаждаясь туманом, *меня ты преследовал: мозговою игрою.*[5]

This *motivation by the subconscious* ensures the "aesthetic status" of all those inconsistencies which then become part of the story. The motivation by the subconscious introduces a *new dimension* into the aesthetic representation. And most likely, the very notion of "mnogoplannost'" means that the destiny of a specific character is represented – at least – from two points of view simultaneously: the "realistic" point of view and the "subconscious" one; the latter is woven into the plot.

This compositional "confusion" seems to convey another meaning in Pil'njak. In his works disparate "patches" lie close to one another, so

[5] Andrej Belyj, *Peterburg*. Roman, 2 vols., Part II (Berlin, 1922), p. 22.

that the main aesthetic effect and interest reside in combining these disparate "patches". The "patches", quite autonomous, form a fairly loose network: any "patch" can yield place to another. In consequence of this looseness, the prose of Pil'njak is, so to speak, a "neutral" medium: most diverse styles and constructions can get along together. He uses the vocabulary and the style of Peter the Great's time; the stylistic manner of old chronicles; the style of a cookbook; official reports, a legislative code, letters, diaries, advertisements, scientific observations; he turns to account journalistic and oratorical style; in *Tret'ja stolica* he even inserts passages, literally copied from Bunin and Vsevolod Ivanov.[6] These works bear the name of novels only for lack of a more adequate term. They represent a sort of literary "inventory".[7] Pil'njak's works lack impermeability ("nepronicaemost'"),[8] so much so that boundaries between individual books tend to vanish. Many episodes of *Golyj god* came integrally from his volume *Byl'ë*; passages from *Golyj god* moved over to *Mašiny i volki*.

This indeterminate capacity (ëmkost')[9] of literary works appears as a principle of construction willingly resorted to at that time. At the end of his *Sentimental'noe putešestvie* Šklovskij reproduces "Rukopis' Lazarja Zervandova". Šklovskij had the same thing printed in another book *Èpilog*. He affirmed that his book *Pis'ma ne o ljubvi* originated by chance, because letters and pages were accidentally shuffled.[10]

So the compositional "confusion" in A. Belyj and Pil'njak offer a marked difference. The elements of *The Bronze Horseman* and – to a lesser degree – *The Queen of Spades* enter into the construction of *Peterburg*. They undergo complete assimilation to Belyj's own style and then emerge as the organic components of the texture in *Peterburg*. That is to say, A. Belyj's style offers a high degree of impermeability: whatever enters into his work undergoes complete assimilation. On the contrary, Pil'njak's prose presents an extremely low degree of impermeability: "patches" and elements from other writers' works enter into his works without any stylistic transformation whatsoever.

So it appears that the actual "mnogoplannost'" requires the representation of subconscious processes. Only this sort of representation can possibly supply a *new dimension* in the verbal construct. This new dimension then motivates broken narrative – the compositional "con-

---

[6]   Vikt. Gofman, *op. cit.*, p. 12.
[7]   *Ibid.*, pp. 9-10.
[8]   *Ibid.*, p. 12.
[9]   *Ibid.*, p. 11.
[10]   *Ibid.*

fusion". Without this "motivation by the subconscious" the compositional "confusion" may become a mere pose, an empty ornamentalism. This situation does not fail to arise in the Serapion Brothers' writings. Apart from certain attempts by Nik. Nikitin and K. Fedin, the Serapion Brothers' prose fiction shuns any form of "psychologism", let alone "subconsciousness". Most frequently the Serapions borrow stylistic manners from either A. Belyj or Pil'njak, avoiding the blunt psychological or ideological motivation proper to these two writers.

"Ornamental style" – which frequently coincides with compositional "confusion" – shows certain noteworthy facets in the works of Nik. Nikitin. Pil'njak may have inspired him in his attempts to adjust and to readjust his creative effort to divers ways of perception, i.e., to modify more or less abruptly his style.

Nik. Nikitin often inserts a *lyrical comment* – a choice and arrangement of words striving for highly emotional effect – opposite the motive of the event depicted or even instead of the motive of the given event. His tale *Rvotnyj Fort* may serve as a relevant basis for illustration.[11]

The lyrical comment betraying the presence of the author creates an emotionally colored setting of the scene, its atmosphere, which after Lubbock one might call "provision of character and energy".[12] This "provision of character and energy" then ushers in the event. For instance, in Chapter VIII Rugaj somewhat treacherously informs Polaga of her husband's being enamored of another woman. Desperate, she gives herself to Rugaj. Now, when it comes to conveying Polaga's despair, the author inserts a lyrical comment:

В голове у Полаги бьется несносное, то – что давно нудилось:
"Ах, так ... ах ... так" ...
Что смотришь там из-под кленового кустика, зайчуха? Счастье твое в овсах. Наше горе по серому кошеному полю, под ночными июньскими небесами.
Тяжело и смутно человечье горе.[13]
Полага наклонилась к Ругаю, разорвала кофту.
– На! Целуй крепче. Все одно.

The device of interweaving the texture of the story with a network of lyrical comments through which the author actively participates in the drama often appears in Nik. Nikitin's works. While introducing the

---

[11]   *Vid.* p. 124 *et seq.*
[12]   Percy Lubbock, *The Craft of Fiction* (New York, 1958), p. 206.
[13]   Nik. Nikitin, *Rvotnyj fort. Rasskazy.* Izd. 2-oe, ispr. i dop. (M., GI, 1926), p. 56.
(The italics are mine.)

author and his – highly emotional – point of view into the story, lyrical comments break the narrative and render it inconsistent. This circumstance may testify to a certain loss of the feeling of the traditional genre: a purely lyrical vein – i.e., the fact of the *author* – mingles with an epic one – i.e., the fact of the *character* in the story. In this connection A. Voronskij said: "[...] теперь прозу пишут стихами, а стихи – прозой."[14]

The author, so to speak, feels *instead* of his characters and thereby he deprives them in his own behalf of those emotions and frames of mind that the characters themselves ought to experience, express and actualize in the story. Here again, one might discover a link between Nik. Nikitin and Pil'njak: the latter tends to transform things in his story into the monologue of the author.

In one of Nikitin's other tales, *Polët*, there occurs such a passage:

Биография их точна, как астрономические выкладки Кеплера.
– ... Когда мы играли детьми ...
– ... Когда мы были в школе ...
– ... Когда мы сидели на одной парте ...
– ... Когда мы учились в университете ...
– ... Когда мы служили в 5-й бригаде и оставляли Брест-Литовск немцам ...
– ... Когда пришла революция ... тут они молчат.
– ... Когда нас забрали в Красную Армию ...
И дальше – уже о дивизионе, о тоске, о красных знаменах, о вечном ветре моей страны, о том – где нет уюта, а только ледяные бугры и снега, о сыром лунном вечере с жестким снегом, когда спотыкаясь о ледяшки возвращались домой Климович и Фирсов.[15]

The narrative material in this excerpt presents a considerable syntactic uniformity. At a certain moment in this jerky enumeration of emotionally significant experiences the two points of view – that of the *author* and that of his *characters* – merge, as indicated by the italicized sequence. Then they part again. This occurs throughout the whole of the tale.

At times, Nik. Nikitin's style approaches that of A. Belyj in its "motivation by the subconscious". For instance in Chapter VII of *Rvotnyj Fort* the author describes a kaleidoscopic delirium attacking the prisoners jailed in the Fort:

[14] A. Voronskij, "Iz sovremennyx literaturnyx nastroenij", *Na Styke* (Moskva-Petrograd, 1923), p. 41.
[15] Nik. Nikitin, *Polet. Povest'* (Berlin, 1924), p. 9. (The italics are mine.)

Тухнут огни. В бреду вспоминают люди неясное.

– Эскадрон! Коли!

– Живи, Митюша, честно …

– Жрать нечего …

– Жидовку одну богатую …

– Именем революции …

– Пустяком живет человек …

Когда луна приходит в одиночные камеры, как невеста на свидание, тогда не уйти от тоски.

Марк Цукер разговаривает с тенью.

– Положим – продал … Дивизии гибнут. Кто просит их гибнуть? Да, продал … Вот на зло продал. Так и надо гибнуть. И я гибну … За идею продал … Слышите, за идею … Не согласен я … Могу я идею?

Марк стучит в мягкие кирпичи.

А в № 8 морской житель, водит, как Беппо сидит на площади … Каменная итальянская площадь. Прожектор-луна крадется вдоль полотняной стены. Но что это – оркестр подымает залу. Подымает … Шум – шум.

Марк стучит.

– Не скажу … Не скажу … К чорту партию! Не согласен … Ничего не хочу.

Шум звенит, что железо.

Монахи дерутся на площади. Красные факелы.

– Именем Христа.

Помертвело у паяца сердце из стружек.

– Ой – не меня, не меня, не меня …

Сейчас лязгнет среди ночи замок, смертельный замок. Потому что прольют холодное, что ледяная вода: не берите вещей, вещей не надо.

– Я продал, я Россию продал. Не надо. Не меня, не меня … Не согласен.

А молитва монахов горда, а молитва торжественна.

– Именем … именем …

In this excerpt isolated motives lie side by side without any immediately perceptible causal link. Most disparate experiences fill the broken narrative so that various semantic planes extend parallel to one another. What attains the perception of the reader is a rhapsody of emotionally charged and disjointed "patches" and of disparate mosaic-like figurations. He must take his stand well back to appreciate the unity of impression which prevails in the picture.

Even so, Nik. Nikitin's style differs from that of A. Belyj in an important respect. However disparate "patches" may be in *Peterburg*, a solidly constructed plot stands as the main unifying principle and "patches" form a functional part of the plot. The destinies of the main

characters spin through states of reality and states of dream. This creates the complexity (mnogoplannost') of the novel. The play with the verbal medium involving the same characters increases this complexity. In Nik. Nikitin complexity is more illusory than real. The author juxtaposes as many various experiences – "patches" – as there are characters, so that each experience pertains to one – secondary – character. "Živi, Mitjuša, čestno" pertains to a greenhorn prisoner. "Židovku odnu bogatuju", to Galka, another jailed malefactor. "Pustjakami živet čelovek", to an old dropsied prisoner. Mark Cuker and still another prisoner also possess their own respective "patches". The complexity is thematic, i.e., the author may have written as many separate stories as there appear "patches". These "patches" do not in any significant degree enter into the plot, meager anyhow. They figure as "ornaments" meant to illustrate the same theme – Rvotnyj Fort – in different stylistic foreshortenings. Moreover they contribute to strengthen the feeling of the unity of the author's personality. On these items too Nik. Nikitin reminds more of Pil'njak than of A. Belyj. A. Belyj creates few characters with many experiences. Nik. Nikitin depicts many characters with few experiences.

Often Nik. Nikitin lets emotionally charged "patches" replace or metonymically convey the motive of event. In Chapter VII of *Rvotnyj Fort* the imprisoned robber Galka attempts to escape from the Fort. His attempt fails and Galka suffers capital punishment. Now, how does the author elaborate this motive? The event itself is not represented, as, say, is the scene of shooting that Pierre witnesses in *War and Peace*. The author lets the context suggest this event. One of the prisoners, Mark Cuker, sees in his mind's eye himself led to his own execution.

Сейчас лязгнет среди ночи замок, смертельный замок. Потому что прольют холодное, что ледяная вода: *не берите вещей, вещей не надо.*[16]

This motive foreshadows Galka's – and not Cuker's – execution. There follows Galka's unsuccessful attempt at flight. And then a motive similar to the previous one – but more sordidly colored – ushers in the motive of Galka's being taken to execution:

Старик, не отвечая, поворачивается к Галке спиной, – и равнодушно, как жирный холощенный кот:
– *Вещей тебе не надо.* А хлеба нету.[17]

---

[16]   Nik. Nikitin, *Rvotnyj fort*, *vid.* footnote 13 of Chapter VII. (The italics are mine.)
[17]   See footnote 16.

Right after this the author points his search-light at another "patch" motive and later adds in a detached manner:

За темным плацем шваркнул выстрел, упал в Свеягу,[18] выплыл и, шелестя травой крутого берега, побежал в лес.
    За первым, догоняя его, мчится второй.

The execution is not depicted but the report of the gun, anthropomorphized, comes and both strikes the ear and catches the eye. The author veils the event by its incidence, or, to be more accurate, the incidence itself acts and reminds one of and ushers in the event.

One may define the position of "ornamental" prose in terms of – at least – two co-ordinates: sense of crisis of the genre and effect of validity. Genre is a certain *conventional* literary category serving as a frame of reference for the aspects of literary works. "The sense of genre is important. Without it words are deprived of a resonator, the effect develops blindly", said Ju. Tynjanov in this connection.[19]

The essential character of literary work is its *artificiality* (in the good sense of the term), i.e., the author's art produces the work; the work is artificial as opposed to natural. The subtle tension between genre (conventional category) and literary work (artificial product) accounts for *literariness*.

Now, the sense of genre weakened in Russian prose after Čexov. The author cared less to construct fictional plots with all their elaborate techniques. The cultivation of the literary hero, a certain idealization of love, the importance attached to landscape, all these and other components of prose fiction lost much of their appeal. The author narrated his own observations, which supposed descriptive details, autobiographic writings, anecdotes and puns. Plotless narration of random scenes, memoirs, chronicles, and epistolary forms had taken the best of it.

At such transitional stage, when the old sense of the genre broke up and the new one has not yet taken root, the boundary between literariness and "non-literariness" grows indistinct or vanishes altogether, so that in the two extreme cases literariness either disappears altogether or everything becomes literariness. This indistinctness of the boundary between literariness and "non-literariness" results from the fact that no new sense of the genre has yet marked the contrast between what is convention and

[18]   *Ibid.*; Svejaga is the name of a river.
[19]   B. Èixenbaum, "V poiskax žanra", *Literatura. Teorija, kritika, polemika* (Leningrad, 1927), p. 292.

artificiality (i.e., what *is* literature and literariness) and what is not.

The trend toward the one extreme found its form in the thinking of the theoreticians of the LEF group. They believed that the resurgence of novels and belles-lettres evidenced *embourgeoisement*.[20] In their thinking fiction should yield place to *document*: reporting, newspaper articles, diary, memoirs. The LEF theoreticians interpreted the focusing on factual material as an epoch-making change in people's comprehension of the world: "high art", "creation", "artistic synthesis" should have faded out to the advantage of utilitarian work.

The trend toward the other extreme affected most strikingly the writings of Pil'njak and, indirectly, such Serapions as Nik. Nikitin and Vsevolod Ivanov. Pil'njak's originality consisted in turning to account the very elements of the crisis. Actually he brought out this sense of crisis with particular force.

Whereas for the LEF people the focusing on document entailed elimination of literariness (convention and artificiality), for the professional writers such as Pil'njak or Nik. Nikitin or Vsevolod Ivanov it represented just another device, a new piece of convention. This focusing on document, or "naked material" (golyj material), peculiarly marked the "ornamental" prose.

Pil'njak did not create a new narrative style, if by creating new narrative style we mean a powerful effort of synthesis, which, so to speak, melts and brings stylistic substances previously disparate into one, individually branded, mass. He applied another method which ensured him originality rather than spirit of innovation. As his narrative texture unfolded, he inserted "unprocessed" stylistic "patches", unbelievably diverse, coming from most various sources. The method vaguely reminds one of centos and Nekrasov's long poems (such as *Komu na Rusi žit' xorošo*). And in order to attain an effect of validity, Pil'njak motivated all these "patches" by the focusing on document, on "naked material". The focusing on document, or on factual material, tends to sharpen the impression of "reality", of "mores" and to discount the impression of literariness. The writer tricks his reader all the more graciously because he "quotes" "documents". The authenticity of this "document", or "naked material" does not absolutely matter. What matters is that the "document", presented to the reader, communicates an *impression* of authenticity. Under these circumstances, a supposed piece of "real life" stands in a contrast to the "literariness" of the work. Such a piece of "real life"

---

[20] Gorelik Abram (A. Ležnev), "Sovremennaja literatura", *Literaturnye budni* (Moskva, 1929), p. 15.

becomes exotic against a "literary" background. Play on this contrast opposing "reality" to "literariness" enhances literary impact.

In Pil'njak this focusing on document holds up entire works. It acquires a structural function. Let me cite one example for the sake of clarity. The title of one chapter in *Golyj god* reads thus:

Глава IV. Кому – таторы, а кому – ляторы
    (Об'яснение к подзаголовку:
        В Москве на Мясницкой стоит человек и читает вывеску магазина: "Коммутаторы, аккумуляторы."
        – Ком-му...таторы, а кко-му...ляторы ... – и говорит: – Вишь, и тут омманывают простой народ! ...)

The chapter consists of several subdivisions, such as: "Provincija, znaete li. – Gorodskie tatory" and "Požar. – Ljatory". Moreover the chapter abounds in "documents" such as: excerpts from private correspondence; a sort of epigraph in the middle of the text; an excerpt from the chapter written by a "loxmatyj popik"; an excerpt from a song; a signboard; titles of books sold at a book-store; notes taken by soldiers during a lecture on politics. The author winds up the chapter repeating the title: "Komu-tatory, a komu-ljatory!" So the whole chapter lodges in a framework of supposed "documents" or "naked material" or "factual material". These "documents" tend to evoke an impression of "real life" and to efface that of "literariness". The use of "documents" such as these:

И солдаты после лекций подавали записки:
    – "А что будет с Гришкой[21] в царствии небесном?" – "Товарищ Лекцир! А што будит с маею женою, если я на фронти буду голосить за есер, а она за Пуришкевича?" – "Прошу тебе об'яснить можно ли состоять вдвух партиев сразу тов. есер и тов. большевиков?" – "Товарищ лекционер! Прошу тебе обяснить при программи большевиков будит штраховаца посев на полях или представляется экспроприация капиталу?" – "Господин товарищ! будут ли освобождаться женщины от восьмичасового дня во время месячного очищения и просим вкратце обяснить биографий Виктора Гюга.
                                                                Тов. Ерзов."[22]

motivates, i.e., renders believable, certain reality and mores just by virtue of their being "documents". The "documents" often elicit comical effect

---

[21] I.e., Griška Rasputin. Boris Pil'njak, *Golyj god* (Moskva-Leningrad, 1929) Chapter IV.
[22] *Ibid.*

because they are written in a curiously illiterate language or jargon. Moreover, the "documents" accentuate stylistic contrast. It grows out of the situation under which the supposedly "practical" language of the "documents" stands out against the "poetical" and "emotional" language stuffing the author's lyrical monologue and highly emotionally colored descriptions.

The same technique of focusing on document, or factual material occurs in Nik. Nikitin and in Vsevolod Ivanov.

In *Rvotnyj Fort* Nik. Nikitin indulges in using such a style when he produces "historical data" about the foundation of the Fort. Here a historian is speaking: he mentions and quotes the "cydulki" – notes – that Catherine the Great supposedly wrote to Lieutenant-General Dondrjukov, the presumed founder of the Rvotnyj Fort. Most likely the author devised these "data" and "cydulki" himself for the purpose of providing the story with a realistic motivation: thus a stamp of historical authenticity validates the story. A similar illusion of historical authenticity arises when the author – for example L. Tolstoj in his novels – "validates" his fictional characters by introducing into the story real historical personalities.

The unfolding of the factual material, that is to say, of the supposedly factual material, opens the course to the aesthetic application of those styles pertaining to official records, minutes, proceedings, transactions, inventories (protokol'nost').[23] Properly used, this "protokol'nost'" turns into a trenchant literary tool. "Protokol'nost'" can motivate any literary construction: the narration in terms of volume, development and succession. Only what is "validated" stands on record. It is up to the reader to intuit the emotional content of the official record and to imagine the living human reality concealed behind this record. The use of laconic *radiograms* in *Courrier-Sud* and *Vol de Nuit* by Antoine de Saint-Exupéry affords an admirable example of this power-packed emotion and poetry.

Whether Nik. Nikitin always used this method with discernment furnishes an occasion for doubt. In his tale called *Noč'*, when summarily describing the breakfast scene in the armored train, he "inventories" the scene as follows:

В классном пили чай: 1) прапорщик Евдокимов, со смятыми погонами – и глаза у него плоские и белые, как доска, 2) генерал

---

[23] Vikt. Gofman, "Mesto Pil'njaka", Collection *Mastera sovremennoj literatury. Bor. Pil'njak* (Leningrad, 1928), p. 25.

Проломов – начальник поезда и 3) жена его – Лида, душистая и хорошо вымытая, – что праздничная икона.

This manner of enumeration reappears farther in a still more curious context:

Сказано было о рассветной мути, о ржавом небе, и рыжей степи и о том, как туман моет камни. А что туман этот не легче камней – об этом еще не сказано. Но это так.
    Об этом сказали броневые, когда проснулись.
    А проснулись они так же, как всегда просыпались.
    Т.-е.:
    1) машинисты давали свисток,
    2) вскакивали дневальные
    3) кто-либо шел помочиться
    4) вестовые бежали на станцию за кипятком и бубликами, а дальше – колесо ползло по заведенному.[24]

Following in the footsteps of Pil'njak, Nikitin to all appearances aims at "ornamentation" through the *stylistic contrast* opposing to one another the sequences of the story. In the second excerpt under consideration the two halves of the passage differ sharply. First, context bears the stylistic mask of a musing melancholy poet. The set of impressionistic images – rassvetnaja mut'; ržavoe nebo; ryžaja step'; tuman moet kamni – convey the representation of an emotion. Then, the context adjust the stylistic mask of a registering clerk. The very fact of itemizing dispels the illusion of literariness at the first stage; at the second, it creates another – supposedly "non-literary" – type of literary illusion. From the point of view of representation, the set of images in the first half of the excerpt and the itemized list of little events in the second contrast with each other as "poetic" effect does with "prosaic".

The more "prosaic" the factual material, the less "poetic" the style: long elaborate sentences, recurring leitmotifs, refrains, all these poetically oriented "ornaments" vanish. In an extreme case the author puts to use the documents of every-day life. So in Nikitin's tale *Polet*, in Chapter VIII, entitled "Dokumenty A. V. Dobroxotova", the life of a suicide is summed up in an itemized list of twenty documents such as food-cards, tobacco-cards, student's matriculation certificate, business trip certificate, letters. And then, the two men who had put themselves to the trouble of reading these scraps, interchanged these remarks:

[24] N. Nikitin, *Noč* in the collection *Bunt. Rasskazy* (Moskva-Petrograd, 1923), pp. 64, 89.

– Всё?

Спросил Климович, мигая от лампы, когда Фирсов свернул в газету пачку.

– Всё. Вот он – весь.[25]

The task of evoking living human reality from these items devolves on the reader.

Vsevolod Ivanov uses a similar method of focusing on documents. He exercises greater restraint in selecting his "factual material". In his novel *Golubye peski*, unlike Nik. Nikitin, he uses the "documents" that motivate an exotic and romantic representation. In epigraph there stand excerpts from a supposed book entitled *Podvigi v poxode protiv Birmana*:

... Орда ринулась в неизвестную пустыню У-Бо. Много дней она шла. Люди, кони и слоны её войск утомились и от утомления даже не могли спать. Смерть и страх приблизились к сердцам. [...][26]

The recitation of incantations acts for the purpose of the same "poetic" – and not "prosaic" – motivation of the story.

In all these cases of "focusing on document" a formally cognitive message – or conative in incantation – loses its initial purpose and performs poetic function.

The purpose of the "ornamental" prose entails, for one, the writer's especial emphasis on bringing out *qualities* characteristic of persons and things. Persons and things will be described or the range of their meaning will be restricted. *Epithets* and *similes* correspond with particular fitness to this "ornamental" purpose. An epithet names the proper quality. A simile compares an object to an image on the ground of a quality common for both the object compared and the image that the object is compared to.

The works of Vsevolod Ivanov – such as his early tale *Sinij zverjuška* [...] (1922), his partisan tales *Bronepoezd 14-69* and *Partizany*, his novels *Cvetnye vetra* and *Golubye peski* – provide the instance of this aspect of the "ornamental" prose. Let us consider the following excerpt from his novel *Cvetnye vetra*, Chapter IV:

В эту ночь дул в Тарбагатайских горах с севера, с далекого моря, синий льдистый ветер. Нёс он запахи льдов и холодил души.

Ныли под ним кедры, били ему в лицо костлявыми и могучими сучьями, хватали за синие волосы и трепали по земле, среди скал и каменьев.

---

[25] Nik. Nikitin, *Polet. Povest'* (Berlin, 1924), p. 44.
[26] Vsevolod Ivanov, *Golubye peski, Sobranie sočinenij*, tom 5 (Moskva-Leningrad, 1929).

И злого, холодного втискивали его в ущелье Исык-Тау, что на Чиликтинской долине – камень широкий и упрямый.

Дул в Тарбагатайских горах синий ветер. А в ущелье Исык-Тау приходил он с запахами кедров, глухих, нечеловеческих болот и необузданный и едкий мял и жёг камни.

А пряталось за камнями двое русских. Прикрывались кедровыми ветками, ноги обложили мхами и молчали, как камни. В эту ночь говорил только ветер, густым и нечеловеческим голосом.

(Сыро дышали камни. Мокрые кедровые ветки не грели. Мох – холодный и жесткий.)

Земля чужая и холодная. Камни чужие, холодные, как эта синяя ночь с синим, льдистым ветром.

Один из беглых – маленький, мягкий – колотил кулаками по камню, ломал ветки, царапал ими тело. Но тело устало и покорно отдавалось ветру, тогда русский ощупывал другого, высокого, жилистого и неподвижного.

Тот, вытянув ноги и руки, лежал за камнем, и только, когда рука маленького щупала лицо, у него яростно сгибались горячие губы.

Утром русские бежали дальше, на юг, камнями.

Ушел ветер, и пахла земля горячими травами. Низко трепыхалось в горных речушках блеклосинее небо, как огромная синяя рыба.

А вершины гор были, как красные утки в синих облаках.

А тело человека просила земля – твердо и повелительно. А душу его просили горы.

Люди же эти, радостно, как хлеб, ели жирные, распадающиеся на губах травы. Но не питала земля, и не было силы двигаться. За кустарники тащили на руках они свое тело. Срывали кустарники одежды, – голыми хотела взять их земля.

Шли русские.

… Схватила с неба земля синюю ночь. Нежно и тепло вздохнули горы …

А еще на другой день ели грибы, били палками шилохвостей в мочажинах. Срывались шилохвости с воды, с хитрым утичьим хохотом, передразнивая горы, спускались в долину.

Никли двое голы, беспомощны и голодны.

А еще шли день. Уже туман в теле, туман – тело слабое и не свое. Манила голая русалка – земля в короне зеленой, с грудью теплой.

Ползли по каменным тропам на юг. В день проползли два рысьих прыжка.

Молчал длинный, жилистый, с твердым, звериным взглядом из-под надвинутых на глаза бровей. Молчал и второй.

А еще в день – на мягкой и рыхлой россыпи отдались земле. Дрогнула радостно россыпь, поползла с горы вниз. Засмеялись переливчато гальки, терлись о людское тело.

Запахло лугами, широкими, хлебными. Проплыла мимо осыпи березка.

А двое – лежали голые, сухие и угловатые – кости. Голыми хотела их взять земля …

In Vsevolod Ivanov's text under consideration there appears a lavish profusion of words indicating *qualities* of both substantives and verbs. Epithets occupy a prominent position. A statistical approach may be taken toward the problem; though rudimentary, it still conveys a certain degree of significance. The text contains 232 declinable words and 85 adjectives, i.e., 36.6% of the total of the declinable words in this text are adjectives – words *naming qualities* attributed to persons and things. There are 130 nouns, i.e., 56% of the total of the declinable words. In other words, for each 1.5 noun there is 1 adjective. Of course, each adjective does not represent an epithet. "Tarbagatajskix" in "v Tarba- gatajskix gorax" performs the function of a logical, specifically geo- graphical, determination. A similar observation also applies to other adjectives: they are "informative" and not "ornamental", i.e., they are not epithets. Allowance should be made for this reservation. None the less, what matters is the signal importance attached to words naming qualities. Epithet holds a distinctive place in this text. One should take into consideration too that *adverbs* modifying a verb fulfill a function equivalent to that of an adjectival epithet: they name the quality of an action, i.e., such words as "nežno" and "teplo" in "nežno i teplo vzdoxnuli gory".

Vsevolod Ivanov's epithets, and speaking more broadly, his imagery elicit vividly *sensuous* effects. The epithets recording *sensuous effects* and particularly those achieving *visual effects of color* characterize the stylistic system of Vsevolod Ivanov. A. Voronskij enumerates the epithets describing Siberia in Vsevolod Ivanov's prose: густой, жирный, теплый, тучный, радостный, медоносный, жизненосный, густопахнущий, тугой, крепкий, смольной, жаркий, красно-оранжевый, синий, упругий, великий, сладостный, острый, стальной, зеленый, бурый, спелый, сладко-пахучий, нежный, тягучий, радужный, кровавый.[27]

In the text that I am analyzing *blue* recurs 9 times. One might almost speak of a "Rhapsody in Blue". *Red* and *green* appear once each. Judging Vsevolod Ivanov, E. Zamjatin refers to Ivanov's "impressionizm obrazov".[28] To interpret one artistic medium in terms of another may prove misleading. Still, Zamjatin's opinion may hold true, insofar as the author apprehends nature and artistic reality through colored surfaces subjectively perceived, applies brightly-colored "dabs", and "paints" out-of-door landscapes, all this in a high key. Vsevolod Ivanov uses

[27] A. Voronskij, "Literaturnye siluèty", *Na Styke* (Moskva-Petrograd, 1923), p. 85.
[28] E. Zamjatin, *Lica* (New York, 1955), p. 197.

more variegated pigments in other places; this excerpt does not so forcefully illustrate the situation.

The epithet "blue" performs fairly divers functions in this text. E.g., in "sinjaja noč'" or "bleklosinee nebo" the epithet appears conventionally ornamental and conforms to a conventionally romantic style. It merely renders explicit the quality implicitly contained in the substantive and therefore does not possess vigorous artistic strength. Its condition changes in the images "sinij l'distyj veter" or "sinie volosy". At the risk of inflating the number of terms transferred from one aesthetic medium to another, we may assimilate this use of the epithet "blue" to an *expressionist* device: the application of the color undergoes a distortion or an exaggeration (as in "sinix oblakax") so that the style carries a sharper emotional impact. So the tendency conduces toward the subordination of the object "ornamented" to the "ornament" itself (i.e., the epithet "blue" in this instance). The "ornament", i.e., the epithet "blue" "infects" the objects which we do not normally expect to be blue. The "ornament" – krasočnyj èpitet – in this instance truly dominates the context stylistically; it communicates such mood as the given "krasočnyj èpitet" may kindle in the reader's mind.

Actually the whole chapter reflects a complex mood. It stands somewhat apart from others. *Cvetnye vetra* is a loosely plotted piece of "bytopisanie" massing divers episodes of the Civil War in Siberia. Now, this chapter does not convey the "plot" of the story: the characters do not appear; no dialogue animates the narrative. Vsevolod Ivanov's manner of reproducing dialogues does not offer any stirring interest. It cannot claim to be an accurate ethnographic "transcription" of popular speech: in *Sinij zverjuška*, Er'ma, the main character, says "ploxa" and "ploxo" in the same breath.[29] Artistically speaking, it scarcely emerges from a certain phraseological monotony and undramatic volubility.

The chapter is, in a sense, a "free motive"[30] the function of which consists in crystallizing the *mood* of the story. It seems to me that J. Steinbeck in the *Grapes of Wrath* similarly "stores" the mood of the story in short, emotionally charged chapters inserted into the body of the unfolding action.

The two starving men are *not* given proper names: the author chooses to leave them unidentified and not to render them more specific than the generic "dvoe russkix". Nature *does* bear proper names: "Tarbagatajskie gory", "uščel'e Isyk-Tau"; "Čiliktinskaja dolina". The purpose seems

---

[29]   *Serapionovy Brat'ja. Al'manax pervyj* (Peterburg, 1922), p. 29.
[30]   *Vid.* p. 123 of this study.

quite clear: the generic appears at a farther remove from the reader's mind than the specific. Here human beings appear generic; nature is specific. Therefore nature forces its presence on the reader's mind more urgently than human beings do. Naming also brings about another aesthetic "by-product": a romantically tinted Oriental exoticism.

Moreover, nature becomes anthropomorphized: "*Nyli* pod nim kedry, bili emu v *lico kostljavymi* i mogučimi suč'jami, *xvatali za sinie volosy...*"; "V ètu noč' *govoril* tol'ko veter, *gustym i nečelovečeskim golosom*".[31] In the last instance, the use of "nečelovečeskim" is quite astonishing: nature (wind), anthropomorphized, refines its "human" quality by appending an "inhuman" epithet.

On the contrary, human beings tend to assimilate to nature, i.e., to objects of nature: "molčali, kak *kamni*"; "Uže *tuman* v tele ..."; "... s tverdym, *zverinym* vzgljadom ..."; "A dvoe – ležali golye, suxie i uglovatye – kosti". Men are crushed by nature. They strive in a losing game, because "... telo čeloveka prosila zemlja – tverdo i povelitel'no". Still worse, "*golymi* xotela vzjat' ix zemlja", i.e., she wanted them utterly humiliated and depersonalized. She keeps at it till men dissolve in nature and establish with nature an impersonal communion, just as beasts, birds, stones and grass. As soon as this dissolution of men in nature is achieved, the picture changes: "Drognula radostno rossyp' [...] zasmejalis' perelivčato gal'ki [...] Zapaxlo lugami, širokimi, xlebnymi. Proplyla mimo osypi berezka". A strong pantheistic mood inspires this picture of Vsevolod Ivanov.

It can be seen that in order to communicate this mood to the reader, the author multiplies and intensifies those ornaments and images that in the picture lend to nature and to objects of nature a character of elementary violence: "sinij l'distyj veter"; "xolodil duši"; "kamni čužie, xolodnye, kak èta sinjaja noč' s sinim l'distym vetrom" and other similar images. The author qualifies his human characters with those epithets and places them in those situations that emphasize their weakness, their dependence on and eventually their surrender to nature: "a prjatalis' za kamnjami dvoe russkix. Prikryvalis' kedrovymi vetkami; nogi obložili mxami ..."; "Ljudi že èti, radostno, kak xleb, eli žirnye, raspadajuščiesja na gubax travy"; "... na mjagkoj i ryxloj rossypi otdalis' zemle".

---

[31]   The excerpt quoted on pp. 67-68 of this study is the Chapter IV of *Cvetnye vetra* by Vsevolod Ivanov in the collection *Partizanskie povesti* (Leningrad, 1932). (The italics are mine.)

III. THE TECHNIQUE OF *SKAZ* IN THE
SERAPION BROTHERS' WORKS

Narrative techniques conform in varying degrees to either of the two functionally different types of narration:

1) "scenic" narration ("die 'szenische' Erzählung");
2) narration proper ("die eigentliche Erzählung").[1]

In the first instance narration serves as a more or less expanded commentarial material binding together elements of dialogue. Dialogue form tends to fulfill the structural function (osnovnoj formoobrazujuščij èlement),[2] whereas narration, as it were, merely links dramatic scenes and thereby provides the epic minimum which prevents the given literary work from turning to pure drama. Here the reader no longer perceives narration as an oral performance. Narration displays distinct written character. It conveys descriptions (for example of nature), characterizations or even philosophic or lyrical digressions. The dramatic and the narrative forms correspond to the "scenic" and "panoramic" presentations of the story.[3] Although the "scene" occupies a less voluminous place than the "panorama" does, it supplies the essential articulation which moves the plot onward in the given literary work. *Madame Bovary* may serve as an example of the well-balanced combination of the "panorama" with the "scene": the first – narration – carries "great spaces of life and quantities of experience";[4] the second – dramatic form – brings about "intensity of life".[5]

In the second instance the *process of oral narration* as such stands in focus, and this process of oral narration forms the dominant component of literary work. Under such circumstances the reader learns the story from the mouth of the narrator motivated for this purpose by the

---

[1] B. Èixenbaum, "Leskov i sovremennaja proza", *Literatura. Teorija, kritika, polemika* (Leningrad, 1927), p. 210.
[2] *Ibid.*, p. 211 *et seq.*
[3] Percy Lubbock, *The Craft of Fiction* (New York, 1958), p. 67.
[4] *Ibid.*, p. 118.
[5] *Ibid.*

author. Focusing (ustanovka) on *telling by word of mouth*, on the *live voice* of the narrator, matters most in such a literary work.

One of the ways of doing so is the *skaz* technique. The author uses this *skaz* technique with a view to setting off the *oral narration* of the person who communicates the story. For this purpose the author selects the proper *lexical* means, he construes the appropriate *syntactical* combinations and he sets the *intonation* in harmony with that of the supposed narrator. This supposed narrator is the subject whose consciousness – whatever the degree of its explicitness may be – both records literary reality and interprets its meaning, estimates it and imparts to it the tonality agreeable to this consciousness' understanding.

Russian authors indulged frequently in viewing the world through the eyes of a rather naive and socially humble person and in describing it with his own words. Puškin's provincial squire Ivan Petrovič Belkin, Gogol''s beekeeper Rudyj Pan'ko, Leskov's "anonymous" narrator of working-class background in *Levša*, Dostoevskij's "poor man" Makar Devuškin, Saltykov-Ščedrin's narrator, all these figures perform a similar function. An abstract and impersonal world assumes a concrete and personally molded shape. And the more the narrator's consciousness is singularized, the more it alters – exaggerating in any imaginable sense – the dimensions of the events and things depicted, eliciting effects of caricature, parody or pathetic experience.

Since *skaz* as an artistic technique demands *direct* speech, the language that the narrator uses acquires an all-pervading force of characterization. While speaking, the narrator betrays his social background, his temperament, his education. In the technique of *skaz*, a peasant, a semi-intellectual, a worker, each of them speaks in an idiom marked by specific social or professional characters.

Moreover the *skaz* practice invariably accentuates *comical* effects. The comical effect attending *skaz* devices results from the fact that, when the writer wants his words to be "palpably felt" – which *is* the very purpose of *skaz* as an oral narrative technique – he reinvigorates them by letting them deviate from and distort the "canonical" literary pattern of language.[6]

As the speaking subject deviates from the norms of written literary language, he adopts other speech habits: a vocabulary colored with unusual dialectal and provincial terms; popular speech and popular etymology; divers jargons; puns and odd syntactic constructions marked

[6] B. Èixenbaum, "Leskov i sovremennaja proza", *Literatura. Teorija, kritika, polemika* (Leningrad, 1927), p. 220 *et seq.*

by bizarre intonations. All these elements, combined, produce comical effect because of their unexpectedness.

This tradition of the comic through verbal effects, traced back to Gogol', rampant in Leskov – such works as *Očarovannyj strannik* or *Levša* – blossoms again in the twenties in the works of the Serapions such as Zoščenko or Vsevolod Ivanov or in the stories of Babel'.

Of course, the comic through verbal effects frequently attends the comic of situations. Either – or both together – may occasion laughter. The motive of a rejected suitor which Zoščenko uses in "Viktorija Kazimirovna" offers nothing particularly laughable. In "Gibloe mesto" the motive of mistaken identities (with the further complication to the effect that the "villain" turns out to be a malefactor of an unexpected kind) *is* funny. Both stories excite laughter by the manner in which the narrator, Nazar Il'ič gospodin Sinebrjuxov – *tells* his stories.

Zoščenko, the most consistent and vivacious practitioner of the comical *skaz* among the Serapions, keeps this purely oral narrative vein throughout many of his works, for example in *Rasskazy Nazara Il'iča gospodina Sinebrjuxova* (1921).

A spice of the grotesque pervades these stories. The term needs qualification. In characterizing Zoščenko's style I use this term with certain reservations. Here is a partial definition of the grotesque from Eixenbaum:

> The style of a grotesque demands that, in the first place, the described situation or event be enclosed into a world – small to the point of fantasticality – of artificial experiences [...], that it be completely fenced off from great reality, from the true plenitude of spiritual life, and in the second place, – that this be done not with either a didactic or satirical purpose, but with the purpose of giving scope to *playing with reality*, to the breaking-up and the free reshuffling of its elements so that usual correlations and connections (psychological and logical) turn out to be not valid in this world built up anew, and any trifle can grow to reach colossal proportions.[7]

A genuine grotesque demands a maximal contrast between very dissimilar styles within the same framework. Moreover, it requires a semantic incommensurability opposing representation to "verisimilitude". It is a kind of aesthetically projected *reductio ad absurdum* which in the reader provokes a sense of alienation from the familiar world. So, in Gogol''s *Šinel'*, the instance of a grotesque,[8] stylistic contrast grows from the alternation of distinct manners of elocution: a comical *skaz* of the

---

[7]   B. Èixenbaum, "Kak sdelana 'Šinel'' Gogolja", *ibid.*, pp. 162-163.
[8]   *Ibid.*, p. 160 *et seq.*

author exploiting divers sound and verbal effects and imitating "ne-brežnuju naivnuju boltovnju"[9] presents a startling contrast with the style of pathetic oratory. The former is to the latter as private friendly chat is to solemn theatrical declamation. The whole construction is topped off – I should rather say artistically over-turned – by the intrusion of an emphatically sentimental and melodramatic declamation.[10] This utter stylistic incommensurability suffices to leave the imprint of the grotesque on the whole story.

Moreover the perspective that Gogol' develops warps hyperbolically all proportions between thematic units. Details are stupendously magnified, so much so that the "reality" – and along with it Gogol''s "realism"[11] – of our everyday experience with its "normal" causal links and its "ordinary" psychological relations breaks down into a fantastic absurd and in its own way consistent world.

The language that the characters speak in the story bears witness of this fantastic world. They do not speak a spontaneous everyday language. It is rather a soulless and impersonal speech of an automaton, of a puppet.[12]

Here may lie the clue to the interpretation of the Šinel' as a grotesque. By means of these theatrical, and even "puppet-theatrical" speeches and situations the author narrows his vision on a *single aspect of life*. The author isolates "some defect" or "ugliness", trivial and accidental.[13] Discarding the universal – the image of universal human nature – the author adopts the particular; emphasizing the latter he misshapes proportion and symmetry, thereby setting in relief the follies and the incongruities of human nature. In this way man stands entirely dominated by a single passion. He appears under the aspect of his limitations; he does not appear under the aspect of the universal. Now, the first is ugly; the second is beautiful and ideal. S. H. Butcher summarized Aristotelian thought on tragedy and comedy in these compact and penetrating terms:

[...] Whereas comedy tends to merge the individual in the type, tragedy manifests the type through the individual. In brief, it may be said that comedy, in unmixed sportive form, creates personified ideals, tragedy creates idealized persons.[14]

[9]   *Ibid.*, p. 158.
[10]   *Ibid.*, p. 157.
[11]   V. Setschkareff, *N. V. Gogol. Leben und Schaffen* (Berlin, 1953), p. 164.
[12]   B. Èixenbaum, "Kak sdelana 'Šinel' Gogolja", *Literatura. Teorija, kritika, polemika* (Leningrad, 1927), p. 158.
[13]   *Aristotle's Theory of Poetry and Fine Art*. Translated and with critical notes by S. H. Butcher (New York, 1951), p. 21.
[14]   *Ibid.*, p. 388.

"Personified ideal" spells – in this context – one-sidedness driven to the extreme. An isolated, exaggerated single quality becomes incarnate in man who thus assimilates to a single-springed puppet. And *this* situation comes fulfilled in the grotesque where the universal or the "natural" – suffers distortion – i.e., hyperbolization of a detail at the expense of the harmonious whole – to the point of reaching ludicrous ugliness. The situation turns out to be ludicrous because there occurs "a transition, a change of mood, resulting in the discovery either of an unexpected resemblance where there was unlikeness, or of an unexpected unlikeness where there was resemblance. There is always a blending of contrasted feelings. The pleasure of the ludicrous thus arises from the shock of surprise at a painless incongruity."[15] In this we discover the polar phenomenon responsible for aesthetic experience: the tension between the "sense of novelty" and the "sense of recognition". I have observed its existence in the technique of *ostranenie*.[16]

Gogol' exploits the "ugliness" of Akakij Akakievič Bašmaškin in this Aristotelian sense of comedy. Moreover, he does so be using his complex play on the *skaz* technique.

The comic in Zoščenko proves to be simpler. His stylistic manner deserves the appellation of the grotesque not because of the world represented but rather because of the unusual twist that Zoščenko gives to his language in his stories.

Zoščenko's characters do not possess sufficient "depth" to develop an "ugliness" to the absurd, which, when done, engenders such a grotesque figure as Akakij Akakievič with his "večnaja ideja buduščej šineli".

Whereas Gogol' achieves the grotesque by juxtaposing and inter-twining several violently contrasting manners of *skaz* Zoščenko's *skaz* unfolds on a single layer: that of the narrative *skaz* of anecdotes.

Nazar Il'ič gospodin Sinebrjuxov lives in a perfectly "normal" three-dimensional world governed by common psychological laws. Nothing particularly grotesque inheres in this world.

The comical effect emanates from the *verbal medium* and not from the representation that the verbal medium comprehends. Let us consider only a very short excerpt from this work. In the introduction Nazar Il'ič gospodin Sinebrjuxov begins to narrate his feats saying:

Я такой человек, что все могу ... Хочешь – могу землишку об-работать по слову последней техники, хочешь – каким ни на есть рукомеслом займусь, – всё у меня в руках кипит и вертится.

---

[15]   *Ibid.*, p. 376.
[16]   *Vid.* p. 40 *et seq.*

А что до отвлеченных предметов, – там, может быть, рассказ рассказать, или какое-нибудь тоненькое дельце выяснить, – пожалуйста: это для меня очень даже просто и великолепно.[17]

This excerpt, although a very small part of the whole, shows that the author means to lend to it an individual "tone" of a spontaneous, slack and muddled oral narration.

Moreover this oral narration creates an irresistibly hilarious impression with the reader because of the character of the language that the narrator "manipulates". It teems with comical "deviations" and "distortions".

The very name of the narrator – Nazar Il'ič gospodin Sinebrjuxov – displays an unexpected character. The "canonical" combination would read "gospodin Nazar Il'ič Sinebrjuxov" in which "Nazar Il'ič Sinebrjuxov" stands as a "primary" word-group, "gospodin" acting as a "secondary" (it does not appear unlawful to adapt Jespersen's terminology to this specific instance).[18] Thus the "canonical" combination would not offer any particularly laughable feature, except the semantic value of the farcical "Sinebrjuxov". "Frustrated expectation" pops up as soon as "secondary" splits the "primary" word-group into two incongruous halves. As soon as the "canonical" pattern breaks up, the "secondary" frees itself from its "canonically" dependent status and enters into a new combination marked by "primary" status and semantic "independence". Then, instead of *one* semantic center (gospodin *Nazar-Il'ič-Sinebrjuxov*) there emerge *two* semantic centers: (1) Nazar Il'ič and (2) gospodin Sinebrjuxov. Hence an effect of unexpectedness, as if the man suddenly cracked asunder: the deadly serious Nazar Il'ič ("Ja takoj čelovek, čto vsë mogu" – "great expectations") facing the irresistibly funny gospodin Sinebrjuxov ("vsë u menja v rukax kipit i vertitsja" – "frustrated expectations"). This "dual personality" of the narrator threads its way through all these stories and accounts for their basic design: the dramatic purpose of the "serious personality" (Nazar Il'ič) is thwarted by the comical phraseology of the "farcical personality" (gospodin Sinebrjuxov).

Such words as "zemliška" in "mogu zemlišku obrabotat'" or "tonen'-koe del'ce" in "kakoe-nibud' tonen'koe del'ce vyjasnit'" leave the imprint of a colloquial spoken language, i.e., they support the oral narrative "dominant" of the excerpt. They contribute to the attainment of this result because of their *expressive* (ėkspressivnyj) "halo".[19] In the word

---

[17] Mix. Zoščenko, *Rasskazy Nazara Il'iča gospodina Sinebrjuxova* (1921) in Zoščenko's *Izbrannye povesti* ("Sovetskij pisatel'", 1937), p. 39.
[18] Otto Jespersen, *Essentials of English Grammar* (London, 1959), pp. 78-90.
[19] B. V. Tomaševskij, *Stilistika i stixosloženie* (Leningrad, 1959), p. 20.

"zemliška" the pejorative suffix -iška ("so značeniem prenebreženija ili snisxoditel'noj ironii")[20] confers a *subjective evaluation* on the word.[21] The same subjective evaluation affects the suffix -ce in the word "del'ce".[22] Both expressive and affective force applies to the adjective "tonen'koe" when the diminutive suffix -en'k- modifies the word.[23]

Words and speech possess different degrees of semantic "commitment". One center of polarization groups "semantically neutral"[24] words and speech, e.g., the word "zemlja" in a sentence such as "mogu zemlju obrabotat'". The other attracts *semantically "committed"* words and speech, i.e., emotionally charged; these words and speech bear a certain degree of "expression" (èkspressija), e.g., "zemliška" in Sinebrjuxov's speech: "... mogu zemliški obrabotat'".

In the first instance the sentence appears to convey nothing beyond its object of communication (although in an artistically intended work a semantically quite neutral speech seems hardly imaginable).[25]

In the second instance in addition to the object of communication the sentence characterizes the *attitude* toward the object of communication. Now, the emergence of the attitude toward the object of communication – endearment, wrath, disdain and other possible attitudes – necessarily brings into the picture a *living concrete* and *strongly characterized subject of speech.*

The confrontation of the two sentences: "mogu *zemlju* obrabotat'" (my hypothetical sentence) "mogu *zemlišku* obrabotat'" (Sinebrjuxov's speech) indicates that nothing is signaled about the speaking subject in the first sentence, whereas the second sentence has a strongly characterized speaking subject indissolubly "committed" to it, owing to this stylistic device of exploiting pejorative suffixes.

Other stylistic devices in this excerpt also reflect the author's purpose to characterize a lively, happy-go-lucky fellow, somewhat glib, rather poorly educated and with a smattering of knowledge. Georgij Gorbačëv describes Sinebrjuxov in terms no less hilarious than those that Sinebrjuxov himself uses in characterizing himself; Gorbačëv unmasks

---

[20] *Sovremennyj russkij jazyk*, ed. by V. V. Vinogradov, *Morfologija* (Moskva, 1952), p. 124.
[21] *Ibid.*, p. 124.
[22] *Ibid.*
[23] *Ibid.*, p. 204.
[24] This expression is from Horace G. Lunt, *Fundamentals of Russian* (New York, 1958), p. 74.
[25] B. V. Tomaševskij, *Stilistika i stixosloženie* (Leningrad, 1959), p. 22.

Sinebrjuxov as a "deklassirovannyj krest'janin, byvšij soldat, čelovek s dušoj lakejsko-meščanskoj".[26]

The phrase "po slovu *poslednej texniki*" is obviously misinterpreted "po *poslednemu slovu* texniki". Zoščenko wrote these stories in 1921, the time when the technological craze set in. And so Nazar Il'ič gospodin Sinebrjuxov pays his tribute of phraseology to the new trend as well as he can. The phrase concretely illustrates S. H. Butcher's interpretation of the Aristotelian view on the ludicrous. A "change of mood" arises from the realization of the fact that an "unexpected unlikeness" supersedes initial "resemblance".

The term "rukomeslo" belongs to popular speech (prostorečie).[27] It appears to derive from two different words: *ruko*delie and re*meslo*. The term "marks" the narrator. Moreover "hands" so emphatically set off ("kakim ni na est' *rukomeslom* zajmus'"; "vsë u menja v *rukax* kipit i vertitsja") may acquire a special significance. Namely, suggesting *gesticulation* which in its turn entertains an illusion of lively oral speech.

Expressive nuances, affecting isolated parts of speech as well as syntagmas and sentences, assume the status of dominant element (formoobrazujuščaja dominanta)[28] and overshadow the object of communication, the representation conveyed by syntagmas and sentences. In Eixenbaum's terminology this means that "form" acts outside "motivation".[29]

Whereas in Gogol' both the representation and the verbal medium are grotesque, in Zoščenko only the verbal medium is grotesque and it is so owing to the continual breaking of the semantically neutral patterns of speech.

Let me also subject to comment an excerpt from the story "Viktorija Kazimirovna" which Zoščenko published in *Serapionovy Brat'ja*, *Al'manax pervyj* (1922). The narrator, Nazar Il'ič gospodin Sinebrjuxov, at war in Poland, fell in love with a Polish girl Viktorija Kazimirovna. Her step-father, a wealthy, decrepit miller, kept secret where he had concealed his treasure. She incited Nazar Il'ič gospodin Sinebrjuxov to try to make the old miller tell his secret. Nazar Il'ič gospodin Sinebrjuxov contrived a ruse:

[26] Georgij Gorbačëv, *Sovremennaja russkaja literatura* ("Priboj", 1928), p. 114.
[27] *Tolkovyj slovar' russkogo jazyka*, ed. by D. N. Ušakov, 4 vols (Moskva, 1935), III, 1403.
[28] B. Èixenbaum, "Leskov i sovremennaja proza", *Literatura. Teorija, kritika, polemika* (Leningrad, 1927), p. 219.
[29] *Ibid.*, p. 220.

И вот придумал я такую хитрость, потому что вижу: красота ее погибает втуне.

Скажу, думаю, старичку, престарелому мельнику, что выселяют из местечка Крево … Он безусловно вынет свое добро … Тут мы и заставим его разделить.

Прихожу на завтра к ним. Сам, знаете ли, бородёнку подстриг, блюзу чистую надел, являюсь прямо-таки парадным женишком.

– Сейчас, – говорю, – Викторичка, всё будет исполнено.

Подхожу к мельнику.

– Так и так, – говорю, – теперь, говорю, вам каюк-компания, завтра выйдет приказ по случаю военных действий выселить всех жителей из местечка Крева.

Ох, как содрогнётся тут мой мельник, как вскинется на постельке.

И сам, как был в нижних подштанниках – шасть за дверь и слово никому не молвил.

Вышел он на двор, а я тихохонько следом.

А дело ночное было. Луна. Каждая даже травинка виднеется. И идёт он приметно, весь в белом, будто шкелет какой, а я за сарайчиком прячусь.

А немец что-то, помню, тогда постреливал. Хорошо. Идёт.

Только прошел он немного, да вдруг как ойкнет.

Ойкнет и за грудь скорей.

Смотрю и кровь по белому каплет.

Ну, думаю, произошла беда – пуля.

Повернулся он, смотрю, назад, руки опустил и к дому.

Да только гляжу – пошел как-то жутко. Ноги не гнёт, сам весь в неподвижности, а поступь грузная.

Забежал я к нему, сам пугаюсь, хвать да хвать его за руку, а рука холодеет и, смотрю, в нем дыханья нет – покойник.

И незримой силой взошел он в дом, веки у него закрыты, а как на пол ступит, так пол гремит – земля к себе покойника требует.

Закричали тут в доме, раздались перед мертвецом, а он дошёл поступью смертной до постельке (sic!) тут и скосился.

И такой в халупе страх настал, сидим и дыханье свое слушать жутко.

Так вот помер мельник через меня и сгинули – аминь во веки веков его деньжонки – капиталом.[30]

One important observation is necessary. For my purpose, I evaluate the characters of narrative form by how close it approaches *oral* spontaneous narration. An element of *stylization* of oral speech colors the *skaz* technique. Zoščenko, however consistent in practising this technique, does not escape this stylization either. Most likely people do *not* talk exactly in this manner. Zoščenko magnifies certain specific characters of popular speech.

[30] *Serapionovy Brat'ja. Al'manax pervyj* (Peterburg, 1922), pp. 10-11.

The lexical means, abundantly scattered throughout this excerpt, lend to the speech of the narrator a distinct expressive (èkspressivnyj) color, i.e., words, becoming "palpable", accentuate the attitude of the speaking subject. Moreover these lexical means "mark" Sinebrjuxov as a possessor of a certain social phraseology[31] which also characterizes the technique of *skaz*.

Terms designated as "colloquial" (razgovornye): ženišok; travinka; sarajčik; skosit'sja; den'žonki; sginuli; prjamotaki.

Terms belonging to "popular speech" (prostorečie): kajuk (kajuk-kompanija is obviously an incongruous distortion of *kajut*-kompanija); šast'; tixoxon'ko; podštanniki; xvat' (as a verbal predicate); pomer; čerez (meaning "because of"); amin'.

Certain terms possess an obsolete nuance (ustarelyj): vtune (which is also bookish); čerez (meaning "because of"); amin'. Obsolete terms, namely church-slavonicisms, in certain literary contexts – in the excerpt under consideration for example – perform a definite stylistic function: they elicit comical effect and thereby linguistically single out the speaking subject.[32]

In addition, words and phrases such as "v nižnix podštannikax", "škelet" (the standard literary term being skelet), "ojknet", also help the context "deviate" from the common literary standard and thereby contribute to give the verbal medium an expressive and comical twist.

From the syntactical point of view, the excerpt likewise bears the stamp of a spoken colloquial and expressive language.

The initial "i vot", a colloquially tinted coördinate phrase, marks transition from the preceding context to the narrated episode and somewhat bluntly recalls the attention of the listeners.

The excerpt is interwoven with parenthetic words, parenthetic phrases and one parenthetic sentence ("parenthetic" not quite successfully translating "vvodnye slova", "vvodnye sočetanija slov", and "vvodnoe predloženie"):[33] dumaju; znaete li; govorju; pomnju; smotrju; da tol'ko gljažu. In extending throughout the narrative material this network of parenthetic expressions the author attains a double purpose. It goes without saying that the author (Zoščenko) does not necessarily reproduce his own personality or his own mental view in the person of the fictitious narrator (Nazar Il'ič gospodin Sinebrjuxov).

[31]   *Vid.* p. 73 of this study.
[32]   All the definitions of the preceding terms are borrowed from *Tolkovyj slovar' russkogo jazyka; vid.* footnote 27.
[33]   *Grammatika russkogo jazyka* (ed. V. V. Vinogradov). Tom I: *Fonetika i morfologija*, Tom II: *Sintaksis* (in 2 parts) (AN SSSR, 1954), II, 2, pp. 142, 148, 163.

On the one hand, the narrator reveals his – frequently emotional – attitude toward and his personal appraisal of the object of communication. Quite naturally, the parenthetic expressions of this type are oftentimes verbal forms of the first person singular since they "mark" the speaking subject. Thus the author makes the reader feel at every turn the presence of a living temperamental – and perhaps somewhat silly – narrator. This circumstance may, incidentally, explain the syntactical status of parenthetic words (vvodnye slova): they indicate the attitude – of evaluation for example – that the speaking subject holds toward the object of communication contained in the sentence; since they do not convey a communication but express an attitude toward the communication held in the sentence, they cannot be syntactically linked with the sentence.

On the other hand, by interspersing his story with parenthetic expressions, the narrator aims ever and anon to engage the attention of the listeners and through his appeals to provoke their response to his communication. No wonder that these parenthetic expressions are verbal forms of the second person plural, since they pertain to addressees. The parenthetic expressions of this type fulfill a function analogous to that of interjections (as "ox" in "Ox, kak sodrognëtsja tut moj mel'nik ..."). They distinctively characterize oral conversational speech.

A still more significant factor in the author's focusing (ustanovka) on lively spoken language is the manner in which he handles *predicative constructions*.

A few times the author resorts to *ellipses*: the verb simply drops out. In the sentence "teper', govorju, vam kajuk-kompanija" the word "kajuk-kompanija" stands as the grammatical subject, "vam", as the indirect object with respect to which the action develops whereas the action itself (the verb) does not show up. Likewise, the sentence "a ja tixoxon'ko sledom" has its verb omitted. Examples of ellipsis also occur in these sentences: "Nu, dumaju, proizošla beda – pulja" and "v nëm dyxan'ja net – pokojnik"; the words "pulja" and "pokojnik" do not link up explicitly with the rest of the sentences. In all these instances the verb or another missing link can easily be retrieved. Now, nothing, perhaps, betokens a spontaneous spoken language more than ellipsis. And the verb slips out most frequently in elliptical constructions because interlocutors immediately understand it from the situation. Ellipsis communicates to spoken language laconism, expressivity, compactness and energy,[34] qualities which, curious fact, exist along with glibness in the speech of Nazar Il'ič gospodin Sinebrjuxov.

[34]   B. V. Tomaševskij, *op. cit.*, p. 267.

Both living oral speech and written language assume meaningful form through the grammatical association of the components constituting the sentence and through word order.[35]

Living oral speech differs from written language by the fact that when the former lacks the grammatical coherence of the latter, it can, in order to compensate for that deficiency, utilize the *intonation*. That is to say, the *variation* of stress, length and pitch respectively and their *relative* position to one another can modify the meaning of the sentence, although the grammatical pattern remains unchanged. So the category of intonation basically represents an *oral, spoken* phenomenon. All these peculiarities pertaining to intonation do not virtually find any representation in writing; punctuation renders them very indifferently. The Serapions indulging in "ornamental" prose – the early Zamjatin, Vsevolod Ivanov, Nik. Nikitin – designed certain experiments in this respect. I do not believe these experiments to be particularly successful.

The ultimate problem that the author tackles when employing the *skaz* technique consists in *imitating the intonation of the oral speech*. The author operates so as to make the reader sense the voice of the narrator. He creates the "postanovka golosa" mentioned already by Leskov.[36]

We should pose the problem in terms of how the intonation affects the communication. In the following sequence syntagmas, pitch and phrase stress can tentatively be distributed in this manner:

a délo / nočnóe bylo // luná // káždaja daže /

travínka vidnéetsja //

"Luna" as it stands in this context and as it appears in a dictionary, performs quite different functions. Here it is a nominal sentence – "odnosostavnoe nominativnoe predloženie".[37] In its dictionary form it is no more than a lexical item. Apart from the context, only *intonation* enables the mere lexical item to bear the name of the subject of thought and maintain the relation of this subject of thought to the given reality.

Let me consider the following sentences: "Ox, *kak sodrognëtsja* tut

---

[35] *Ibid.*, p. 263.
[36] Boris Èixenbaum, *op. cit.*, pp. 224-225, and Vsevolod Setschkareff, *N. S. Leskov. Sein Leben und Sein Werk* (Wiesbaden, 1959), p. 163 *et seq.*
[37] *Grammatika russkogo jazyka* (*vid.* footnote 33), *ibid.*, p. 57.

moj mel'nik, *kak vskinetsja* na postel'ke" or "tol'ko prošel on nemnogo da vdrug *kak ojknet*" (the italics are mine, H.O.).

These colloquial[38] predicative constructions, formed by means of the intensive particle "kak" and the perfective future form of the verb, designate suddenly occurring actions *in the past.*[39] Now this appears to "violate" the semantically neutral pattern.

The perfective present does not indicate whether E^n precedes E^s or not, and when used in its narrowed, nuclear meaning, it intimates that E^n does not precede E^s, and thus its envisaged completion is posterior to E^s: *futurity* [the italics are mine, H.O.] is the most usual meaning of the perfective present...[40]

This "most usual meaning" I believe to be the semantically neutral one. Everything happens as if the speaking subject displaces the speech event back into the past: the actual moment of the speech event yields awhile to the fictitious. Along with this "violation" of the semantically neutral pattern there emerges an *expressively* (èkspressivno) colored attitude of the speaking subject toward the object of communication. In speech this expressively colored attitude brings about automatically the situation in which the syntagma "kak + perfective future of the verb" (and possible proclitics and enclitics) carries the *intonational cadence* (intonacionnaja kadencija): a sharp rise of the tone, a heavy phrasal stress and a lengthening of the stressed syllable. The tentative pattern is this:

kak sodrognĕtsja   kak ójknet   kak vskínetsja

      ↗ ↘   ↗ ↘   ↗ ↘

And finally let me discuss these predicative constructions: "I sam kak byl v nižnix podštannikax – *šast' za dver'* (1) i slovo nikomu ne molvil"; "Ojknet i *za grud' skorej* (2)"; "Povernulsja on, smotrju, nazad, ruki opustil *i k domu* (3)"; "Zabežal ja k nemu, sam pugajus', *xvat' da xvat' ego za ruku* (4), a ruka xolodeet ..."

In the examples (1) and (4) the predicate is conveyed by *interjectional* expressions derived from verbs. *Šast'*: familiar term of popular speech (prostorečie and familiarno) means "vnezapno vošel, vyšel, probežal".[41]

---

[38] *Tolkovyj slovar' russkogo jazyka* (*vid.* footnote 27), I, 1285, #2.

[39] *Grammatika russkogo jazyka* (*vid.* footnote 33), II, 1, p. 398, § 482.

[40] Roman Jakobson, *Shifters, Verbal Categories, and the Russian Verb* (Harvard University, 1957), p. 6 (E^n stands for "a narrated event"; E^s stands for "a speech event").

[41] *Tolkovyj slovar' russkogo jazyka*, ed. by B. N. Ušakov, 4 vols (Moskva, 1935), IV, 1322.

Xvat': term of popular speech, means "xvatil".[42] These interjectional expressions, used by way of a predicate, mark out an instantaneous past action. They very typically characterize colloquial language and invest it with a strongly *expressive* (expressivnyj) color.[43]

The examples (2) and (3) represent "incomplete sentences" (nepolnye predloženija)[44] in which verbs are missing altogether. They offer a certain analogy with elliptical constructions. Just as ellipses, these verbless "incomplete sentences" emphasize in colloquial speech an expressively rendered energetic action or movement. In (2) the effect of colloquial speech is even enhanced by intensive "skorej" instead of more literary "skoree". These constructions communicate to the narrative a character of dynamically unfolding action.[45]

The more expressively (èkspressivno) colored the given predicative construction, the less precise and definite the meaning. This applies especially to the terms of popular speech.[46] Referring to our examples, we can feel that "*šast'*" means some violent rapid motion but what precise concrete meaning the term represents we do not grasp. The contrast can be felt by comparing "*šast'* za dver'" with "*vybežal za dver'*": in the first instance a general idea of rapid motion (expressively colored) prevails; in the second instance the motion is *named*.

Things happen as if the thickening expressive "halo" surrounding the verbal medium veiled the mental representation of the real phenomenon. Under the impact of expression (èkspressija) the term has its relation to reality weakened. Intonational pattern concomitantly varies with more accentuated expression.

All these observations lead me to assume tentatively that in the *skaz* under consideration there emerge two "poles".

One "pole", more likely to attract *morphological* means of predication, tends to strengthen the relation of predication to reality, thereby elucidating meaning and bringing representation into focus. Then the attitude – namely the emotional one – toward the object of communication tends to disappear and thereby the presence of a *living* narrator is not felt.

The other "pole", more likely to attract *intonational-syntactical*

---

[42] *Ibid.*, IV, 1140.
[43] A. N. Gvozdev, *Sovremennyj russkij literaturnyj jazyk*. Part I: *Fonetika i morfologija*; Part II: *Sintaksis* (Moskva, 1958), I, pp. 400-401.
[44] *Grammatika russkogo jazyka* (ed. V. V. Vinogradov). Tom I: *Fonetika i morfologija*; Tom II: *Sintaksis* (in 2 parts) (AN SSSR, 1954), II, 2, p. 88.
[45] *Ibid.*, pp. 102-104.
[46] B. V. Tomaševskij, *Stilistika i stixosloženie* (Leningrad, 1959), pp. 21, 22.

(intonacionno-sintaksičeskie)[47] means of predication, lends an expressive (èkspressivnyj) color to the object of communication, thereby emphasizing the *attitude* toward this object of communication. Then the relation of predication to reality tends to weaken, meaning grows elusive and representation comes out of focus. *Spoken oral word* then captures the attention of the reader, thereby emphasizing the *presence of the living narrator*.

The technique of *skaz* emerges from the tension between these two "poles".

Limitations due to the very principle of this technique restrict the range of its aesthetic effectiveness.

There are two aspects of this *skaz* principle. First, a *definite phraseology* "marks" the narrator. Second, a *sole point of view* apprehends reality. Aesthetic effectiveness of *skaz* depends, it appears, directly on the narrowness of both the phraseology reproducing reality and the point of view apprehending this same reality. As both the phraseology and the point of view narrow, the gap between the "sense of novelty" and the "sense of recognition" with the reader widens; which accounts for aesthetic impact on the reader. Now, "narrowness of phraseology" in the given contextual situation means practically that the author limits the number and restricts the diversity of the verbal means to the quantity necessary for an adequate characterization of the narrator. The "pure" *skaz* technique prevails insofar as the narrator, endowed with a definite phraseology and a distinct point of view, stands as the *sole* intermediary between literary reality and the reader. The author may or may not motivate the narrator. In Zoščenko's *Rasskazy Nazara Il'iča gospodina Sinebrjuxova* the narrator is motivated by a footnote.

If the author exceeded the quantity of verbal means necessary to characterize the narrator, he would contravene the principle underlying the *skaz* technique. In such an instance the predominance of *one* phraseology and *one* point of view would vanish.

World, things and persons are, in their mimesis, reduced to a common phraseological denominator in a "pure" *skaz* representation. Things are adapted to phraseology (Zoščenko); phraseology is not adapted to things (as in Puškin). The narrator re-shapes the world in the terms prompted in his case by his social, psychological and occupational background.

This situation stands out in relief when the narrator comes to rendering

---

[47]   *Grammatika russkogo jazyka, vid.* footnote 44, II, 1, p. 82.

the *dialogue* carried on between the characters of his story. In the style of *skaz*, dialogue does not at all characterize the interlocutors, as, for example, it does in L. Tolstoj's novels. It still less performs a dramatic function, as in drama. The speech that the characters use carries the narrator's – and not their own – expression (èkspressija) and style, for the obvious reason that all dialogues are conveyed by and woven into the texture of the *narrator's monologue*. In Zoščenko's story that I have analyzed the narrator – Nazar Il'ič gospodin Sinebrjuxov –, reproducing the speeches of other characters, simply puts his own phraseology, his own speech twist into their mouths, so that different characters share common features of speech. The old miller, Viktorija Kazimirovna, ensign Lapuškin and the old general, all of them speak an identically colored expressive language which does not characterize them individually. Even the raven, for want of human language, exhibits the same – anthropomorphized – attitude in his conduct as Sinebrjuxov does in his speech:

[...] только, смотрю сверху на меня ворон спускается.
Я лежу живой, а *он может думает, что я падаль* и спускается.
Я на него тихохонько шикаю.
– Ш, – говорю, – *пошел, провал тебя возьми*.
Машу рукой, а *он, может быть, не верит* и прямо на меня наседает.[48]

The narrator's style completely absorbs the speech peculiarities of the characters bustling about in the story. Therefore characters do not possess any "depth" with Zoščenko; the expression (èkspressija) of the narrator divests them of all speech individuality. This observation can also apply to the other stories of Zoščenko.

A still more enlightening example we find in Leskov's *Levša*. The anonymous narrator of the "legend" (as the author calls his story) comes from the milieu of Tula working folk. The narrative wears the corresponding expression. Here again the narrator reproduces all the dialogues himself through his own voice. It is not always clear when the narrator speaks himself and when he reports other characters' speech: the characters' dialogues and the narrator's monologue do not sharply contrast with one another syntactically and such parenthetic words as "de", "govorit" add to confusion.[49] As for lexical means, they are identical in both the narrator's monologue and the characters' dialogues. Therefore the czar, the "donskoj kazak" Platov, the Englishmen, the left-handed smith himself and the armorers of Tula, all of them wield an

---

[48] *Serapionovy Brat'ja. Al'manax pervyj* (Peterburg, 1922), p. 17.
[49] V. V. Vinogradov, *O jazyke xudožestvennoj literatury* (Moskva, 1959), p. 124.

identically colored and "distorted" speech.[50] They all etymologize foreign words so as to assonate them with Russian words, thereby eliciting in-congruous effects of pun.[51] They equally infringe on"canonical" literary pattern when speaking. This "deviation" from the linguistic standards proper to the educated turns out to be particularly unexpected in the case of the czar and his entourage.

This "legend" also presents interest from another angle. The "point of view" of the *narrator* – the fictitious Tula laborer – does not pre-dominate throughout the whole story. From Chapter IV on there slips in the "point of view" of the *author*, i.e. of Leskov himself.

Each of these two "points of view" – that of the narrator and that of the author – shows in a distinct "syntactical design" and a distinct "intonation".[52] The shift from one "point of view" to another manifests itself clearly in Chapter VI.[53] The author's literary narrative, more or less ironical, as well as the style of a moralizing commentator enframe the actual *skaz* of the "non-literary" narrator. This dynamic inter-relation, binding the two "points of view" and blending the two verbal spheres, forms the aesthetic purpose of the story. Because the two "points of view" undergo changes in their interrelation, the function and the significance of the *skaz* varies throughout the story. Although at the initial stage in the story the illusion of a narrator may prove complete, it turns out soon that the lively oral speech of a simple-minded narrator is but a conventional form of the author's, i.e., Leskov's narrative. Whereas Zoščenko does not usually dispel the illusion of an actual narrator, Leskov chooses to do so. Leskov sweeps away this illusion of an autonomous narrator and under such circumstances *skaz* turns into somewhat ostentatiously applied "humorous quotation",[54] incidental in the author's speech.

At this point the limitation of the *skaz* technique betrays itself. In exploiting the *skaz* technique the author purposes to create the character of a narrator coherent and valid in terms of stage impersonation (sceni-českij obraz). And insofar as focus is on rendering the verbal medium "palpable", the author "violates" the literary "canonical" pattern of speech by resorting to the phraseology of an unsophisticated narrator. Now, in order that the effect of coherence and validity attend upon the

---

[50]   *Ibid.*, p. 126.
[51]   *Ibid.*, p. 126 and Vsevolod Setschkareff, *N. S. Leskov. Sein Leben und Sein Werk* (Wiesbaden, 1959), p. 165.
[52]   V. V. Vinogradov, *op. cit.*, p. 128.
[53]   V. V. Vinogradov, *op. cit.*, p. 128.
[54]   V. V. Vinogradov, *op. cit.*, p. 128.

mentioned stage impersonation, the "point of view" of the narrator must predominate. As soon as the author introduces his own "point of view" the effect of coherence and validity attendant upon the stage impersonation of the narrator is destroyed. Then the reader does not believe any longer that the oral narrative, as a whole, flows from the mouth of a living narrator. The reader does not feel the actual presence of the latter. And the *skaz* material itself, however expressive (èkspressivnyj) or linguistically peculiar, enters as any other component, into a broader literary construct and performs most various functions. In the instance of *Levša* the *skaz* material, perhaps I should rather say the would-be *skaz* material, frequently becomes an object of an ironical verbal overplay by the author.

Zoščenko's instance pertinently exemplifies how the technique determines the genre. He most consistently uses the *skaz* technique, i.e., the phraseology and the "point of view" of the narrator completely predominate. In order to render the verbal medium "palpable" the author shapes an unsophisticated narrator – Nazar Il'ič gospodin Sinebrjuxov. Now, an unsophisticated narrator apprehends world, persons and things in an unsophisticated way. The complexity of relations and the manifold significance of thought cannot permeate his mind. They filter into his mind ludicrously simplified. Or, trivial notions pop into his mind absurdly exaggerated. But in both instances the mechanism remains the same: the mind distorts the proper scale of things. So, Nazar Il'ič gospodin Sinebrjuxov speaking about one miserable gun – morskaja pušečka Gočkis – says: "*Germanii* ona dosaždala".[55]

Such a narrator, by definition, sees neither far nor deep. Complex literary constructs cannot reach the reader through the sole mind and the sole phraseology of a Nazar Il'ič gospodin Sinebrjuxov because a Nazar Il'ič gospodin Sinebrjuxov's mind cannot grasp complex relations and manifold significance of thought, which a large literary construct involves.

Therefore the pure *skaz* flourishes in smaller genres such as *anecdotes*. No wonder that Zoščenko with his unadulterated *skaz* succeeds best in *short anecdotes*, only formally connected by the same narrator.

As soon as literary construct extends, the "point of view" of the author must needs interfere in order to sharpen the myopic vision of the unsophisticated narrator. But then the character of the narrator in the story loses its autonomy and its validity. The narrator *helps* the author tell the story but he no longer tells it himself. So it happens in Dostoev-

[55] *Serapionovy Brat'ja, vid.* footnote 48, p. 13.

skij's *Besy*. The narrator of this novel – "G-v" – turns into "living italics".[56]

The *skaz* technique, widely practised in the early twenties, is but one of the possible ways in which writers solved the problem of the narrative form and that of narration. A full account of this technique should include not only Gogol' and Leskov, but also such a "natural" writer as Dal' or such an "ethnographic" author as A. Mel'nikov-Pečerskij. Moreover the same strain of *skaz* threads its way through the tales of Remizov, Zamjatin, the sketches of Prišvin and the writings of the Serapions Vsevolod Ivanov, Fedin and Nik. Nikitin.

[56] Il'ja Gruzdev, "Lico i maska", *Serapionovy Brat'ja. Zagraničnyj Al'manax* (Berlin, 1922), p. 228.

PART THREE

THE REPRESENTATION

IV. THE PROBLEMS OF CHARACTERIZATION

"Characterization" is one of those notions that show at what a dis-advantage the literary scholar stands when attempting to define literary concepts. We currently manipulate a fairly ponderous apparatus of critical terminology. We resort frequently to such terms as "description", "incident", "character", "dialogue" and many others in our literary study of a text, as if all these terms expressed unalloyed limpid elements. They do not, of course. Henry James said in this connection:

[...] I cannot imagine composition existing in a series of blocks, nor conceive, in any novel worth discussing at all, of a passage of description that is not in its intention narrative, a passage of dialogue that is not in its intention de-scriptive, a touch of truth of any sort that does not partake of the nature of incident, or an incident that derives its interest from any other source than the general and only source of the success of a work of art – that of being illus-trative. A novel is a living thing, all one and continuous, like any other organism, and in proportion as it lives will it be found, I think, that in each of the parts there is something of each of the other parts. [...] What is character but the determination of incident? What is incident but the illustration of character?[1]

However, we cannot but use these rather fluid terms, for want of any more adequate.

The term of characterization, spontaneously, suggests the devices em-ployed for the purpose of shaping human persons in literary work. These devices pertain either to the description of how men act in their environ-ment, or to what men say and how they say it.

It seems convenient for my purpose to view the problem from two different angles. On the one hand, characters affect the theme and the fable. They maintain a relation to history and to life. It matters to find out what personality types fill the works of the Serapion Brothers. On

[1] Henry James, "The Art of Fiction", *The Portable Henry James* (New York, 1956), pp. 404-405, pp. 391-418.

the other hand, characters present interest for literary judgment, insofar as they enter into the plot of the given story. Their changing reciprocal relations as well as their own development affect the purpose and the over-all construction of the story. This aspect of the problem of characterization matters even more than the preceding because "*homo fictus*"[2] emerges only in relation to the plot. Lën'ka Panteleev was a Leningrad robber (nalëtčik), famous at the beginning of the NEP period.[3] In relation to history and to life this Lën'ka Panteleev is not of intrinsically literary interest. As a theme of a fable artistically elaborated by the plot, this personality type's life acquires literary value. The actual sordid robber interesting the criminologist becomes the fascinating character of a work of fiction: a Šmerl Tureckij Baraban or a Saša Barin in Kaverin's tale *Konec Xazy*.

The mind of Lën'ka Panteleev, a character of history, remains hidden from the criminologist; it is the major task for the latter to discover the method of seeing through the mind of the former. On the contrary, a Šmerl Tureckij Baraban or a Saša Barin, characters of fiction, have no secret from the novelist, their creator. There lies the difference between the characters of history and life and the characters of fiction. In the world of history there occur accidents and unpredictable circumstances. In the world of fiction everything is purposeful and planned.

1

The "ornamental" short story charged with high-pitched emotional tone was the dominant literary form approximately from 1921 to 1924. During this post-revolutionary period the prevailing themes dramatized in Soviet literature dealt with the events of the Civil War. The characters peopling the literary works of the early twenties contrasted with those which the pre-revolutionary literary tradition had habitually drawn. The pre-revolutionary writers focused their creative efforts on the "upper part" of man. Now, the Revolution was a violent process. It stripped men of their routine attitudes and values. Only basic drives and most deeply rooted cultural universals remained with man. The depiction of the elemental forces of the Revolution (revoljucionnaja stixija) characterized the stories of this period. In these works the biological man emerged

---

[2]   E. M. Forster, *Aspects of Novel* (New York, 1954), p. 55.
[3]   V. Sajanov, "Put' V. Kaverina", which is an introduction to V. Kaverin, *Konec Xazy. Povest'*. Tome I of V. Kaverin's *Sočinenija* ("Priboj", 1930), p. 9.

with more dominating prominence than the socio-cultural. The "lower part"[4] of man was portrayed. The Serapion Brothers' works, in keeping with the literary trend, reflected this curious mixture of romantic pathos and crude naturalism, e.g., such works as *Bronepoezd 14-69, Partizany, Cvetnye vetra, Golubye peski* by Vsevolod Ivanov; *Rvotnyj Fort, Pës, Noč', Polët* by Nik. Nikitin; *Sentimental'noe putešestvie* by Šklovskij; *Čortovo koleso, Šestoj strelkovyj, Komissar vremennogo pravitel'stva, Lavrovy* by Slonimskij.

The Marxist critic Poljanskij blames the Serapion Brothers for ignoring the proletariat on their "large and small canvases".[5] Another Marxist critic Gorbačev objects to their predilection for a purely external description of the Revolution and for the uncomplicated personality types with elementary attitudes and motives.[6] Their criticism contains a grain of truth, although the political bias influencing Poljanskij's and Gorbačev's criticism adds nothing valuable to literary judgment.

The Serapion Brothers possessed enough aesthetic culture not to let ideology crudely interfere with literary performance. In their characterization, i.e., artistic recreation of people, they did not side emphatically with any class. In Nik. Nikitin's *Noč'*, a story about the encounter of two armored trains, both the Whites and the Reds display equal senselessness, cruelty and humanity. Prolomov, the White general, loves Russia in his own way and prays for Russia (in the bath-room), while his wife Lida is unfaithfull to him with ensign Evdokimov, an alcoholic and cynical officer. Sosyx, the Red commissar, spices his revolutionary activity with a dubious love affair with his American secretary. So Nikitin favored neither side.

Many of these stories actually dealt with one or several incidents, related in a hurry, devoid of any serious attempt at a more thorough analysis of characters. Ležnev, referring to works of this period, spoke about "bezgerojnost'" and "èpičeskaja massovost' scen bor'by".[7]

All this crooked and clumsy humanity shuffling around in the Serapion Brothers' stories strikes the reader by a certain flavor of exoticism. One might speak, in this connection, about a thematic *ostranenie*. A certain "specialization" in the painting of characters marks each Brother.

[4] Vladimir Pozner, *Littérature russe* (Paris, 1929), p. 334.
[5] Valer'jan Poljanskij, "Serapionovy Brat'ja", *Voprosy sovremennoj kritiki*, pp. 156-162 (Moskva-Leningrad, 1927), p. 158.
[6] G. Gorbačev, "Serapionovy Brat'ja", *Sovremennaja russkaja kritika (1918-1924)* (ed. Innokentij Oksenov), pp. 63-83 (Leningrad, 1925), p. 66.
[7] Abram Gorelik (Ležnev), "Xudožestvennaja literatura revoljucionnogo desjatiletija", *Literaturnye budni* (Moskva, 1929), p. 254.

Vsevolod Ivanov wrote most conspicuously about peasants and partisans. The Civil War and Siberia served as an exotic background against which these rugged, beastly and brave men fought, loved and died. No idealization prettifies the image of the peasant. Some of these peasants show senseless cruelty and callousness. In *Partizany*, one of the pesants, Anton Seleznev, says:

[...] Ничего нет легче человека [...] убить ... [...] Человека – что его, его всегда сделать можно. Человек – пыль. [...][8]

But the author did not deprive them of all humaneness either. The same peasant, Anton Seleznev, who so easily disposes of human life, professes deep-rooted love for the earth, for his peasant's duties:

– Землю, парень, зря бросать нельзя. Нужно знать, когда её бросить ... – твердо сказал Селезнев. [...] – От Бога заказано землю любить. [...] – Надо, паря, в сердце жить [...]

At times Vsevolod Ivanov somewhat overdraws his pictures of the "philosophizing" peasant. Zoščenko cleverly parodied this both voluble and "simplified" theology in the mouth of the peasant.[9]

An entire lack of "sophistication" characterizes these men. They respond only to immediately perceptible motivation; they do so spontaneously both in good and in evil.

[...] Мозги, не привыкшие к сторонней, не связанной с хозяйством мысли, слушались плохо, и каждая мысль вытаскивалась наружу с болью, с мясом изнутри, как вытаскивают крючок из глотки попавшейся рыбы, [...]

says the author about these peasants.[10] The characters do not reveal their psychological experiences. Or rather they do not know how to do so in a conventional, analytical way. Only an outward, primitive sign of it transpires.

This lack of "sophistication" manifests itself with particular force in matters pertaining to sex. In the Serapion Brothers' works that I mentioned above there is not a single example of "romantic" love. Vsevolod Ivanov's characters shook off the chains of civilization. Perhaps it would be more adequate to say that they had never worn them. They race through an elementally sensuous life, coarser and less civil than the

---

[8] Vsevolod Ivanov, *Partizany* in his *Partizanskie povesti* (Leningrad, 1932), pp. 134-136.

[9] Mix. Zoščenko, "Družeskie parodii", II. Vsevolod Ivanov, "Kruževnye travy", *Literaturnye Zapiski*, 2, p. 9.

[10] Vsevolod Ivanov, *op. cit.*, p. 136.

virile uninhibited peasants of Giono but not as degraded as those of Caldwell. Pozner, another Serapion, did not quite miss the truth when he said about Vsevolod Ivanov that "Son œuvre est la glorification du ventre et du sex".[11] Whereas the pre-revolutionary writers – Pozner remarked – would infect their characters with "noble" diseases such as tuberculosis or insanity, Vsevolod Ivanov willingly let his men come down with diarrhoea or syphilis.

The language that people in the story manipulate conveys their individual characterization. For the purpose of typification the writer selects certain terms drawn from dialects, slang and jargon. He does so with restraint because, insofar as he aspires after literariness, he must not deviate too markedly from the language considered as the literary norm of the period, lest the reader fail to feel the author's writing as art. Now, Vsevolod Ivanov frequently contravenes this principle of good taste. He lapses into linguistic naturalism for linguistic naturalism's sake and not for the sake of individual characterization. His lavishness of manner does not at all compare with Čexov's artistic economy and with the restraint that Čexov exercises in using profanity for the purpose of typification. And still, Čexov's peasants are more humanly convincing in their debasement. In order to realize the difference it suffices to confront two female peasants occupying thematically similar positions: Fekla in Čexov's *Mužiki* and Agrippina in *Cvetnye vetra*. Virtually all Vsevolod Ivanov's peasants, male or female, speak almost continually in this key:

– Батя, опять хороводишься тут? ... Мочи с тобой нету, по волости всей послух – блядун, бают, у те отец-то ... Наложниц завел, хахаль, едрена мышь![12] [...]
– Воспода! ... Да ведь тебе, почесть, шесть десятков – в монастырь надо, душу спасать? ... А он бабу в дом вводить удумал? Мало нас баб-то в дому? Мать-то в гробу переворачивается, поди! ... И диви бы каку ... А то блядь! С каким она солдатом не спала. Митьку возьми! ...
Дмитрий захохотал:
– Приходилось! ... У нас раз-раз – и в дамки ... Жива-а.
– По всей волости, воспода! ... В городе таскалась-таскалась ... В деревню с голодухи приперлась. Всех мужиков испоганила. И телеса-то поганые, голые, почесть, по телу ни волосика. Бабы в бане видели. Позарился тоже на мясо, прости ты меня, владычица и богородица! ...[13]

[11] Vladimir Pozner, *op. cit.*, p. 334.
[12] Vsevolod Ivanov, *Cvetnye vetra*, in his collection *Partizanskie povesti* (Leningrad, 1932), p. 154.
[13] *Ibid.*, p. 168.

The situation reminds one of the anecdote related by C. Coquelin about a mountebank, a peasant and a sucking-pig. A mountebank imitates the squeal of a sucking-pig and reaps applause. A peasant takes it upon himself to squeal as well. He holds a real sucking-pig concealed under his cloak and pinches the beast secretly. The sucking-pig squeals but the peasant is booed. And Coquelin adds:

[...] Le cochon criait fort bien sans doute; mais il criait sans art.
    Et voilà l'erreur du naturalisme: il veut toujours faire crier les cochons.[14]

The utterances quoted from *Cvetnye vetra*, though plausible, characterize more the attitude of the author than they artistically reproduce a type. Vsevolod Ivanov's attitude to "transcribe" reality does not necessarily represent an attitude oriented to art. "Transcript" of reality should not be mistaken for artistic imitation of reality. The former is a bare copy of reality and therefore not art. The latter transcends the bare reality. The artistic imitation gives a reality free of accident and removed from both the transient and the particular. Now, the verbal medium in Vsevolod Ivanov's works often becomes too transient, too particular and too much steeped in accident. Artistic imitation endures owing to its adequately reproducing "the universal element in human life".[15]

The strongly naturalistic approach adopted by Vsevolod Ivanov and other Serapion Brothers resulted from the influence that the depicted reality exerted on the manner in which the writers elaborated their thematic situations. The Civil War unleashed the elemental violence of the mob. Slaughter, putrifying corpses, rape, famine and attendant barbarity became the thematic material *par excellence*. The "rough speech of the millions", as Majakovskij said[16] invaded the central avenues. It undoubtedly affected the post-revolutionary generation of young writers and set the fashion of using substandard forms of language in literature. It was Gor'kij's merit to have reacted against this misuse of the linguistic medium.

The amorous man of three score years referred to in the quotation above is a queer person. Vsevolod Ivanov named him Kallistrat Efimyč and rough-hewed him into one of those truth-seeking peasants whom many a Russian writer made wander all over the wide world in quest of the true "faith". Apparently Ivanov did not quite know what to do with

[14]   C. Coquelin, *L'Art du Comédien* (Paris, 1894), p. 56.
[15]   *Aristotle's Theory of Poetry and Fine Art*. Translated and with critical notes by S. H. Butcher (New York, 1951), p. 150.
[16]   Vladimir Majakovskij, "Kak delat' stixi" (1927), *Polnoe sobranie sočinenij* (Moskva, 1959), t. XII, pp. 81-117; the quoted expression on p. 84.

him. Kallistrat Efimyč does not bask in the naive, quaint and gnomic wisdom of Turgenev's Kas'jan ("Kas'jan s Krasivoj-Meči", *Zapiski Oxotnika*); nor does he evoke the impression of gentle folk poetry as the latter. He does not possess the restless and extravagant mind with which Leskov endowed his "enchanted wanderer", a bird of passage so eager for peregrination and so forgetful of wisdom. He does not struggle in the "metaphysical hysteria" (the term belongs to Berdjaev) as the "bogoiskateli" of Gor'kij whom the latter depicted in his *Ispoved'*. Compared with these and other humble wanderers in the quest after "truth" whom Russian writers portrayed, Kallistrat Efimyč seems only sketchily outlined. He lives with his family persevering in an amorous affair with a woman reputed of easy virtue (described in the preceding quotation). His sons set afloat a rumor about his being a visionary and thaumaturge in order to make profit out of the credulity of the simple people. Then, in company with his ladylove, he leaves his family and happens to join the Red partisans. At the end he settles down to till the land. The motive – doubtless symbolic – of his breaking bread winds up the story. Kallistrat Efimyč may well characterize the searching soul of the peasant who both anxiously and hopefully believes that he finds his "truth" with the Bolsheviks.

We need not read "deeply" Vsevolod Ivanov's stories. His characters do not, it seems, convey any powerful artistic generalization. His stories border upon journalistic reports, vivid, perceptive and somewhat rallying (as the farcical scene in *Bronepoezd 14-69* where the peasant partisans spare no pain to convert a captured American to communism, using, as a last resort, an Orthodox catechism in which the picture of Abraham's sacrificing Isaac with God hanging on the clouds provides the vehicle of communication understandable for both parties). This manner entails the sketchiness of his characters: a few sharp features, exaggeration and no psychological content to give depth to the design. But within these rather narrow limits the characters manifest a refreshing liveliness. They share a revolutionary *élan*. It causes them to strive, and in the fight they display their good manly quality. So Veršinin, the partisan leader in *Bronepoezd 14-69*, accepts sacrifice and danger for the sake of his hope "Budut že posle nas ljudi xorošo žit'".[17] In the fight too they lapse into an icy repellent callousness. An innocent man has just been shot; the executioners are playing cards:

---

[17] Vsevolod Ivanov, *Bronepoezd 14-69*, in the collection *Partizanskie povesti* by Vsevolod Ivanov (Leningrad, 1932), p. 55.

Выпрямил Никитин сухую спину и ровной походкой пошел к амбару.

– Постановление исполнено?

Мужики харчисто сплевывая, играли в карты. Рыжебородый доиграл банк и, тасуя карты, отвечал:

– Ето обязательно!

И, подымая колоду для снимки, спросил:

– Тебе сдавать, Микитин?

– Нет.

– Ладно... Во-от ба-анк!... Четыре керенки! Но кто?[18]

What the Revolution actually is they understand rather vaguely. The author depicts different personality types with varying degrees of political and social awareness. The uncomplicated ones – and these appear most attractive in Vsevolod Ivanov's works – have not substantially outdistanced the brave revolutionary peasant in *Golyj god* who declared that he was enthusiastically supporting the Bolsheviks and the Soviets against the Communists.[19]

The task of leadership, naturally, falls to the men more aware of the end that the Revolution pursues and of the means that it demands. Let me consider the following three characters wielding the revolutionary leadership: Nikita Egoryč Veršinin in *Bronepoezd 14-69*; Nikitin in *Cvetnye vetra*; Vas'ka Zapus in *Golubye peski*. They are more or less tough organizers attempting to impose discipline upon the rebellious and anarchy-ridden peasants. They attempt to channel an elemental outburst of energy so that it may serve political purpose and achieve social efficiency. Humanly, they quite differ from one another.

Nikita Egoryč Veršinin, the chairman of a revolutionary committee, is among these leaders the most "peasant". The author had refashioned this tale throughout its successive editions in order to adjust it to the ideological requirement of the moment. So the character had changed from edition to edition. In early editions, Veršinin's political mindedness does not stand out conspicuously. He draws his motivation for action basically from the intense will to defend the peasant's land from any usurper. He behaves toward his men more like a severe and loving father than the "iron communist". In private life he is even henpecked by his wife.[20]

---

[18]   Vsevolod Ivanov, *Cvetnye vetra, ibid.*, p. 234.

[19]   Boris Pil'njak, *Golyj god*, in his *Sobranie sočinenij*, tom I (Moskva, 1929), p. 221. Vsevolod Ivanov confesses that he himself in his youth was poorly prepared for political activity and, at the outbreak of the Revolution, had a very insufficient political education (*vid., Sovetskie pisateli. Avtobiografii v dvux tomax*, Moskva, GIXL, 1959; t. I, p. 436).

[20]   A. M. Van Der Eng-Liedmeier, *Soviet Literary Characters* (The Hague, 1959), p. 21, note 32.

(This motive disappeared in later editions.[21]) These features give him sympathetic human touch.

Nikitin far more emphatically evokes the image of the "iron communist". This man is a fanatic, presumably a Red Army man, committed to the "cause". His harsh and unrelenting activity enables the peasants to launch an organized revolt against the Whites. In the case of Nikitin the author tried to embody the ideal of the Bolshevik party worker: a rigorist, supremely self-disciplined, hard-driving, exacting toward both himself and his subordinates, imbued with revolutionary ethics which oblige him to employ any means to attain the end. Nikitin does not hesitate to have an innocent man executed if revolutionary expediency so demands: "Kto-to ubil, kogo-to nado ubit'. Ub'ëm!" says he.[22] He vindicates the bloodshed that he prepares saying: "Mne ne nado [i.e., bloodshed]. Ja dlja vsego mira. Poslednjaja krov'".[23] The author makes this character act energetically and speak peremptorily. But on the whole, the author fails to render Nikitin sufficiently convincing. Vsevolod Ivanov succeeds in those characterizations that lie inside the spontaneous world of uninhibited picturesque peasants sprinkled with linguistic *couleur locale*. Therefore, such a character as Veršinin appears artistically rather convincing because he is one of those who belong to this world. Nikitin does not appear artistically convincing: he moves in this world as an alien word mass.

Among these three leaders Vas'ka Zapus is the most "romantic". This Party commissar, a former sailor, succeeds eventually in combining purposeful discipline with his naturally tempestuous daredevilness. His ideological enemies characterize him in these terms:

Сволочь, зверь. Но мечта и огонь. На многие подвиги способен человек. [...] Подвижником ему быть в другие времена.[24]

Even the enemies speak of this strong personality with a tone of admiration. Zapus performs his revolutionary mission with as much initiative and drive as Nikitin. Unlike Nikitin, he wins over the wavering workers to his side also by using his personal charm. There is about his personality a sort of "romantic" recklessness (bessabašnost') which compels people's sympathy and which, by the way, turns the heads of women. Contrary to Veršinin, a solidly married man, and unlike Nikitin, who appears a

---

[21] *Ibid.*, p. 21, note # 32.
[22] Vsevolod Ivanov, *Cvetnye vetra*, vid. footnote 18, p. 233.
[23] *Ibid.*, p. 238.
[24] Vsevolod Ivanov, *Golubye peski* in *Sobranie sočinenij*, t. 5 (Moskva-Leningrad, 1929), p. 186.

frowning man and a confirmed bachelor, Zapus is a philanderer. The reader could hardly expect him otherwise. Olimpiada, the wife of his archenemy Artemij Trubyčev, falls head over heels in love with him. So does Fioza Semenovna, the wife of a local notable. Among them all only Zapus knows firmly what he wants. His philandering and pranks do not divert him an inch from his course and when time comes for him to die, he dies bravely, leader of his men, fighting for his cause literally to the last drop of his blood.

These three characters might create the impression that in them Vsevolod Ivanov attempted to carve the image of the "positive hero", whose cult stands out so prominently in the Soviet literature. The impression would be erroneous. The concept of the "positive hero" as contemplated by the communist thinking derives its origin from the dogmatic view that literary performance must primarily subserve a normative function. Such prototypes of the "positive hero" as Klyčkov in D. Furmanov's *Čapaev* or Levinson in A. Fadeev's *Razgrom* serve as a standard of excellence to be imitated by the reader. The aesthetic design, instead of existing in its own right, must strengthen the convincingness of this standard of excellence. The "positive hero" that Soviet literary critique advocates must be notable for "the preeminence of conscious self-discipline, awareness of the public consequences of every private act, and a capacity to subordinate every personal emotion to the political program of the Party".[25] Insofar as the "positive hero" comes into the world as something more than a still-born stereotype, his prime value resides in the habit of unsparing self-examination resolved into action.

Vsevolod Ivanov's characters – at least in his works of the early twenties – are quite different. The underlying intention in his stories is at variance with that which lies at the root of the cult of the "positive hero". Partisans, peasants and soldiers serve as models for literary representation. The author does not exert any special effort to put into his literary representation an ethical or political norm.

Moreover, the inner psychological tension from which the "positive hero" derives his strength does not affect his characters. In any case Vsevolod Ivanov does not choose to show it. Critics, namely A. Voronskij, labelled this trend in Vsevolod Ivanov's works as "antipsychologism".[26]

[25] Rufus W. Mathewson, Jr., *The Positive Hero in Russian Literature* (New York, 1958), p. 235.
[26] A. Voronskij, "Literaturnye siluèty", *Na styke* (Moskva-Petrograd, 1923), p. 104.

Mixail Slonimskij stood, thematically, to a certain degree, in opposition to Vsevolod Ivanov. Whereas the latter willingly depicted the peasants and soldiers fighting for the Revolution, the former "specialized" in reproducing its waifs and strays. A. Voronskij criticized him saying "The Revolution has turned only one of its sides to him – blood, death and people who had served their time.[27] However, this affirmation holds true only partially. Slonimskij was one of the first "fellow-travelers" who attempted to outline the figure of the communist "positive hero".

In his early stories Slonimskij described the impact that the war and the Revolution had exerted on army men. The war spreads a corrupting influence on the bizarre human fauna bustling about in his stories. For example, his *Čortovo koleso*, *Šestoj strelkovyj*, *Komissar vremennogo pravitel'stva* (all written in 1922) form rather homogeneous thematic series. The officers and soldiers of a regiment battered in actions are idling away their time in their winter quarters. A desolating war, brute and paltry life make these men yield to increasing demoralization. The incidents, asinine and barbarous, occur against this background.

In the story *Čortovo koleso* all officers breathe one characteristic atmosphere – that of demoralization. It determines the behavior of all of them. The officers, with Lieutenant-Colonel Priluckij at their head, seek oblivion in excessive drinking and gambling. Only Priluckij, *pro forma*, professes his faith in the victory of Russia whereas his subordinate, ensign Penčo, openly voices his disbelief. "Čortovo koleso" – the "devil's wheel" – is a sort of very primitive merry-go-round assembled of a sleigh, a beam and a circular revolving platform, which one of the officers, ensign Penčo, set up on the ice-covered pond. This "devil's wheel" links all the characters of the story – Lieutenant-Colonel Priluckij, engineer, ensign Penčo and others – in an ungracious, and eventually, fatal experience. There is a sinister symbolism in that "devil's wheel": their drunken demoralization produced this imbecile entertainment and the latter kills Lieutenant-Colonel Priluckij, officer who sponsored the entertainment.

Плясало по льду, подскакивая и мотаясь, тело подполковника Прилуцкого. А прапорщик Пенчо стоял посредине пруда и крутил колесо.
– Крутись, чортово колесо! Круши черепа! Мели кости! Рви мясо! Полосами сдирай кожу! К чорту! [...][28]

---

[27] Quoted from E. F. Nikitina, *Russkaja literatura ot simvolizma do našix dnej* (Moskva, 1926), p. 222.
[28] Mixail Slonimskij, *Povesti i rasskazy* ("Sovetskij pisatel'", 1937), p. 37.

Such is the senselessly cruel mind of the officers whose demoralization Slonimskij describes.

The atmosphere of demoralization grows even more oppressive in the story *Šestoj strelkovyj*. Four types of service-men enter into collision. First, there appear the "villain" officers of the old school who oppressed with impunity the rank and file reduced by the spirit of discipline to blind obedience. Such is Colonel Budakovič imbued with *esprit de corps* which does not leave him to his very death. He tolerates injustice inflicted upon the rank and file for the sake of preserving solidarity among officers. It is not a time for quarrels, he says, because the discipline in the army is faltering. The reader may infer from the development of the story that when the old regime had collapsed, Colonel Budakovič received the order to establish with the rank and file new relations based on democratic principles. Even at such a crucial moment Colonel Budakovič cannot suppress his *esprit de corps*. Instead of adopting a conciliatory attitude toward the riflemen, he acts and speaks quite irrationally.

> Полковник Будакович взмахнул рукой:
> – Господа стрелки!
> Стихло дыхание.
> – Господа солдаты!
> Стрелки слушали. Полковник Будакович оглядел толпу молча и спросил негромко:
> – Кто сказал: курица?
> И прибавил:
> – Курица – не птица. Прапорщик – не офицер. [...]
> – Господа солдаты! – сказал он. – Ваша очередь спасать Россию! Господа солдаты![29]

Thereupon he sabered to death the rifleman standing next to him.

Lieutenant Taul'berg impersonates the type of officer in a sense opposite to Colonel Budakovič. The latter, speaking to the former, says:

> – Упрямый немец! Хочет, чтобы всё гладко было. Не уговорить.[30]

To the narrowly officer's outlook of Colonel Budakovič Lieutenant Taul'berg opposes another, more comprehensive. In Colonel Budakovič's thinking – in which he makes such a poor showing – whatever serves officerdom is unobjectionable. Lieutenant Taul'berg worries about others' interest too. He is the only one who protests when the officers

[29]   *Ibid.*, p. 56.
[30]   *Ibid.*, p. 44.

appropriate the gifts sent to the rank and file. Unlike all his other equals, he forbids depriving peasants of their chattels for the benefit of the officers. This lieutenant stands firm on his duty and, prompted by his sense of justice, he does not hesitate, even to his own disadvantage, to denounce the unfair treatment of the rank and file. None the less, he behaves even more irrationally than Colonel Budakovič. He is arrested by the latter because of the firm stand that he takes for the ill-treated riflemen; he breaks loose from the guard-room (the author does not say who killed the sentry); he joins another deserter, rifleman Fedosej; he escapes from the deserter's village and thinks to return to his regiment forgetting that he has slumped to the status of a deserter; he appears suddenly at the headquarters of the division; taken for an officer who has joined the Revolution, he is dispatched back to the regiment at the head of a company. Then he commits suicide lest he should be killed by the riflemen of his regiment as an officers' spy. Taul'berg's thoughts sound, at the end, in a minor key:

[...] Жизнь – дремучая, как лес, и страшная, как топь. Не знают люди, как жить нужно. Всё неправильно. И он, поручик Таульберг, неправильный человек. Не стоит сорванный погон человеческой жизни.[31]

Another type of serviceman is represented by the quartermaster Gulida. The two preceding types respect an officer's code of honor, however short-sightedly they may behave. On the contrary, Gulida ignores any code of honor whatsoever. He does not actually fight but abuses his position and sordidly exploits the men at war:

Гулида скопил уже шесть с половиной тысяч и отложил их в банк в Петрограде, чтобы купить по окончании войны дом.[32]

This shifty rascal worms his way into all places and offices; he insinuates himself into unsuspecting people's favor. Gulida, a petty provincial Iago, survives in any predicament, where other worthier men perish. When really forced into an action, he feigns death before he is wounded (in *Komissar vremennogo pravitel'stva*). Gulida exemplifies the type that Nik. Nikitin called "jackals of the Revolution".[33]

And finally there emerges the crowd of rank-and-file soldiers. In the

[31] *Ibid.*, pp. 49-50.
[32] *Ibid.*, p. 40.
[33] N. Nikitin, at the end of the story *Noč*', in the collection *Bunt. Rasskazy* (Moskva-Petrograd, 1923), pp. 59-111.

story under consideration they are riflemen. Slonimskij probably sur-
passes all his fellow Serapions in reconstructing the stark horror of
hand-to-hand fighting in his close-up descriptions. He does not dilute
the intense potency of his picturing by lapsing into exaggerated lyricism
as Vsevolod Ivanov does in his early works. Slonimskij also succeeds
best among the Serapion Brothers in painting the drab and desperate life
of the rank and file, both at the front and in the barracks. An important
autobiographic element is doubtless infused in the works in which he
describes all these experiences. For example, in his story *Gibel'* the
combat rages near the village of Edinorožec, which he also mentions in
his autobiography.[34] The autobiographic elements stand out even more
prominently in his novel *Lavrovy*. The young hero of the novel, Boris
Lavrov, lives through a grueling experience of a fighting man and of a
private in the sixth field-engineer battalion. This battalion took an active
part in the bloody rebellion of 27 February. Now, Slonimskij himself
was a private in the sixth field-engineer regiment in Petersburg when the
Revolution broke out: "I met the Revolution in Petersburg as a soldier
of the sixth field-engineer regiment. The regiment rose in rebellion on
the 27th of February in the morning (half an hour after the riot; the
barracks were located next to ours). Over half of the officers were
killed."[35] So the description of the violence and the duress in Slonimskij's
works must have come from first-hand knowledge.

The rank and file in Slonimskij's writings conveys the image of an
eternal underdog, defenseless against his superiors. This underdog serves
as cannon fodder at war and as a vulnerable scapegoat at peace. The
degrading situation in which the underdog stands continuously breeds
universal brutality, the more savage because it is blind. Woe to him if
he falls into the hands of a man like Kozlovskij, a non-commissioned
officer depicted in the novel *Lavrovy*:

Он всегда радовался всякому ухудшению: это подтверждало его
твердое убеждение в том, что счастливая жизнь невозможна. Горе
тому, в ком он заподозревал мысль о возможности счастья на земле!
Козловский замучивал такого человека всеми способами, какие
только имелись у него. А способов этих у взводного было немало.
[...][36]

---

[34] "Mixail Leonidovič Slonimskij", *Pisateli. Avtobiografii i portrety sovremennyx
russkix prozaikov*. Ed. by Vl. Lidin (Moskva, 1926), pp. 285-286; the reference is
on p. 285.
[35] *Ibid.*
[36] Mix. Slonimskij, *Lavrovy* (Moskva, 1936), p. 60.

In the character of this Kozlovskij, who especially enjoys beating his orderly on the neck with his boots, Slonimskij treats the theme of brutality in literary representation, of – to quote the words of Ivan Karamazov – "naslaždenie istjazaniem bit'ja".

Slonimskij clipped off from his soldiers whatever romantic halo may have glorified other soldiers in other literary works. His soldiers are as far from incarnating the heroic tradition of soldiership as the poles are apart. His soldier weeps, when a shell smashes his hand, not so much with physical pain as because of awareness that he no longer will return to his civilian life of, say, a shoemaker: "– Čem že ja rabotat' budu, bratcy!" says he.[37]

In the works such as *Šestoj strelkovyj* and *Lavrovy* Slonimskij shows the rank and file taking their revenge on their masters. The rebellion is, by way of reciprocity, bloody and senselessly cruel.

2

The critics of the twenties entertained, it appears, contradictory notions of either "psychologism" or "antipsychologism". It was mentioned above that A. Voronskij styled the early works of Vsevolod Ivanov as "antipsychological".[38] He did so with a tone of commendation. Voronskij said: "[...] The reader now is not kept long in the stifling cages of psychologism"[39] and added that the Serapion Brothers were working just in this direction. Six years later, in 1929, Ležnev remarked, also with a tone of commendation, that prose had returned to serious "psychologism".[40]

Both terms – "psychologism" and "antipsychologism" – when scrutinized, prove to be elusive. Just as the term of "characterization", they do not lend themselves to an analysis that would isolate them completely from other categories. In a story, anything said or done – omitted or concealed – in some way tells the mind of both the character and the author. If so, anything can become psychological material. No rigid standard prescribes that one type of word mass does convey "psychologism" and another type does not.

[37] *Ibid.*, p. 114.
[38] *Vid.* p. 102.
[39] A. Voronskij. "Iz sovremennyx literaturnyx nastroenij", *Na styke* (Moskva-Petrograd, 1923), p. 43.
[40] Abram Gorelik (Ležnev), "Xudožestvennaja literatura revoljucionnogo desjatiletija", *Literaturnye budni* (Moskva, 1929), p. 254 *et seq.*

The problem that "psychologism" poses in fiction seems to boil down, speaking very schematically, to determining that upon which the author lays his emphasis in his work. The emphasis may accentuate man acting in his environment and ignore the "atmosphere of the mind"[41] of man, i.e., his inner experience. In this case, one may speak of a low degree of "psychologism". Or, the emphasis insists on blending the external reality with the internal, on weaving the flow of mental experience into daily life (byt). This situation represents a high degree of "psychologism". It attains its abundant fulfillment in L. Tolstoj. Or, finally, the emphasis may be shifted inward, inside the mind. If so, story and plot lose their significance to the advantage of a direct contemplation of mental experience. The inward reality intercepts the outward. The pioneers who added this dimension to prose fiction are obviously Proust, D. M. Richardson and Joyce.

Among the three possible emphases mentioned, the third, it seems, is absent in the Serapion Brothers' works. The Serapion Brothers ignored "psychologism" insofar as this term stands for the "stream-of-consciousness" technique of the modern fiction. They did not render the flow of inner experience pulsating with evanescent sensations. At most, they reported this inner experience in the traditional way: internal reality was projected into a plotted story molding the external world. Inwardness of experience did not matter *per se*. It characterized men acting in their environment at the given moment.

In one of his stories entitled *Sad*, K. Fedin brings out one of the significant features of "psychologism" in prose fiction: the change and the development of the character's mind in the course of time under the impact of incidents. In this instance, the method of the psychological characterization of the hero seems to consist in observing economy of means and exercising restraint.

The author narrates the life of a gardener, Silantij, who had been employing all his living force in cultivating the orchard that his master and himself had planted together. When the Revolution broke out, the master deserted his manor house, his orchard and Silantij. The manor house and the orchard were allocated by the new regime for a children's home. Silantij, vegetating for some time, and unable to adapt himself to the new masters, set the manor on fire.

[41]   Henry James, "The Art of Fiction", *The Portable Henry James* (New York, 1956), pp. 391-418, p. 401.

All the elements of the narrative seem geared to actively shaping the "atmosphere of the mind" with the gardener.

A marked emphasis stresses the significant details of the character's environment, namely, the changing aspect of the orchard. Its birth, its sappy bloom, its blighting, calls forth a response each time from Silantij and thereby unbares his mind. As it were, he has grown into the orchard. The author has obviously to emphasize this "orchard motive" so effectively because these environmental details, as so many barometers, record and predict the "atmosphere of the mind". For example, one significant circumstance illustrating the changing aspect of the orchard arises when the boys break the bough of an old apple-tree: this breaking of the bough decides Silantij to take the final drastic action.

The author constructs the same "external" approach in his sketching the character's appearance and action. In order to describe the character he uses those words and expressions that emphasize the material and palpable aspect of nature. The author does not name an emotion, or does so very sparingly. Here is a part of Silantij's tenor of life:

Он жил как медведь. Зимой тянулась долгая спячка. Вдоль изгороди наносило сугробы снега, и сад был в безопасности от людей, скота, бурана. Силантьева жена с утра до вечера топила печь, и сам он сидел или лежал на печи и ждал весны.

Медленно, грузно перекатывался он с печи к столу, как гранитная глыба, необточенная, безмолвная и холодная.

А когда приходила пахучая весна, гранит неожиданно обретал в себе теплоту и, отогретый, начинал постепенно вливаться в форму, которая покинула его с последним лучом осеннего солнца.

Медведь просыпался вместе с садом...[42]

Not a single word pertains to Silantij's emotions in this excerpt. Appearance and action take over the function of suggesting inward life.

Midway in the story, there is a short scene in which the author depicts the gardener sitting on a bench, motionless and in silence beholding the orchard for a long while:

Потом сел на скамейку и просидел до вечера, не шевелясь, глядя в окно, откуда виден был залитый солнцем неподвижный сад.

А когда стемнело, вздохнул и сказал самому себе:
– Пускай гибнет. Не для кого хоронить...[43]

This short scene divides the whole story into two even parts. The first part is "constructive": the gardener asserts his will to keep cultivating

---

[42]   Konst. Fedin, *Povesti i rasskazy* (Moskva, 1936), pp. 350-351.
[43]   *Ibid.*, p. 357.

the orchard, to resist the change, expecting the return of his former
master. The second part is "destructive": Silantij's will power droops; the
orchard goes to rack and ruin; his hope of seeing the return of his master
collapses. His despair, his inability to adapt himself to the new reality
and his hatred for it motivate the *dénouement* of the story: he sets fire
to his master's manor. Now, the quoted short scene forms the hinge on
which the story turns. Nothing apparently happened as Silantij was
sitting on the bench. And still, just at that moment he broke down
psychologically; there he lapsed from hope into despair. The author
dramatizes this scene most sparingly: only three words – не шевелясь,
неподвижный and вздохнул – possibly signal this inward breakdown.
They stand out against the contextual word mass as verbal sign-posts
pointing discretely to the inner emotional process.

The author intersperses the narrative with significant comments *interpreting* the characters. This method is less dramatic than that of consistently *showing how* they would actualize this comment; namely, it is
not so dramatic as reproducing the characters' monologues and dialogues.
As a matter of fact, the author resorts to all these methods. Quoted
conversations *showing* the characters themselves alternate with the
author's comments *upon* the selfsame characters. For example, at the
beginning, the author comments upon Silantij and his master's reciprocal
friendship in these terms:

Уважали они друг друга, казалось, за немногословие и неуменье
что-нибудь переделывать. У обоих было: сказано – сделано. А
делали оба крепко, основательно, с толком.[44]

There immediately follows a dramatic scene showing both men:

Когда молодой сад принялся, ни работник, ни хозяин не судачили,
а только ходили от деревца к деревцу, щурились на снежную белизну
цветочков, усеявших худые ветки, да исподтишка косились друг на
друга.
    – Должен пойти! – утвердительно спросил хозяин.
    – Отчего ему не пойти, – сторожко согласился работник.[45]

And then there again follows the author's interpretative comment upon
the characters:

Были они тогда оба молодые и сильные и закладывали в этом
саду каждый свою жизнь.[46]

[44] *Ibid.*, pp. 349-350.
[45] *Ibid.*, p. 350.
[46] *Ibid.*, p. 350.

The author uses these conversation scenes sparingly. He does so for two reasons. On the one hand, each dramatic scene, in order to be efficient, requires an adequate preparation. Now, the story is too compact and short to allow extensive word masses to serve as preparation for dramatic scenes. On the other hand, the very purpose of the characterization in this instance demands exiguity of conversation because the gardener and other persons in the story represent taciturn characters.

It is characteristic that the author does not submit to analysis the very working of Silantij's mind. The actual process of Silantij's thinking, his sensory and emotional experiences manifest themselves only in external signs; they are not apprehended from inside. All the elements in the story – such as description of the character's environment; detailing of the character's appearance; commenting upon the character; quoted conversations – converge in order to *suggest* a consistent mental and emotional process. But this mental and emotional process itself does not evolve before the mind's eye of the reader. Fedin avoids saying more about the character than warranted need dictates. He tends to set forth significant details changing in time. Thus he strongly reminds one of Čexov who, in constructing his story, pursues the sole purpose of revealing in that way the inner quality of a character.

Vsevolod Ivanov's writings present a clear contrast to the type of work that I have just analyzed. In Vsevolod Ivanov's stories characters continually speak their minds. However, these works hardly deserve the title of "psychological". "Psychologism" involves a certain complexity of narrative elements the integration of which leads to creating a convincing character of fiction. The novelistic experience of a modern reader has deepened his sense of personality in his evaluating the characters of fiction. He expects a certain degree of continuous correspondence between the outward and the inward world because this correspondence accounts for character-development. The modern reader's taste is, so to speak, both dramatic and epic, i.e., in addition to the gradual disclosure of the character through successive actions, the modern reader wants to *see how* the change occurs in the mind of the character. Butcher remarked pertinently:

[...] The ancient stage furnishes us with no such complete instance of character-development as we have, for example, in Macbeth. It is the peculiar delight of the moderns to follow the course of such an evolution, to be present at the determining moment of a man's career, to watch the dawning of a passion, the shaping of a purpose, and to pursue the deed to its final accomplishment. We

desire not only to know what a man was, and how he came to be it, but to be shown each step in the process, each link in the chain; and we are the more interested if we find that the gradual course of the dramatic movement has wrought a complete change in the original character. [...][47]

The excerpt refers to modern drama but it can apply as well to the art of modern fiction. This "dialectics of the soul"[48] seems desperately missing in Vsevolod Ivanov's works in particular and in the Serapion Brothers' in general. The outward daily reality – however sordid it may prove to be – is not concretely woven into the tissue of man's psychological experience. The prose fiction of Vsevolod Ivanov lies on the level of inefficiently motivated incidents.

This emphasis on *external incidents* – such as death, fight, robbery – to the detriment of their psychological motivation quite typically characterizes the majority of the Serapion Brothers' works. The drawback of this is that it precludes the presence of more complex human types. The latter turn out to be artistically unconvincing and not understandable, if some motivation or some psychological explanation in the literary context does not account for their behavior.

The trend toward operating with unmotivated incidents assumes a particularly marked form in the works of Mixail Slonimskij. Discussing the type of servicemen who appear in Slonimskij's stories, I pointed out their erratic behavior and their incoherent speech.[49] There is little action willed and promoted by the characters depicted. Things and events happen "spontaneously": incidents prevail over their psychological motivation. Erraticism of behavior and incoherence of speech would preserve their artistic convincingness if they flowed from demonstrated or suggested emotional experiences. But Slonimskij does not care to establish this functional connection between behavior, speech and emotional experiences. Therefore his characters have no "depth" and do not "evolve".

Another conspicuous example illustrating this point can be found in Slonimskij's story *Mašina Èmeri*. In this story the author narrates the events through which several persons live together in a small town and in a near-by salt-mine in Southern Russia. Olejnikov, the director of the salt-mine, marries a girl, Franja by name. The marriage, un-

---

[47]   *Aristotle's Theory of Poetry and Fine Art*. Translated and with critical notes by S. H. Butcher (New York, 1951), p. 365.
[48]   A. Skaftymov, "O psixologizme v tvorčestve Stendalja i L. Tolstogo", *Stat'i o russkoj literature* (Saratov, 1958), p. 282, p. 282-294.
[49]   *Vid.* p. 103 *et seq.*

sentimental and matter-of-fact, appears a failure from the very outset'
Franja is a sister of Olejnikov's best friend and old brother-in-arms,
Griša. The latter does not appear in person. The reader learns of him
from the letter that Griša sent to Olejnikov. It turns out that Olejnikov
had an episodic liaison with Franja. Griša, who committed suicide,
explained in his letter his reasons: he was unable to reconcile the ruthless
ideology of the Revolution with his "pity" for human beings. Moreover,
aware of the liaison, he begged Olejnikov to marry Franja who, ever
since their liaison, has been harboring an apparently unrequited love for
cold-hearted Olejnikov. Granting Griša's request without delay, Olejnikov marries Franja but, as the author says

[...] за ужином с Франей разговаривал так, словно это была не
молодая его жена, а служащий конторы.[50]

Franja, out of disappointment, looks for comfort and help from the
painter Ljutyj, her rejected suitor. Not quite aware of what she wants,
she brings Ljutyj to the salt-mine and while they are walking through an
inderground gallery he is accidentally killed. Ljutyj's tragic end gives
rise to the false news of Franja's death. After Olejnikov learns that his
wife has perished in the accident, upon his coming home, he falls into
a faint.

The thematic purpose is to imagine the behavior of a man receptive
only to one kind of motivation, so that all other human attitudes tend to
disappear. As a matter of fact, the author apparently takes pleasure in
emphasizing his hero's "automaton-like" attitudes. Olejnikov impersonates the type of an ideological fanatic absorbed by his technological
ideal and his "builder's complex". The whole story consists of mechanically linked incidents. Those links of motivation that prepare and introduce actions tend to vanish. The very beginning of the story illustrates
the author's drift toward depicting incidents removed from their context
of motivation and emptied of their emotional content:

Утром, в конторе управляющему соляным рудником Олейникову
подали только что пришедшее с почты письмо. Олейников вскрыл
конверт, прочел письмо и сунул его в бумажник. И, как в бумажник,
в кипу других приказов он спрятал приказание: приготовить ему на
завтра к восьми часам утра лошадь для поездки в город.[51]

The letter in question is the one that Griša wrote to Olejnikov before
committing suicide. Not a single detail reveals the dramatic significance

[50]   Mix. Slonimskij, *Mašina Èmeri* (Leningrad, 1924), p. 62.
[51]   *Ibid.*, p. 45.

of this motive for the protagonist of the story. Perhaps it can in life
occur that a man marries his former chance mistress at the written
request of her brother who happens simultaneously to be his friend. And
if the man is business-minded, why not take the peremptory decision to
have the nuptial knot tied at 8 a.m. of the day immediately following
the receipt of his former chance mistress' brother's written request to
marry the lady? The difficulty, of course, does not reside in the fact that
a character, Olejnikov in this instance, depreciates his own marriage to
the level of the most insignificant detail of the daily routine. The difficulty
does not grow out of the character's one-sidedness, it arises from one-
sided representation by the author. This one-sidedness of representation
derives from the fact that the author consistently answers an unwarrantable number of "why's?" inadequately, or does not answer them at all.
Now, when the author answers an unwarrantable number of "why's?"
inadequately, he fails to bind the story stuff in firm causal chains, i.e.,
he does not organize a believable story. The author's unwillingness – or
inability – to answer the "why's?" entails the dislocation of the plot
because he then does not adequately motivate the development of action.
The whole situation in the salt-mine is a case in point. The author
desperately needs some circumstance which would awaken a human
response in inhuman Olejnikov. So he resorts to bizarre, artistically in-
operative means. Franja and Ljutyj come to the salt-mine, only faintly
realizing their purpose. The visit turns into a sort of subterranean sight-
seeing tour. And after the author makes Ljutyj utter cries and admire the
echoes, after he makes him dance an abortive walse hundreds of feet
beneath the surface of the earth, the author has him killed: a block of
salt drops onto the head of Ljutyj and buries him and Ljutyj, not unlike
the operatic devil after carrying out his assigned task, vanishes forever
from the story. Thereupon, the guide who shows Franja and Ljutyj
around the salt-mine, is in such a hurry to impart to Olejnikov the news
of Franja's being killed by a slide that he does not even ascertain whether
she actually perished. Both men – the guide who purveys the ill news and
Olejnikov – display what appears to be supreme self-control. Here is
the scene:

На земле он[52] твердым военным шагом пошел в контору. Бывшему
начальнику партизанского отряда не приличествует скрывать свою
вину.
     Олейников был в конторе.
     Он поднял глаза от бумаг на Белебея, и брови его сдвинулись.

[52]   *Ibid.*, pp. 79-80; the guide Belebej.

– Что случилось?
Белебей отрапортовал по военному:
– Товарищ управляющий, ваша супруга погибла по неосторож-
ности. Произошел обвал. Виновник – я, потому что оставил их
одних на минуту.
– Почему вы ее оставили?
– Надо было передать ваше распоряжение десятнику.
– Тогда вы не виноваты. Она сама виновата. Никто не виноват.
Олейников встал и вышел из конторы.

Again, the author chooses to clip off all emotional response and to
reproduce in the character of Olejnikov a sort of rational automaton.
From that moment on, Olejnikov becomes quite "automaton-like". He
walks home:

[...] Он шагал домой, как автомат, держался прямо, не сутулясь.[53]

Along Olejnikov's path the author arrays environmental details such
as this:

[...] Из ворот следующего домика выскочил огромный белый пес,
распахнул пасть, и, словив муху, побрел назад.[54]

Olejnikov's "march of death" reminds one of another rendez-vous with
death, although the two motives do not absolutely stand any quantitative
or qualitative comparison. When Anna Karenina rambles about town
in her carriage and eventually rides to the railroad station, the flow of
her meditation is continually disrupted by small incidents, such as the
two boys buying ice-cream or the drunken factory worker conducted
somewhere by the policeman. Now, these details weave themselves into
the flow of her meditation and thereby create an extraordinarily convincing illusion of living emotional and reflective process. Nothing of
the kind in Olejnikov's case. Another "why?" remains unanswered. The
environmental details dangle purposelessly, without in any way depicting
or showing or shaping the character of his mind. And then, as a finishing
touch of absurd inconsistency, Olejnikov, upon his coming home, falls
into a faint. By this motive it is revealed that a feeling beyond Olejnikov's
control and stronger than a cold sense of duty attaches him to his young
wife. Now, anything can happen in life: perfectly illogical and inconsistent actions still stand because they are of life. Properly speaking,
they only appear illogical and inconsistent. They do so for the reason
that in life we do not have at our command all the means necessary for

[53] *Ibid.*, p. 80.
[54] *Ibid.*

tracking all motives of people's behavior. On the contrary, everything cannot, i.e., should not happen in a good work of fiction. What action is to life, plot is to fiction – this slightly modified observation of Aristotle's holds true today as well as it did at his time. Plot means a minimum of organization and consistency. And insofar as the convincingness of characters in a high degree depends on that of the plot, a distorted plot engenders distorted characters. This situation arises in *Mašina Èmeri*: the motives, far-fetched, transparent and thrust in too mechanically, distort the plot. Therefore the characters lose their convincingness. It is quite significant that the only live and believable character in the story happens to be Griša, the one who, committing suicide in time, stays outside the plot.

This unconvincingness of the whole impairs another aspect of the story. The two men – Olejnikov and Ljutyj – symbolize opposite philosophies. One is the advocate of technical and economic utilitarianism. The other represents – not too adequately – sensitivity to art and beauty. This antagonism is but dimly figured in the story. Whereas the two opponents do not actually collide upon sentimental ground, they do so upon ideological. The author lets the "utilitarian" win all along the line. However, the unfolding of the plot does not convey this ideological dialogue with sufficient vigor. The author chooses to represent the painter as a feeble and unconvincing advocate of aestheticism. First Ljutyj agrees to paint vapid pictures *lucri causa*. Then he refuses to do so in order to comply with Franja's whim. The ideal of beauty and art is never the driving force of his behavior as technological ideal is for Olejnikov. The author may, of course, pit a weakling against a strong man. But the play becomes unattractive in this case, since the outcome of the play is too obviously determined in advance. Ljutyj is only a pale and abortive figure when compared with Kaverin's Arximedov in *Xudožnik neizvesten*.

This trend toward exiguity of motivation leads to what we may call – adapting professor Roman O. Jakobson's terminology to our purpose – metonymic[55] representation of the character. The author disintegrates the complexity of the depicted personality and its environment and gives a part for the whole. The technique opens an unlimited number of possibilities and derives from a long literary tradition. I need not carry

---

[55] Roman Jakobson and Morris Halle, *Fundamentals of Language*, namely the chapter "The Metaphoric and Metonymic Poles" by R. Jakobson (The Hague, 1956), pp. 76-82, p. 76 *et seq.*

on my investigation beyond E. Zamjatin, the spiritual father of the Serapion Brothers.

E. Zamjatin, probably, goes further than anyone of the Serapion Brothers in this metonymic representation of the characters. He operates by means of synecdoche:[56] some distinct quality, some individual trait or physical detail of appearance signal the whole personality of the character. In his story *Ostrovitjane* (1917) he causticly satirizes certain aspects of English life, such as religious smugness. The author carefully selects some significant detail with each character conceived. He brings it into so sharp a focus that this significant detail bounces into prominence and overshadows the character itself. Thus the significant detail turns into a label, and the label acquires its own existence and metonymically represents its bearer. Mr. D'juli, the vicar of the town in which the story unfolds, announces his presence and evinces his emotion by means of the gold crowns on his teeth. They are eight in number. Zamjatin had been a naval engineer, i.e., an exceptionally good mathematician, before he devoted himself to literary craft. It would be quite in the spirit of Zamjatin's literary technique to draw a diagram showing the correlation between the variation of the number of the gold crowns displayed by Mr. D'july when he grins and the qualitative intensity of his mood.

On a Sunday in March, as Mr. D'juli returns home from church, he witnesses an accident: a car knocks a man off his feet, just in front of Mr. D'juli's house. Mr. D'juli wants to avoid having the injured man carried into his house for medical care but he feels it awkward to evidence such hardheartedness toward an injured fellow creature in the presence of his fellow citizens. Grudgingly, he admits the injured man: *four* gold crowns emerge and his mood drops to +4.

– Несите же в дом! – кричал четверорукий. – Чей это дом? Несите...

Тут только викарий Дьюли очнулся, ответил себе: мой дом, схватился за квадратные башмаки и стал помогать пронести раненого – мимо двери. Но маневр не удался.

– Гелло, мистер Дьюли! – кричал четверорукий джентльмэн. – Ваше преподобие, вы разрешите, конечно, внести его к вам?

Викарий *радостно* показал *четыре золотых зуба*:

– Ах, О'Келли, вы? Конечно же – несите. Эти автомобили – это просто ужасно! Вы не знаете – чей?[57]

---

[56] Vladimir Pozner, *Littérature russe* (Paris, 1929), p. 320.
[57] Evg. Zamjatin, *Ostrovitjane. Povesti, rasskazy, teatr. Sobranie sočinenij*, t. 3 (Moskva, 1929), pp. 9-10.

The injured man – his name is Campbell – stays, taken to bed, for some days in vicar D'juli's house. His presence disrupts the time-table that has regulated the clock-like life of the D'juli family and makes the vicar feel a growing resentment: only *two* gold crowns are displayed and Mr. D'juli's mood drops still lower to +2.

За завтраком миссис Дьюли, глядя куда-то мимо викария – может быть, на облака – вдруг неожиданно улыбнулась.
    – Вы в хорошем настроении сегодня, дорогая... – викарий показал *две золотых коронки*. – Вероятно, ваш пациент, наконец, поправляется?

Mrs. D'juli tells him that the patient, restored, will leave shortly: at once *eight* gold crowns shine forth – the mood shoots up to +8, the maximum on vicar D'juli's barometer.

– О да, доктор думает, в воскресенье ему можно будет выйти...
    – Ну вот и великолепно, вот и великолепно! – викарий *сиял золотом всех восьми коронок*. – Наконец-то мы опять заживем правильной жизнью.[58]

In other circumstances Mr. D'juli's crowns exhibit completely negative intensity of mood, which appears from either the application of a suitable epithet or the meaning attached to the immediate context. The situation arises when anything contravenes those principles that vicar D'juli has expounded in his monumental book *The Precepts of Compulsory Salvation*. O'Kelly, a jovial and somewhat loose Irishman, ever causes vicar D'juli's barometer to sink. At a social gathering at D'juli's, in an atmosphere particularly pleasing to the host, the company is backbiting O'Kelly, when the latter calls in person. The spite of the whole company against O'Kelly culminates in vicar D'juli's laying bare his *two* gold crowns. The mood drops to −2.

Викарий был уже спокоен. Он вновь был автором "Завета Спасения" и *благосклонно показывал золотые коронки*:
    – ... Единственная надежда – на благотворное влияние среды. Я не хочу приписать это себе, но вы знаете – прихожане Сэнт-Инох стоят на исключительной высоте, и я надеюсь, что мало-по-малу даже О'Келли...
    – О'Келли? Да, не правда ли, ужасно? – заволновались голубые и розовые дамы, и быстро закивала футбольно-круглая голова. [...]
    – О'Келли? Ну как же: за кулисами в "Эмпайре" ... Ремингтонистки? Ну ка-ак же! Четыре ремингтонистки... [...] Мистер
[58]   *Ibid.*, p. 18.

Мак-Интош занимал пост секретаря Корпорации Почетных Звонарей прихода Сэнт-Инох и, следовательно, был специалист по вопросам морали...

Вы знаете, я бы таких, как этот О'Келли... – воодушевился Мак-Интош. Но, к сожалению, приговор его остался неопубликованным: обвиняемый явился лично, а приговоры суда по вопросам морали об'являются заочно.

– А мы только что о вас говорили, – викарий показал адвокату *два золотых зуба*.[59]

At another juncture the negative maximum is reached. This negative maximum occurs when, as the author says: "Velikaja mašina vikarija D'juli ostanovilas'."[60] The disaster occurs on account of Campbell: his above-mentioned accident has for a while annihilated the order that leads vicar D'juli to "compulsory salvation". No wonder then that, in view of such threatening development, the vicar cannot smother his resentment in the face of the injured man's unwillingness to co-operate (Campbell does not want to undress lest the D'julis discover that he does not wear any shirt). *Eight* gold crowns emerge and Mr. D'juli's mood toboggans to −8.

[...] Время завтрака – четверть второго – давно уже прошло, и викарий в библиотеке ломал голову над временным расписанием. Если, в самом деле, всё передвинуть на три часа, то обед придется в одиннадцать вечера, а посещение больных – в час ночи. Положение было нелепое и безвыходное. [...] Мистер Дьюли с ненавистью глядел на тяжелый, квадратный подбородок Кембла, упрямо мотавший: нет.

– Послушайте, вы же, наконец, в чужом доме, вы заставляете всех ждать... – Мистер Дьюли улыбнулся, *оскалив золото восьми злых зубов*.[61]

Other characters in the story also have their personalities stamped with some significant detail, although these details do not, perhaps, stand out so "diagrammatically". Among the participants are a pince-nez (Mrs. D'juli), huge square shoes (Campbell), worms (i.e., Lady Campbell's lips which stand for her) and the sky-blue ones and the pink ones (in this case, the color of dresses metonymically represents those who wear them – the ladies).

It would not be difficult to show that Zamjatin employs, with varying degrees of emphasis, the same method of characterization in his other works.

[59] *Ibid.*, pp. 22-23.
[60] *Ibid.*, p. 10.
[61] *Ibid.*, pp. 10-11.

There is something cinematographic about this method. The continual shifting of the depth of field splits up the totality of the picture into small, apparently unrelated, fragments. Zamjatin shallows his depth of field so much so that only those objects appear sharp that lie at the very point on which the camera focused. Everything before or behind this point blurs down. Thus are constructed – I should say "photographed" stories such as *Peščera*, *Mamaj*, to a certain degree *Rasskaz o samom glavnom*.

Nowhere does, perhaps, this "estranging" (ostranjajuščij) mechanism of metonymic representation achieve a more uncanny effect than in Zamjatin's very short story *Drakon*:

Люто замороженный, Петербург горел и бредил. Было ясно: невидимые за туманной завесью, поскрипывая, пошаркивая, на цыпочках бредут вон желтые и красные колонны, шпили и седые решетки. Горячечное, небывалое, ледяное солнце в тумане – слева, справа, вверху, внизу – голубь над загоревшимся домом. Из бредового, туманного, мира выныривали в земной мир драконо-люди, изрыгали туман, слышимый в туманном мире как слова, но здесь – белые, круглые дымки; выныривали и тонули в тумане. И со скрежетом неслись в неизвестное вон из земного мира трамваи.

На трамвайной площадке временно существовал дракон с винтовкой, несясь в неизвестное. Картуз налезал на нос и, конечно, проглотил бы голову дракона, если б не уши: на оттопыренных ушах картуз засел. Шинель болталась до полу; рукава свисали; носки сапог загибались кверху – пустые. И дыра в тумане: рот [...]

Дыра в тумане заросла: был только пустой картуз, пустые сапоги, пустая шинель. Скрежетал и нёсся вон из мира трамвай.

И вдруг – из пустых рукавов – из глубины – выросли красные, драконьи лапы. Пустая шинель присела к полу – и в лапах серенькое, холодное, материализованное из лютого тумана.

– Мать ты моя! Воробьёныш замерз, а? Ну, скажи ты на милость!

Дракон сбил назад картуз – и в тумане два глаза – две щелочки из бредового в человечий мир.

Дракон изо всех сил дул ртом в красные лапы, и это были, явно, слова воробьёнышу, но их – в бредовом мире – не было слышно. Скрежетал трамвай.

– Стервь этакая: будто трепыхнулся, а? Нет еще? А ведь отойдет, ей-Бо ... Ну ска-жи ты!

Изо всех сил дул. Винтовка валялась на полу. И в предписанный судьбою момент, в предписанной точке пространства серый воробьёныш дрыгнул – еще дрыгнул – и спорхнул с красных драконьих лап в неизвестное.

Дракон оскалил до ушей тумано-пыхающую пасть. Медленно картузом захлопнулись щелочки в человечий мир. Картуз осел на

оттопыренных ушах. Проводник в Царствие Небесное поднял винтовку.

Скрежетал зубами и нёсся в неизвестное, вон из человеческого мира, трамвай.[62]

The pity for a freezing little sparrow stands out with a particularly incisive vigor against the background of a bleak foggy "dragon world" which the author depicts in the story.

The strength of such a representation consists in the fact that "*dehumanized*" metonymic means of representation, by sheer contrast, enormously magnify the quality of the *human* response that they convey.

[62] Evg. Zamjatin, *Ostrovitjane. Povesti i rasskazy* (Berlin-Peterburg-Moskva, 1923), pp. 159-160.

V. THE PROBLEMS OF PLOT

Let me first analyze certain terms pertaining to this problem. The discussion is based on B. Tomaševskij's theory of literature[1] as well as on Austin Warren's chapter "The nature and modes of narrative fiction".[2]

First, we wonder what the work is about. We look for its *theme*, i.e., we determine the axis that maintains the unity and the consistency of meaning in the work. The theme in a sense summarizes the whole work – "Понятие темы есть понятие суммирующее".[3]

Three different approaches lead to the comprehension of a work of prose fiction. First – the notion of *fable*. Second – that of *plot*. Third – that of *narrative structure*.

Fable shows what actually happened. What matters from this point of view is a chronological unfolding of events. The period of time that encompasses the totality of events strictly corresponds to its calendar value. The fable as such is not a fact of art. It is, if I may use Warren's expression in a different context, the "raw material" of a fiction work.

Artistic purpose discloses itself on the level of the plot and the narrative structure, i.e., when the author *organizes* his "raw material".

The plot may be defined as the "скрытая форма" of the work (this term is used by Il'ja Gruzdëv, one of the Serapion critics, in a somewhat different context).[4] The plot implies the causal unfolding of the work, i.e., the selection of those reciprocally conditioned and motivated events logically necessary to impel the action onward. It is the interpretation of the meaning – i.e., search for causes and effects – that the story-stuff presumably embodies.

The narrative structure produces the form whereby the reader learns

---

[1] B. Tomaševskij, *Teorija literatury* (Leningrad, 1925), pp. 133-158.
[2] René Wellek and Austin Warren, *Theory of Literature* (New York, 1956), pp. 201-215.
[3] B. Tomaševskij, *op. cit.*, p. 137.
[4] Il'ja Gruzdev, "Utilitarnost' i samocel', *Sovremennaja russkaja kritika (1918-1924)*, ed. by Innokentij Oksenov (Leningrad, 1925), pp. 245-250, p. 250.

the story. It actually implies all the artistic devices at play. These artistic devices are understandable only within the framework of the narrative structure.

A *motive* represents the ultimate element of the narrative structure, i.e., it is any of those indecomposable units the combination of which conveys the thematic unity and consistency of the whole work of fiction. Tomaševskij's and Warren's terminologies betray a certain fluctuation in this respect. We may wonder whether the notion of motive comprehends anything intrinsically different from other categories of work of fiction. What differentiates these categories is our scale of perception which we apply to the narrative structure. Whereas theme binds in unity the whole work of fiction, motives are smaller themes integrated within the work of fiction and binding in unity smaller parts of the work of fiction. Therefore the narrative structure is none other than the totality of motives presented in the very sequence which appears in the book. What consequently matters is the introduction of a given motive at the moment when this motive achieves the greatest aesthetic effect, disregarding the chronological and causal sequence of the same motive.

Confronting the notion of plot and that of narrative structure we discover that the totality of motives functionally falls into two categories: one category includes *bound* motives, i.e., those motives that the development of the plot cannot dispense with. The removal of these motives would break the causal link between events. The other category covers *free* motives. These may incur omission without breaking the causal link between events. They form a part of the narrative structure.

Each motive should perform a definite function within the framework of the narrative structure. The totality of purposes deposited in motives constitutes a system of motivation.

The term *motivation* has two different meanings. On the level of the fable, motivation provides credible reasons for people's behavior. For instance in Kaverin's *Konec Xazy* the episode of Pineta's kidnapping is motivated by the malefactors' will to have him crack the safe for them. On the level of the plot, motivation means that the author uses the same episode for the purpose of constructing the plot. For example, the motive of Pineta's kidnapping contributes indirectly to the fulfillment of the requirement of the theme. The author may have used this same motive in order to give a design of caricature to his story.

A *situation* means relations between the characters of a fiction work at a given moment. Insofar as relations between characters change and evolve, the situation changes and evolves too.

Relations between characters bring into view their conflicting – or concurrent – interests. Each situation gives an account of the *collision* – or the concurrence – of interests at play. An initial situation – *nœud* – originates an antagonism of interests. The struggle results in a collision of these opposing interests and eventually resolves in a final situation – *dénouement*. The more intense the struggle, the greater the *tension* of the situation. The over-all process of struggle bears the name of *intrigue*. The plot may be defined analytically as a complex of intrigues.

How to analyze the Serapion Brothers' works from this point of view? The degree of elaboration in plot construction offers a convenient method of commentary. It would appear logical to commence this study by analyzing those works in which concern for plot construction seems least conspicuous. Then we may focus our attention on the works in which concern for plot construction appears more conspicuous.

It can be observed that the "Eastern" wing of the Brotherhood[5] – Nik. Nikitin, Zoščenko, Vsevolod Ivanov – does not concern itself too eagerly with the problems of plot construction. The "Western" wing[6] – Kaverin, Lunc and Fedin to a degree – takes much deeper interest in these problems of plot construction.

Let me analyze the tale *Rvotnyj Fort* of Nik. Nikitin (the "Eastern" wing of the Brotherhood).

The theme of the tale deals with the destiny of a Soviet northern fort – called Рвотный Форт – during the Civil War, its capture by the enemy and the individual destinies of persons connected with the Fort.

The "ornamental" prose, typical for the period of "revolutionary romanticism", weakened the vigor of articulation in the literary work of that time in general and in plot in particular. "Бытописание" of a peculiar type resulted from this weakening of articulation. Integrating a well-characterized man into the tightly articulated frame-work of a dramatic play did not interest the authors of this "ornamental" prose trend.

Insofar as the plot construction of the *Rvotnyj Fort* is concerned, reciprocal involvements between characters of the tale mark a multifarious pattern. One "triangular" relation involves Puškov, the chairman of the local Soviet, his wife Polaga and Taja Pazova, the girl that Puškov fell in love with ("one-man-two-women" triangle). Another

---

[5]   This expression is quoted from Evg. Zamjatin, "Serapionovy Brat'ja", *Literaturnye Zapiski*, 1 (May 1922).
[6]   See footnote 5.

"triangular" relation: Rugaj, a communist propagandist, and Polaga and Puškov ("two-men-one-woman" triangle). In both cases a love motivation underlies people's actions. This situation, emotionally motivated, merges with another situation required by the life in the Fort, namely Dondrjukov, the commander of the Fort, Katja, the female investigator, Fedja, the barber, prisoners, and others. The author has all these characters converge upon the Fort, which accounts for manifold relations. E.g., the destiny of Rugaj, the communist propagandist, is moving along two lines of motivation. On the one hand, an "ideological" line: his commitment to communist activity, his dialogue with Dondrjukov. On the other hand, a "sentimental" line: his love for Polaga and his abortive fatherhood.

Thus the author depicts a whole original constellation of actors, their reciprocal relations, and endows the actors with quite a pithy and humorous characterization. Weakness discloses itself when it comes to articulating the plot structure: the plot structure fails in the sense of purpose. For instance, Puškov impersonates a character who motivates the lines of conduct of at least three other characters in the story: his wife Polaga, a bourgeois girl Taja, and the communist propagandist Rugaj. Each of these characters "depends" on Puškov. His estrangement for his wife Polaga disrupts the even tenor of her life. His faint romance with Taja must have decided her – at least partially – to tumble into the vortex of the Revolution. Rugaj, eager to win Polaga's heart, succeeds only when her husband's indifference drives her to despair. They are not episodic characters, they are central. Therefore, if the author wanted his plot to prove artistically convincing, he should have shown – once he set them agoing – how the relations between his main characters evolve and how they resolve in a final situation. Now, the problems of plot posed by these relations are not solved. The author let Puškov foment all these disturbances and then cast him light-heartedly back into oblivion. What happened to Puškov-Taja relations? We do not know because Puškov simply vanished from the story without saying good-bye. What befell Rugaj and Polaga? We do not know either since Rugaj as may be presumed, ran away without leaving a trace. Insofar as plot structure is concerned, the author fails to create a convincing illusion of relations between these characters because he eventually handles main characters in an episodic way. Dondrjukov, the self-abusing commander of the Fort, appears to be the only main character in the story who in terms of plot enacts his part consistently to the end.

Among the Serapion Brothers V. Kaverin evinced the liveliest interest for "sjužetnaja proza", i.e., for literary works in which plot constructing is the dominant preoccupation of the author. His very early stories, such as *Odinnadcataja aksioma* (1920), *Pjatyj strannik* (1921), *Ščity i sveči* (1922), *Xronika goroda Leipciga za 18. . god* (1922), *Mastera i podmaster'ja* (1923) and *Bočka* (1923) are works of bewildering fantasy and unrestrained phantasmagory. Rampant experimentation marks these stories. They do have their particular significance, though.

In his autobiographic sketches[7] Kaverin relates how curiously his very first story – *Odinnadcataja aksioma* – came into existence. Preparing his examination in logic, Kaverin, a freshman at the University of Leningrad, acquainted himself with the principles of the geometry of Lobačevskij. He was particularly struck by the fact that Lobačevskij had not accepted the eleventh axiom of Euclid which posits that parallel lines never meet. In Lobačevskij's own system of geometry parallel lines meet at infinity. This geometrical concept inspired Kaverin in concocting his first story:

Лобачевский свёл в пространстве параллельные линии. Что же мешает мне свести – не только в пространстве, но и во времени – два параллельных сюжета? Нужно только, чтобы независимо от места и времени действия между героями была внутренняя логическая связь.

Придя домой, я взял линейку и расчертил лист бумаги вдоль на два равных столбца. В левом я стал писать историю монаха, который теряет веру в Бога, рубит иконы и бежит из монастыря. В правом – историю студента, проигрывающего в карты последнее достояние. Действие первого рассказа происходило в средние века. Действие второго – накануне революции. В конце третьей страницы – это был очень короткий рассказ – две "параллельные" истории сходились. Студент и монах встречались на берегу Невы. Разговаривать им было не о чем, и автор обращался к природе и Петербургу, пытаясь с помощью Медного всадника изобразить всю глубину падения своих героев.[8]

Although immature, the story was awarded a small prize in a literary contest sponsored by *Dom literatorov*.[9] It is significant that the nineteen-year old Kaverin at the very outset of his literary career experimented with the category of time and causality. As his primary means of representation Kaverin adopts a certain organization of time, namely, he dislocates chronological sequences. He disregards the laws of "normal" causality. Now, the sense of "engineering" of time category in literary

---

[7] V. Kaverin, *Neizvestnyj drug. Povest'* (Moskva, 1960).
[8] *Ibid.*, pp. 238-239.
[9] *Sovetskie pisateli. Avtobiografii v dvux tomax*, (Moskva, GIXL 1959), I, pp. 496-498.

representation means sense of plot constructing. So, Kaverin, even before breathing the atmosphere of the "plot-minded" fraternity[10] of the Serapion Brothers, showed his liking for the manipulation of plot. In this respect his literary temperament differed very markedly from that of Zoščenko or Vsevolod Ivanov. Whereas the latter derived their literary dynamism from effects of the verbal medium, Kaverin derived his from the "intellectual" framing of his stories.

There cannot be, in literary creation, any radical opposition between characterization and plot-making. It is the character that produces action. Now, "action-producing" quite obviously enters into the plot. The two notions correspond to the two artistic perspectives in which one and the same creative process is viewed.

The Serapion Brothers do not seem to have always succeeded in keeping both efforts of characterization and efforts of plot-making in equilibrium. Now, a story has a greater artistic value when the two components – convincingly living characters and solidly articulated plot – appear simultaneously, because a greater number of aesthetic elements are integrated.

In one case characterization tends to predominate to the detriment of plot-making. Then, there ensue stories – in fact, more or less extended *anecdotes* – the interest of which lies in the fact that various characters are delineated. Such are, for example, the stories of Slonimskij, Nik. Nikitin or Vsevolod Ivanov. Certain of these stories have been considered elsewhere in the present study. Characters thus depicted are *"flat"* (the term belongs to Forster):[11] they do not evolve psychologically; they lack complexity; they do not change throughout the story. The character is "assembled" around a *single trait* that prevails over everything else. That is why the Serapion Brothers' representations lapse so easily into *caricature*. Earlier in this study[12] an attempt was made to grasp the significance of this hyperbolization of a detail at the expense of the whole.

In another case the purely *experimental* value of plot deprives characters of all verisimilitude. This is particularly true of the early works of Kaverin. In them, characters are but puppets, or even geometrical phantasms which the author's imagination manipulates and arrays in its toying with what Zamjatin called "arxitekturnymi, sjužetnymi massami".[13] More consistently than any other fellow Serapion, Kaverin responded to

---

[10]   *Vid.* pp. 47-49 of this study.
[11]   E. M. Forster, *Aspects of Novel* (New York, 1954), p. 67.
[12]   *Vid.* p. 116 *et seq.* of this study.
[13]   Evg. Zamjatin, "Serapionovy Brat'ja", *Literaturnye Zapiski*, 1 (May, 1922).

Lunc's appeal to learn the art of plot constructing, i.e., to experiment.

In his story *Xronika goroda Lejpciga za 18 . . god* the only real and verisimilar character is the narrator. Even so, the latter is not real in terms of circumstantial verisimilitude: the narrator cannot, obviously, hold council with his own fictitious characters as it happens in this story. The narrator is convincing in the reader's consciousness with his consistent, ironical and bantering *tone* of narration. In such a case characters do not appear for their own sake. The author does not take much interest in producing them as symbols meriting consideration in their own right. He rather displays them as conventional sign-posts which show the way through the labyrinth of plot combinations, and which permit the reader to identify situations in their succession and to tell them from one another, to confront motives and to operate the mechanism of intrigues. In order to feel this preponderance of plot-making concern over characterization, it suffices to compare the above-mentioned story with the later work of the same author, *Xudožnik neizvesten*. In both works Kaverin betrays his liking for "toying" with the plot. The first story shows little beyond rampant experimentation with plot construction and with fusing fantasy and reality. In the second work, in addition, there emerge impressive and convincing characters and not mere logical symbols as in the first story.

This experimentation with plot virtually forced Kaverin to use a purely conventional romantic material devoid of concrete social reality and of realistic motivation believable in terms of circumstantial verisimilitude. Only such abstract material figuring algebraic symbols rather than living characters could enable the author to mold the forms of plot to his fancy, with sudden changes in points of view, in place or time. Such is his collection of stories *Mastera i podmaster'ja* (1923). Since the material represented in the work has its relation to reality distorted, characters live in an artificial world and become utterly grotesque, like the character that has only two dimensions – breadth and height – whereas the third dimension is missing altogether (the story "Inžener Švarc" in *Mastera i podmaster'ja*).

When Kaverin chose to have the relation to reality strengthened in plot-constructing, then, of course, material represented resisted phantasmagory, and imposed limitations on the author's inclination to experiment with the forms of plot.

Such a change in Kaverin's attitude occurred in his tale *Konec Xazy* (1924). In this tale, characters are no longer conventional, in the sense in which are conventional in his previous stories the monk, tormented

students of old, mediaeval scholastics, masters, clowns and soldiers. Likewise, the very conventionally romantic mediaeval Germany yields place to the post-revolutionary Leningrad. Still, Kaverin does not remain immune from a somewhat conventional romanticism of the "lower depths" of the NEP period. This partially accounts for the superficial characterization of the individuals represented.

The analysis of *Konec Xazy* may illustrate the manner in which Kaverin attempts to meet the requirement of plot construction of Western type.

The *Theme*: The decline and the destruction of a gang of Leningrad malefactors.

The *Fable*: A gang of Leningrad malefactors (nalëtčiki) planned a daring robbery: to break the safe of the State Bank. The leader of the gang, Šmerl Tureckij Baraban, wanted the robbery to be carefully organized and smoothly executed entreprise. For that purpose he and his accomplice Saša Barin kidnapped Pineta, a man whom they believed to be a steel specialist thoroughly acquainted with the construction of bank safes. Pineta would, according to their plans, make all the technical contrivances necessary to crack the safe. They committed a blunder in kidnapping Pineta: he was but the namesake and nephew of the true safe specialist. The actual safe specialist Pineta that they were looking for had died.

The gang also lured away a girl stenographer Ekaterina Ivanovna Molotova. They presumably needed her for secretarial work. It appeared soon that the leader of the gang Šmerl Tureckij Baraban took a passionate interest in her. One of the gang, Aleksandr Leont'evič Frolov, who appeared to have gained her love, betrayed her and helped Šmerl Tureckij Baraban abduct her. The gang kept both Molotova and Pineta in confinement in their den.

Before her treacherous abduction Molotova wrote a letter to her former friend Sergej Veselago in which she notified him that she was breaking off her relations with him. Sergej Veselago, a political prisoner, after reading the letter, escaped from his jail and came to Leningrad in order both to wreak vengeance on Frolov and to meet Molotova. He challenged Frolov to a duel and killed him. Two letters put Veselago on the trail of Molotova. He found one in Frolov's pocket-book. The landlady of the house in which Molotova lived showed him the other: the letter was addressed to Molotova and contained an offer of secretarial employment. The same man, namely Tureckij Baraban, wrote both letters. Veselago came to the right conclusion that Tureckij Baraban and

his gang had abducted Molotova. Veselago finally succeeded in finding trace of her. While haunting different saloons he met a prostitute Suška who was connected with the gang of Tureckij Baraban. Suška agreed to help Veselago in coming to the rescue of Molotova. Suška, Veselago and Suška's friend who stayed at the malefactors' den planned Molotova's escape.

While the gang went on a spree on the eve of the safe-breaking, Suška's lover Pjatak, one of the gang, got an inkling that Suška was being won over by another man. He shadowed Suška and Veselago while they were heading for the gang's den to carry out their plan of rescuing Molotova. Pjatak realized that Suška had betrayed the gang and himself. He decided to kill her. There occurred a fateful confusion: as Molotova was leaving the malefactors' den, Pjatak, mistaking her for Suška, lodged a knife in her back.

Veselago, carrying the corpse of Molotova, reported to the police and disclosed all that he knew about the gang of Tureckij Baraban. Veselago was arrested: the police realized that he was a runaway prisoner. On the basis of his testimony the police raided the malefactors' den. The whole gang fell into the hands of the police.

The *Plot*: This is a conflict or collision plot of a "triangular" type, which means that relations and reciprocal involvement between the three main characters develop into a final clash – a collision which solves the accumulated contradictions.

This type of plot occurs frequently in the Serapion Brothers' works. Its degree of complexity varies: the main plot, i.e., "two-men-one-woman" triangle, with its system of motivation, e.g., love-hatred relation, may take sub-plots and collateral motivation. It affects the onward movement of the action with varying intensity. Whereas in a tale such as *Polët* by N. Nikitin the two-men-one-woman triangle creates considerable tension of situation, tension is practically inexistent in Vsevolod Ivanov's novel *Golubye peski*, in which situations revolve around the "two-women-one-man" triangle.

The interpretation of the plot depends on the point of view that the author adopts toward the theme. In the tale under study the theme is "the decline and the destruction of a gang of Leningrad malefactors". Such an understanding of the theme leads us to conclude that the story is assembled around the triangle Molotova + Veselago + Baraban. Reformatskij calls such a configuration "trexčlennaja novella": $a_1 + b + a_2$ (on + ona + on),[14] i.e., Veselago + Molotova + Baraban. Now, it might

[14] A. A. Reformatskij, *Opyt analiza novellističeskoj kompozicii* (Moskva, 1922), p. 8.

be possible to consider the theme from another angle, e.g., to view it as "the tragic love of a political prisoner". Then the interpretation of the plot would change: the purpose of the story would consist in dramatizing not "the end of the gang" but the sentimental life of a political prisoner, i.e., the point or the emphasis of the story would change. In this case the story would turn into what Reformatskij calls "četyrexčlennaja novella": $b + a_1 + a_2 + a_3$ (ona + on$_1$ + on$_2$ + on$_3$),[15] i.e., Molotova + Veselago + Frolov + Baraban. As a matter of fact, if the story betrays a certain weakness of construction, it is precisely because there occurred a confusion of these two different thematic interpretations.

In order to meet the requirement of the theme the author builds his plot by juxtaposing two systems of motivations: (1) the will of the gang – and its leader Šmerl Tureckij Baraban – to survive and to extend its activity; (2) the passion of two men for one woman. Therefore the plot unfolds along two lines: (1) the author builds a series of intrigues involving the activity of the gang that wants to crack the safe at the State Bank; (2) the "two-men-one-woman" triangle: Baraban, leader of the gang, and Veselago, a runaway political prisoner, are striving to capture and to recapture the love of Ekaterina Molotova.

The plot appears to present a somewhat unbalanced pattern. The problem posed by the theme is solved almost outside the main field of the theme. The theme requires "the end of the gang". We should expect a main collision between "pro-gang" and "anti-gang" interests. Actually situations are never such that the two main characters – Veselago and Baraban – confront each other, the first in order to destroy the gang, the second, to defend it and to render the antagonist harmless. As a matter of fact, they do not confront each other at all. The "end of the gang" does not come as a result of a dramatic play between "pro-gang" and "anti-gang" interests. In this respect the plot betrays a certain weakness. The first system of motivation – survival of the gang or its death – corresponds to the purpose of the theme. Therefore it is basic. Now, when it comes to tying a *nœud*, to carrying out an intrigue and to bringing about a *dénouement*, in one word, when it comes to propelling the plot, the author abandons the first – the main – system of motivation and resorts to the second – the collateral – system of motivation. For example, the motive of kidnapping Pineta belongs to the main system of motivation. Apparently this is a bound motive: Pineta was to crack the safe and a successful safecracking was, that is to say, should have been the "happy" *dénouement* of the play from the point of view of the gang's interests. In fact, the

[15]   *Ibid.*, p. 9.

motive is not absolutely necessary for the development of the plot. The failure of the whole intrigue with Pineta did not entail any collision required by the theme, it did not bring about a new situation.

In order to impel the action onward – to its dramatic end – the author introduces another similar motive: the abduction of Ekaterina Ivanovna Molotova. This motive belongs to the collateral system of motivation. And still, it is a bound motive: without this motive of abduction nothing would have happened. It necessitated a "middle-man" in the abduction; for this purpose Frolov stepped into the play. The presence of Frolov determined the behavior of Molotova: she took to Frolov and broke off her relations with Veselago. This sentimental frustration brought Veselago on the stage. He tried to wrench Molotova out of the hands of Tureckij Baraban. "The end of the gang" came only as an accidental consequence of a sentimental experience quite alien to "gang business".

Plot spells awareness of the mechanism that keeps the story moving. In this perspective, both the author and the reader view the story from an intellectual and logical angle. Only the understanding of the "bare devices" matters.

The *Narrative Structure*: Narrative structure consists – if I may use the following phrase inspired by the Russian Formalist thinking – in hiding and screening the "bare device". For example, the story commences with this panorama:

В дни, когда республика, сжатая гражданской войной, голодом, блокадой, начала, наконец, распрямлять плечи, изменяя на географической карте линию своих очертаний, в Петрограде, который только что остыл от схватки с мятежным Кронштадтом, на Лиговке, единственной улице, до сих пор сохранившей в неприкосновенности свои знаменитые притоны, из дома, принадлежавшего когда-то барону Фредериксу, министру царского двора, где живут, главным образом, учительницы музыки и иностранных языков, те самые, что по праздничным дням носят на груди часики, приколотые золотой булавкой, из антресолей, которыми зовется в этом доме второй этаж, – 12-го сентября, в 9 часов утра, ушла и не вернулась обратно стенографистка Екатерина Ивановна Молотова.[16]

In this huge, one-hundred-word long period ushering in the story, only the nine last words in fact contribute to the construction of the plot: the inverted complete subject (stenografistka Ekaterina Ivanovna Molotova), the compound predicate (ušla i ne vernulas') and the adverbial modifier (obratno). These nine words convey the motive essential to the plot: the

[16] V. Kaverin, *Konec Xazy. Povest'*. Tome I of V. Kaverin's *Sočinenija* ("Priboj", 1930), p. 17.

abduction of Molotova. It is a bound motive, indispensable for the plot, because without it the *dénouement* could not occur under the circumstances that, by the author's choice, determined the organization of the story.

Consequently, 91 % of the word mass in this introductory panorama is the fact of the narrative structure. The latter communicates human interest to the algebraic "bare device". At the beginning, apart from the statement about Molotova's leaving her home and not returning, the author withholds any other information about the disappearance and thereby he injects an element of mystery and suspense into the story. Then, as the story progresses, the author gradually supplies the missing information. At the end, the author contrives a dramatic *coup de théâtre*: Pjatak, one of the gang, stabs to death the person whom he has believed to be Suška, the prostitute. The person slain turns out to be Molotova whom Pjatak has mistaken for Suška. Now, all these motives pertaining to the description of environmental details, all the ironical comments of the author, all this unfolding vitalizes the abstract plot design and, so to speak, invests the skeleton with flesh and blood. The narrative structure integrates all the motives presented in the very sequence that appear in the book.

The *Motives*: In *Konec Xazy* Kaverin attempted to work out a novel of adventure. The novel of adventure has never patently succeeded in Russian literature. Kaverin's attempt falls short of the intelligent and thrilling manner in which R. L. Stevenson constructed the plot in his mystery and adventure stories. Nor does Kaverin exhibit the phantasmagorial verve of such a story-teller as Alexandre Dumas Père.

Kaverin avails himself of the stock motives that have traditionally actuated novels of adventure: abduction and kidnapping; escape from prison (for woman's sake); mistaken identities; duel (for woman's sake); the help of a compassionate prostitute.

All these stock motives are spared the stereotype by Kaverin's ironical vein and his parodying treatment of them.

The spectacular escape in *Le Comte de Monte-Cristo* may well set a standard of prison-breaking in this kind of thrill literature. Is it not aristocratic, when the prisoner earns his freedom at the frightful price of letting himself be mistaken for a corpse, enshrouded in a winding-sheet and flung into the primeval billowy sea? Now, Veselago, Kaverin's hero, makes his escape ungraciously via the latrine. On his way to freedom, Veselago does not have to survive the test of the sea. He must only swim across the river "[...] v kotoroj po celym dnjam baraxtalis' mal' čiški,

i baby poloskali bel'ë".[17] There is an obvious purpose of parody in Kaverin's treatment of this motive of escape. He ridicules the whole romantic tradition of prison-breaking in these terms:

В первые дни заключения Сергей, как всякий арестант, придумал десятки разных планов побега; среди них были планы с переодеванием и гримом, план с обольщением сестры милосердия в тюремной больнице; каждый из них удался бы только Лейхтвейсу, и то при отсутствии часовых.[18]

Likewise, the author rallies the stock motive of abduction. This motive has throughout centuries endured most diverse treatments in most varied contexts. Let us cite a random example: elopement-abduction of Isabella by Heathcliff in *Wuthering Heights*. The motive is mounted into a fairly romantic and traditional setting: a dark dramatic and eventful night, galloping horses, a young lady with a cloak about her face, and the "lover". In this instance, of course, the somewhat romantically conventional setting provides an utterly unconventional description of devastating, fierce emotions.

Kaverin modernizes the motive: the fair young lady with a cloak about her face, eloping on horseback, yields place to a girl stenographer "looking for a job", preferably a well-paid one. A girl on a hunt for remunerative secretarial employment goes to the address indicated in the offer that her prospective employer has held out to her and walks straight into the trap: the gang abducts her. The irony penetrating the situation betrays certain subtlety. For example, the personality of the employer himself, S. Kačerginskij, *alias* Šmerl Tureckij Baraban. The very contrast of the two names elicits comical effect. The same personality lurks beneath the disguise that the two disparate names provide. The two different "numerators" – "S. Kačerginskij" and "Šmerl Tureckij Baraban" – possess a "common denominator", namely, the same type of orthographic mistakes that both S. Kačerginskij and Šmerl Tureckij Baraban commit in their letters. Therefore the disguise comes easily to be unmasked. This Šmerl Tureckij Baraban represents a "modernized" version of Benja Krik, the superb and generous "King" of *Odesskie rasskazy* of Babel'. And here lies the irony at which Kaverin seems to have aimed in shaping both the character and the motive. On the one hand, Kaverin attempted to transplant the traditions of plot-making and motivation

---

[17]   *Ibid.*, p. 33.
[18]   *Ibid.*; the adventures of Lejxtvejs, a gallant gentleman, are described in the book *Peščery Lejxtvejsa* which Veselago is reading in jail.

prevailing in Western novels of adventure and fantasy (e.g., his fantastic story *Bočka*). On the other hand, this "avtor bestolkovyx romantičeskix novell" (as Lunc called him)[19] directed the edge of his irony at this very same West, namely at those bustling ones who succumb to the cult of mechanical efficiency. The author also pierces with irony those infected with the superficial – and often insincere – civilization of modern times. Viewed in a broader perspective, the two motives – abduction of Molotova and kidnapping of Pineta – acquire ironical significance. The author derides Šmerl Tureckij Baraban's craze for "organizing" or "engineering" affairs "on a large scale" with all the attendant paraphernalia that the modern technology of organization provides. One may wonder why Kaverin, when tackling the theme of "organizing", chooses no better "organizers" than robbers? And why the only two actions bespeaking this spirit of "organization" turn out to be, on the one hand, the kidnapping of a supposed steel expert so that he may contribute to bringing about an "affair on a large scale" ("delo bol'šogo masštaba" as Tureckij Baraban says),[20] i.e., cracking the safe of the State Bank, and, on the other hand, the abduction of a girl stenographer, presumably, for the purpose of writing letters of extortion? Šmerl Tureckij Baraban may well stand for many an "organizer" from other walks of life.

The motive of duel, likewise, is "lowered". In Romantic tradition, duel was a gentleman's affair surrounded with aristocratic sense of honor, courtesy, bravery and beautiful ladies, as in N. F. Pavlov's tale *Jatagan*. In *Konec Xazy* there are two malefactors and one girl stenographer. The two apprentice duelists do not quite know how to act in a duel. After abusing each other verbally they get down to business and the whole duel unfolds in this unaristocratic key:

– Кому первому стрелять? – спросил Сергей.
– Стреляй ты, если хочешь. Твоя выдумка.
– Ты вызван; стало быть, первый выстрел за тобой.
– Иди ты к чортовой матери.[21]

The ineptness of the duel appears the more comical because the author refrains – as the Serapions usually do – from giving any "Vorgeschichte" which might elucidate the antecedent relations between Veselago and Frolov.

Kaverin's irony transforms all the stock motives characterizing novels

---

[19]   *Vid.* p. 27 of this study; "an author of confused romantic short stories".
[20]   V. Kaverin, *op. cit.*, p. 27.
[21]   *Ibid.*, p. 58.

of adventure and renders them inconsonant with their traditional function and significance.

Things happen as if Kaverin, still faithful to the Serapion literary program, undertook, at this stage of his literary development, the difficult task of integrating contemporary subject matter and realistically motivated characters into a complex and absorbing plot. This task he must have had in mind when, in 1924, he said in his autobiography:

[...] On the 8th of May 1924 my best friend, Lev Lunc, who had shared my ideas, died. He thought that verbal ornament was out of date. He was dedicated to the work of the creation of a prose in which plot would be of paramount interest; but he died at the age of twenty-two and did not have time to develop his work.
I want to carry on this work and I think that only in the complex concreteness of the plot[22] built on the powerful thoughts of the present time we can look for a way out of the impasse in which Russian prose has now found itself.

His novel *Devjat' desjatyx sud'by* (1925) to some extent realizes his ambition. The subject matter of the novel deals with the most critical days of the Bolshevik revolution. Kaverin depicts the scenes of fighting in Petrograd, military moves, tense days and nights in the revolutionary and the counter-revolutionary headquarters. Against this background unfolds the personal destiny of a man – Šaxov – who joined the Bolshevik revolution from its very early days. A mystery surrounds the past of Šaxov. As another character in the story, Goloveckij, observes, Šaxov irretrievably missed "one tenth of his destiny" – the most important fraction of it – which has weighed heavy on his conscience and has continually threatened to ruin his life. As the plot unfolds, the reader penetrates the mystery and in a final *coup de théâtre* learns the truth, the missing one tenth of Šaxov's destiny.

Whereas in his previous works Kaverin maneuvered conventional

---

[22] In the Russian text: "... 8 мая 1924 года умер мой лучший друг и единомышленник, Лев Лунц; он думал, что словесный орнамент отжил свой век; он был предан работе создания сюжетной прозы, но умер 22-х лет и не успел развернуть своего дела.
Я хочу продолжать эту работу и думаю, что только в сложной конкретности сюжета, построенного на мощных обобщениях современности, можно искать выхода из того тупика, в котором очутилась теперь русская проза."
("Вениамин Александрович Каверин", *Писатели. Автобиографии и портреты современных русских прозаиков.* Ed. by Vl. Lidin, Moskva, 1926, pp. 133-134; the excerpt quoted is on p. 134).
This reference to Lunc and Kaverin's statement of intending to continue Lunc's work are missing in Kaverin's autobiography of 1959 (*vid. Sovetskie pisateli. Avtobiografii v dvux tomax*, Moskva, GIXL, 1959, pp. 496-510).

characters cloaked with a functional mask, in this novel he attempts to portray three dimensional believable characters. Still, Šaxov remains a pale figure. The "mystery" that he carries with him does him more harm than good, artistically speaking. Šaxov as a character succeeds little in "infecting" the reader with any intense, emotional or intellectual, human experience.

Both the fact of one-sided weak and superficial characterization and the fact of experimentation with plot mean that the Serapion Brothers shared little concern for creating a *human type*. They did not assume the task of what Aleksej N. Tolstoj proudly and somewhat rashly called "čelovekotvorčestvo".[23]

Not unexpectedly does this concern for human type remain true for Fedin, since this writer has basically perpetuated the grand narrative tradition of the XIXth century. Andrej Starcov of *Goroda i gody* engages interest in various respects.

A character in a sense predetermines the patterns of plot. The representation of an *undramatic* character such as Starcov even more effectively emphasizes this reciprocal dependence of both characterization and plot. Plot spells action. And action results from the volition of a *will-endowed* character. Now, Starcov lacks will power: with him, no faculty puts intention into effect, no controlling agency transmutes emotion into deed. Such a situation precludes the possibility for man's personality to achieve dramatic expression. If so, plot construction comes to nothing.

The fact that the author operates with an undramatic character compels him to construct a "binary" plot: Starcov and Kurt Wahn act as a "team", Starcov being "undramatic" and Wahn, "dramatic". It is Wahn's task to supply the volition absent in Starcov. As it were, the "strong" one pushes the "weak" one to act. In fact the two great experiences of Starcov's – "Western" German experience and communist experience of Semidol – occur under Wahn's energetic impact on Starcov. It may well be that the author staged Wahn's extravagant conversion from a jingoistic nationalist into an ecstatic communist only with a view to having Wahn "push" Starcov into the communist experience which will lead Starcov to his doom.

So the choice of an undramatic protagonist beforehand prescribes the design of the plot. It is not "triangular" or "multiangular", because there comes up no real conflict, no veritable collision that would oppose

[23] Aleksej Tolstoj, "Literaturnye zametki. Zadači literatury", *Pisateli ob iskusstve i o sebe. Sbornik statej*, 1 (Moskva-Leningrad, 1924), p. 15.

the protagonist to other characters. The design is "linear", figuring not pursuit, but flight. Starcov uses Wahn – and in smaller measure Mari Urbach and Von Schönau – as a prop, or as a reservoir of volition which he so badly needs in his would-be dramatic course. Therefore the choice and the distribution of other characters in the plot also derives from the initial purpose of characterization. Because of this accessory role, perhaps, the other characters do not seem so convincingly living.

It is a debatable question whether there is any need to attribute the character of Starcov to the line of the "superfluous men". Turgenev applied the phrase to the idealistic and inefficient older generation impersonated in such a character as Rudin (*Rudin*, 1856). Why should we automatically tag all the speculative and undecided minds of Russia with this pseudo-sociological stereotype?

The novel brings us to grapple with another question. Fedin breaks the normal chronological sequence and rearranges the segments of time in a way which sets off certain values of the narrative structure. In terms of fable, the novel occupies the period of time from the summer of 1914 to the summer of 1922. The sequence that appears in the book is unusual. The author *first* gives *dénouement* taking place in the summer of 1922 ("Glava o gode, kotorym zaveršen roman"). Then he switches back to the winter of 1919 ("Glava pervaja o devjat'sot devjatnadcatom"). Only afterward, in the third chapter, does the author start narrating the events from their absolute chronological beginning (the summer of 1914). The last chapter of the book refers to the year 1920.

Displacement of time sequence does not represent, of course, anything conspicuously new in epic tradition. One of the distinguishing characteristics of the epic genre consists in the fact that artistic convention opens the possibility of expanding and contracting the time of fiction. For example, the tradition of commencing the narration *in medias res* dates far back and has emerged reinvigorated in the works of Byron. The novel *Goroda i gody* does not really start *in medias res*, since it begins with the end. But it opens in a very bewildering manner: a crackbrained one is delivering a wild speech from a window overlooking the courtyard of an apartment house:

– Дорогие соседи, добрейшие обыватели, почтенные граждане! Я высунулся из окна с заранее обдуманным намерением: мне скучно, дорогие соседи, меня грызет тоска, почтенные граждане, сердце мое ссохлось и свернулось штопором, как лимонная корка на раскаленной солнцем мостовой.

– Почтенные обыватели! Это верно, что на дворе тысяча девятьсот двадцать второй год.

– Передо мной восемьдесят пять окон, не считая двух чердачных, одного подвального, одного, искусно нарисованного на стене маляром довоенного времени, и того, в котором все вы можете различить верхнюю часть моей фигуры. ...[24]

Such an abrupt start, dispensing with initiatory "Vorgeschichte" or preliminary descriptions, whips up the reader's interest and rudely awakens his curiosity.

This "inaugural speech" bears a curious resemblance to the "Prolog" of *Peterburg* ("Vaši prevosxoditel'stva, vysokorodija, blagorodija, graždane!" ...).[25]

And the resemblance may well not be accidental. In both cases the initial address immediately compels the reader to turn his attention toward the story. Moreover, Belyj's impact may have worked in another way. In his novel Fedin succeeded in blending the grand narrative style of the XIXth century with "ornamentalism" which can be traced back to A. Belyj. "Ornamentalism" means amalgamation of disparate styles, such as the signboard style that Fedin integrates into the narrative structure of his novel; e.g., in the chapter "O kom dumal General-Fel'dmaršal Fon Gindenburg?" a whole page is filled with signboards such as "Tol'ko dlja velosipedov", "Tol'ko dlja pešexodov", "Tol'ko dlja verxovoj ezdy", "Vospreščaetsja njan'kam s det'mi sidet' na lavkax", "Ne raskovyrivat' dorožek zontami i palkami". These signboards create a very special atmosphere in this chapter.[26] It has been mentioned already that the author compensates the lack of dynamism resulting from the presence of the undramatic protagonist by employing auxiliary devices. Now, one of them pertains to Belyj's stylistic tradition: amalgamation of disparate styles, i.e., stylistic contrasts entertain the illusion of drama and motion in the novel.

And finally the novel draws its dramatic convincingness from the very displacement of time sequences. In novels the climax usually occurs before the end of the book. The plot ends, i.e., the *dénouement* takes place, before the narrative structure winds up the story, and the novel tapers off in an "epilogue", or a "Nachgeschichte".[27] In a short story there is usually only one "knot" to unravel; therefore it can be done at

---

[24] Konst. Fedin, *Goroda i gody* (Moskva, GIXL, 1959), p. 7.
[25] Andrej Belyj, *Peterburg*. Roman, 2 vols (Berlin, 1922), I, p. 9.
[26] Konst. Fedin, *op. cit.*, p. 145.
[27] B. Èixenbaum, "O. Genri i teorija prozy", *Literatura. Teorija, kritika, polemika* (Leningrad, 1927), pp. 166-209; p. 171 *et seq.*

one stroke, at the very end of the story, which accounts for the unexpected and "spectacular" end in short stories. A novel usually includes
several "knots". For this reason the author cannot but disentangle them
one by one, since the narrative process permits communicating only one
item at a time. All the accumulated suspense is not released at one blow
as usually happens in a short story. Suspense wanes gradually, in
proportion as "knots" come to be consecutively untied, i.e., as relations
between characters reach their respective *dénouements*.

The novel under consideration follows such a pattern. The respective
dénouements bringing to a climax the relations of Starcov with other
characters come in succession. First, with Mari. Then, by repercussion,
with Rita. Then, with Von Schönau. And at last, with Kurt. In this
train of dramatic situations the moment of the highest tension comes
when Mari, Rita and Starcov meet and realize the misery that has fallen
to the lot of each of them. Mari sees that the man for whom she has
sacrificed everything has not had the courage to remain faithful to her.
Rita, about to give birth to Starcov's child, understands that he has
always loved another woman. And Starcov becomes aware that he has
lost, that he has missed everything in life. The next *dénouement* – the
letter from Von Schönau – acts as a sort of amplifier for the preceding
situation. It places the whole development in a broader perspective. The
point of view shifts: it is the enemy who portrays this final view. Whereas
the climax is viewed by the unprejudiced, earnest and forgiving eye of
the narrator, Von Schönau's letter, subsequent to the climax, illuminates
the same situation with a cruel, cool and inexorable light. The narrative
structure, i.e., the book as it appears to the reader, ends in this ruthless
key. The author interrupts the narrative structure at the moment of its
most impellingly modulated impact on the reader. And in this, it seems
to me, lies the author's skill. The chronological end of the story, although
pathetic, lacks dramatic tension. It should be so because the moment of
the highest tension comes when Rita, Mari and Starcov meet; Von
Schönau's letter only amplifies this situation without changing it.
Throughout the whole subsequent development, tension subsides.
Starcov's physical death does not, in fact, present any dramatic interest,
because as character he ceases to be of further dramatic importance at
the preceding climax. The situation before the climax conveys as much
significance toward the situation after it as the lifetime of action of a
great man does toward his genteel funeral.

The author relegates this "point of weakening",[28] so to speak, back

[28] *Ibid.*

to the beginning of the narrative structure and thereby he achieves several strikingly artistic effects. The book comes to a close at its most dramatic point. Therefore the reader avoids the frustration attendant upon an epilogue, or a "Nachgeschichte" or any other factitious end. The point of weakening stands at the beginning of the narrative structure and, owing to this position, it actually becomes a "point of strength", because it aesthetically "capitalizes" on its powerfully estranging (ostranjajuščij) position. An incoherent declamation uttered by a lunatic from the window of an apartment-house ("Reč'"); a pathetic letter written by one Andrej to some lady called Mari ("Pis'mo"); a meeting of a committee at which a certain comrade Wahn confesses that he killed a person, his former friend, guilty of disloyalty ("Formula perexoda"); these three situations, torn off from their circumstantial context and placed at the beginning of the book (in "Glava o gode, kotorym zaveršen roman"), excite the reader's expectations through the very fact that they appear bewilderingly incomprehensible. At this initial point of the narrative structure the reader cannot realize that these three mysterious situations disclose the miserable end of a weakling. So, by moving the absolute chronological end of the story – i.e., the position of "frustration" – over to the beginning of the narrative structure – i.e., the position of "expectation" – the author turns "frustration" into "expectation". This transformation in itself is not a negligible *tour de force*. And there is more to it. I have presumed that the plot develops a "linear" design. The attribute is, of course, only an approximation which somewhat metaphorically accounts for the unfolding of the plot relations in time. Now, the dislocation of time sequences that I have discussed stirs our sense of time in the novel to the effect that we conceive of the development not as a straight line with a beginning and an end but as a *circle* without either beginning or end. This subtle sense of continuity does not have about it anything mysterious. It is a matter of the psychological experience of the reader. When he reads the book through, he returns to the beginning and rereads at least the two first chapters in order properly to understand the story, and, by the by, only then does he comprehend why Starcov says at the end of the second chapter ("Glava pervaja o devjat'sot devjatnadcatom"): "– Ètogo ja nikomu ne mogu skazat'. Nikomu." Now, as soon as the reader begins rereading the book, he psychologically sets out on the journey again and – what is particularly astonishing – while reading the *end* of the story he enters upon the initial "expectation" stage of the journey through the book. That is to say, the impression of the end in the novel vanishes. Such a *tour de force*, of course, demands of

the author the equilibristic skill of a tight-rope dancer, or else, for want of consistency, the whole structure would disastrously crumble. My feeling is that Fedin has performed his feats of equilibristic skill adequately.[29]

While dislocating time sequences the author may also choose to dissolve the logical links connecting the motives in the plot. Or the author may simply *withhold* from the reader at the outset those motives that are necessary for the correct interpretation of the plot and disclose them only toward the end. Mystery or detective types of plot invariably cling to this pattern.

A similar type of plot shapes Nik. Nikitin's tale *Polet*. The author withholds the initial motivation that gives occasion to the development of the plot. The plot is "triangular": it involves ex-lieutenant Klimovič, ex-lieutenant Firsov and a lady, Valentina Petrovna. The author does not say at the outset that Firsov was jealous of *Valentina Petrovna*, because her appearance and her affair with Klimovič threatened to disrupt the friendship between Firsov and Klimovič. This initial situation comes to light only at the end of the story, in Firsov's notes:

[...] Вам известно, что меня связывала с Климовичем долгая и тесная дружба. Эти годы школы, университета, войны, – пролетели, как дым, и жить бок-о-бок друг с другом стало для нас не только привычкой, но необходимостью, часто нас тяготившею, как тяготит двух рабов галера, к которой они прикованы и когда один опускает правое весло в воду, другой обязательно подымает из воды левое. Рабы не смотрят друг на друга, молчат, но раскуйте их и выпустите из галеры на землю, они упадут друг другу в об'ятия, или убьют друг друга. Это я понял здесь, в тюрьме. Что касается нас, то нечто

---

[29] I would like to observe one curious inconsistency in the distribution of the chronological sequences in *Doctor Živago*. I have not found this item mentioned in the critical literature that I have read on the novel. It appears to me from a careful study of the text that Živago was kidnapped by Red partisans in the summer of 1919. He had stayed with them, sharing their tribulation, until the winter of 1920-1921, when he escaped and returned to Jurjatin. Circumstances attest that Živago came to Jurjatin early in 1921 and then one summer had passed before Komarovskij came to see Živago and Lara in the winter. Now, Komarovskij's two visits positively must have taken place in the winter of 1921-1922, because his visits would have been materially impossible during the winter of 1920-1921 whereas in the spring of 1922 at the beginning of the NEP Živago was already in Moscow. In other words, Živago positively was in the Urals in the winter of 1921-1922 and he was in Moscow in the spring of 1922. So, he must have made the whole trip from the Urals to Moscow *between the winter of 1921-1922 and the spring of 1922*. Now, speaking of this very trip of Živago, the author describes an *autumnal* scenery, which, obviously, is chronologically inconsistent (*vid.* p. 480 of *Doktor Živago* by B. Pasternak, Ann Arbor, Mich., 1959).

похожее соединяло меня с Климовичем, мы даже стали меньше
разговаривать друг с другом, больше молчать, но это не избавляло
нас от соседства, мы понимали друг друга по жестам. Однажды
вечером, Климович проговорился мне о любви, но, с тех пор,
как-то замолк, часто виделся с ней, но со мной об этом не разговаривал, и отсюда разыгралась во мне ревность матери, очень
скупой правда, очень сухой, матери-мужчины, если можно так
выразиться. Это было ненормально и желчно и, еще хуже, то, что
ни одним словом я не мог об этом с ним перемолвиться, т.к. мне
первому стало бы стыдно. Мне пришлось примириться с мыслью,
что для Климовича опять наступил этот период угара и приклю-
чений с женщиной, но тут я стал бояться, что теперь то он от меня
уйдет, что здесь будет кончена его длинная победная эпопея, которой
в тайне я частенько завидовал.[30]

The traditional pattern of plot in which two men fight for a woman grows
later out of this initial situation.

The plot includes a motive which, when fully disclosed, gives the plot
– retrospectively – an unexpected turn: the motive in question is the
suicide of a rejected lover. This motive screens another: that of the
premeditated murder of a suitor by his competitor. On the face of the
plot – before the final "explanation" given by Firsov – things happen as
if Klimovič had committed suicide out of disappointment in love and then
Firsov married Valentina. In fact, Firsov premeditated a murder in
order to get rid of a troublesome rival. So, what the author holds out
on the reader is the initial motivation – Firsov's jealousy of Valentina –
and the motive of a premeditated murder. Both become known at the end.

Still, it remains unclear whether Firsov actually premeditated and
committed the murder of his friend Klimovič. This motive is ushered in
by Firsov himself, i.e., from the point of view of a character in the story.
Firsov acknowledges his felony in his "confession". Now, at this point,
the author takes pleasure in introducing an additional complication:
Firsov wrote his "confession" being already in a state of an incipient
mental derangement. In fact, Nikitin attempts, not quite unsuccessfully,
to produce a psychologically convincing character. This motive of incipient mental derangement with Firsov considerably weakens the
"murder" interpretation of the plot. Therefore the reader does not know
whether he can unreservedly give credit to Firsov's "confession". The
author chooses to leave the reader in a state of uncertainty as to the
essential motive of the tale: suicide or murder?

[30]   Nik. Nikitin, *Polet. Povest'* (Berlin, 1924), pp. 101-102.

Suspense results from this initial incomplete knowledge. It challenges the intelligence and the memory of the reader. In a sense, it also tricks both his intelligence and memory. Edgar A. Poe is said to have written his stories backward.[31] Aleksej N. Tolstoj calls this technique "process mngnovennoj logiki s konca k načalu".[32] These apparently extravagant opinions suggest, it seems, that the writer ("producer") operates "deductively", whereas the reader ("consumer") has to react "inductively". The processes can be reduced to the following formulas:

WRITER (producer)	Plot		
deductive process	A – B – C – D basic motive	... motives logically deduced from basic motive	Z

READER (consumer)	Narrative structure		
inductive process	# basic motive is not revealed at outset	b – c – d ... or any other combination of intermediate motives (they become incomprehensible, hence suspense)	Z/A basic motive given at the end. The reader has *retrospectively* to reconstitute the plot. Suspense is released because the reader comes to acquire full knowledge

The author selects a *basic* motive, i.e., a drug changing man's personality (in *The Strange Case of Dr. Jekyll and Mr. Hyde*) and then he deduces all other motives logically following from the basic motive, e.g., mysterious appearance of Mr. Hyde, murder of Sir Danvers Carew and other motives. The reader learns the story in a logically inverted order, i.e., he learns – without comprehending them – all consequential motives first, and the basic motive at the end. The final "frustration" that the reader may suffer ensues from his feeling of incongruity between his "sweat and tears" and the cause that has given occasion to them. But in this kind of literature, the author may claim all the more spectacular merit *because* the reader experiences the feeling of incongruity between the suspense

[31]   B. Èixenbaum, *op. cit.*, p. 174 *et seq.*
[32]   Aleksej Tolstoj, *op. cit.*, p. 10.

and its cause. The reader may well have a doubtful merit: he swallows
the whole fantastic story hook, line and sinker and then, belatedly, he
realizes that the mountain has brought forth a mouse. Now, the author's
merit is inversely proportional to the reader's: the author has caused the
mouse to bring forth a mountain. Such a feat requires a special enchant-
ment of creation. And it would not be surprising if the story were true
that Eugène Sue, when jailed "pour n'avoir pas monté sa garde",[33]
threatened to stop writing his *Mystères de Paris* and that the maréchal
Soult, himself a keen reader of the *Mystères*, hastened to have him
released.

This anecdote, whether authentic or apocryphal, amusingly illustrates
the idea that literary performance partakes of the nature of *play*.
J. Huizinga defines play in these words:

Summing up the formal characteristics of play we might call it a free activity
standing quite consciously outside "ordinary" life as being "not serious", but
at the same time absorbing the player intensely and utterly. It is an activity
connected with no material interest, and no profit can be gained from it. It
proceeds within its own proper boundaries of time and space according to
fixed rules and in orderly manner. It promotes the formation of social groupings
which tend to surround themselves with secrecy and to stress their difference
from the common world by disguise or other means.[34]

Both E. Sue and the maréchal Soult participated in such an activity: a
play having literary representation for its substratum. In this connection
the notion of the "rules of the game" becomes paramount. If any
participant ever so little ignores or violates a "rule of the game", the whole
"play-world"[35] crumbles away immediately. The "spoil-sport"[36] deprives
the play of its *illusion*. Had E. Sue abruptly stopped writing his *Mystères
de Paris*, he would have violated the "rules of the game": the game would
not have "played itself out", order – another essential feature proper to
play – would have been disrupted, illusion would have crumbled at once
and in consequence the game would have become void and "ordinary
life"[37] would have brutally superseded the spell that the game had cast
over the reader. So, the initiative displayed by the maréchal Soult repre-

---

[33]   Ch.-M. Des Granges, *Histoire Illustreé de la Littérature Française des Origines
à 1930* (Paris, 1933), p. 884.
[34]   J. Huizinga, *Homo Ludens. A Study of the Play-Element in Culture* (London, 1949),
p. 13.
[35]   *Ibid.*, p. 11.
[36]   *Ibid.*
[37]   *Ibid.*, p. 21.

sents the reflex of a player who wants to preserve the game that he shares. This leads me to observe that play betrays itself most patently when it is abruptly interrupted. Then the "play-ground"[38] forfeits its "hallowness", the notion of time specific to play yields to that of the time of "ordinary life" and the "play-mood" melts into "seriousness".[39] Illusion, proper to play, vanishes; it is quite significant that the word *illusion* literally means *"in-play"*, from *inlusion, illudere* or *inludere;*[40] *"disillusion"* then means "the act or the condition of lacking 'in-play'", "play" as defined by J. Huizinga.

The awareness of "play" grows particularly acute when the game comes to be abruptly "spoiled". This notion of "spoiling the game" – Zamjatin calls it "igra v razoblačenie igry"[41] – has left its mark on some of the Serapion Brothers' works. It distinctively characterizes the early works of Kaverin. For example, his tale *Pjatyj strannik* (Oct.-Nov. 1921) – which he dedicated to the Serapion Brothers – apparently renders a puppet performance. However, the puppet performance imperceptibly changes into "human comedy" so that the reader comes to believe all these toylike figurines to be quaint human beings. The characters in the tale remind one of those Japanese figurines which fit into one another so that the larger figurines contain the smaller. The characters, so to speak, occupy different concentric circles with the result that the figurines standing closer to the center are more "puppet-like", and those farther away from the center are more "human-like", and, moreover, the same figurine appearing "human-like" with respect to the character located farther within appears "puppet-like" with respect to the character in the outer circle. For example, Pickelhering is a puppet and the "charlatan" seems "human-like" with regard to Pickelhering, but the same "charlatan" appears "puppet-like" to the "human-like" spectators and the hostess, who, in their turn, may be mere puppets with regard to the anonymous "fifth wanderer", apparently the only human being in the whole tale. The frontiers marking off the world of puppets from the world of men melt away and the reader feels at a loss to ascertain which world he is contemplating. Johann Faust, doctor and master of philosophy; Oswald Schwerindoch, a scholastic and master of many sciences; Hanswurst, a clown; Kurt, artisan of the guild of glaziers; all these odd fellows, always on the move in their phantasmagorial world, acquire human dimension.

[38] *Ibid.*, p. 10.
[39] *Ibid.*, p. 21.
[40] *Ibid.*, p. 11.
[41] E. Zamjatin, *Lica* (New York, 1955), p. 199.

Thus, Oswald Schwerindoch, "scholastic and master of many sciences", wanders about mediaeval Germany in quest of the means enabling him to endow with life his only hope, the Homunculus that he keeps in his flask. Schwerindoch happens to stay at the house of the burgomaster of Cologne as preceptor of the burgomaster's son. He makes up his mind to steal the burgomaster's soul and to transplant it into his Homunculus. He carries out his treacherous plan: he plucks the burgomaster's soul out of his mouth by means of sugar tongs. However, the Homunculus does not want the burgomaster's soul because it is too big for its stature. Now, what will happen to unfortunate Schwerindoch at this dramatic moment? The reader will never learn because at this moment the author chooses to break the spell, to "spoil" the game:

И тогда Освальд Швериндох вновь закупорил колбу, застегнул свою тогу и, даже не успев одеть на голову колпака, отправился на дно кукольного ящика, не получив даже от бургомистра платы, следуемой ему за уроки, которые он давал сыну бургомистра, Ансельму, школьнику.

И пятый странник захлопнул за ним крышку ящика и промолвил [...][42]

Man with his curious passions turns out to be a sad dead puppet thrown to the bottom of the puppet chest. And so it goes with all "wanderers". The author creates an illusion, then he destroys it, then he creates it again.

Another story of Kaverin, *Ščity i sveči*, appears even more phantasmagorial than *Pjatyj strannik*. A shoemaker, a joiner, a dumb man and a soldier (Landsknecht) are playing cards, namely a card game called landsknecht. At the same time the cards stage their own play: the king of clubs convenes a senate at which all the card kings meet. The action in the story shifts from one setting to another. The one who serves as a link between the two settings seems to be the soldier. As a Landsknecht he joins in the game along with the three other gamblers. Landsknecht is also the name of the card game played; therefore the card nobility takes the soldier (Landsknecht) as their Emperor. This story is still more of an experimentation with plot construction than the preceding. A new element comes into play: *phantasmagoria*. Under the impact of phantasmagoria words and stories cease corresponding exactly to empirical reality. Zamjatin called it "stojkie splavy iz fantastiki i real'nosti".[43]

To a degree Kaverin owes his vein of phantasmagoria to the influence

---

[42] V. Kaverin, *Konec xazy. Povest'*, t. I of V. Kaverin's *Sočinenija* ("Priboj", 1930), pp. 277-278.
[43] E. Zamjatin, *op. cit.*, p. 199.

of the German Romantics. In his autobiographic accounts Kaverin good-humoredly owns to this Romantic influence when he refers to his "ogromnyj rvanyj plašč"[44] – in his own mind romantically metamorphosed into a "dlinnyj rycarskij plašč" in *Xudožnik neizvesten*[45] – as to a "dan' uvlečenija nemeckimi romantikami".[46]

The theme of "spoiling the game" is another treatment of the Romantic motive of the play *within* the play. The German Romantics used this motive with a view to represent artistic reality in some special perspective, namely, the motive of the play within the play enabled them to impress upon the world represented the stamp of the grotesque.

In Bonaventura's novel *Nachtwachen* (in the Night Watch Fourteen) there is a following episode narrated: in a madhouse the narrator met a woman, an actress, who, while enacting Ophelia, had entered so much into her role that she had actually gone insane and had not been able to leave her role to resume her normal, sane, personality. The narrator had happened to enact Hamlet with her and in the madhouse they both continued acting Hamlet and Ophelia. The episode may signify that "play" reality dwells in the realm of sanity, whereas "serious" reality pertains to insanity. Is madness the only essential reality, whereas our familiar reality is only an unsubstantial play? Such an assumption, fleeting as it may, suffices to elicit an uncanny sense of alienation of our world. Such appears to be the underlying "hellish" purpose in the writings of Jean Paul. In so far as he is the writer of the grotesque E. T. A. Hoffmann attained to the grotesque mainly through what might be called a recurrent motive of metamorphosis: typically, the sense of alienation and surprised horror in the reader is provoked by an inanimate object which is brought to life or which imitates human beings, e.g., the prophesying weird automaton in the story *Die Automate*; or a man is deprived of his personality by a double (*Die Doppelgänger*); or a world of puppets and dolls, displacing for a while the human world, becomes the only genuine world, as in *Nussknacker und Mausekönig*.

In his early experimental works Kaverin occasionally borrows these Romantic paraphernalia of horror more or less pungent. However, the horror-provoking motives in his representation turn out quite innocuous. In *Pjatyj strannik*, for example, the theme is potentially grotesque. The confrontation between puppets and human beings, or puppets metamorphosed into human beings and then back into puppets, or a puppet

---

[44] *Sovetskie pisateli. Avtobiografii v dvux tomax*, (Moskva, GIXL, 1959), I, p. 503.
[45] V. Kaverin, *Xudožnik neizvesten* (Leningrad, 1931), p. 119.
[46] *Sovetskie pisateli, ibid., vid.* footnote 44.

show throughout – these are situations artistically favorable for the grotesque in the spirit of the German Romantics. Oswald Schwerindoch wanted to bring to life his Homunculus, a doll that he had made up. This might have become the horror-provoking theme of the "artificial man", a monster, that can live only to the detriment of a human personality. Indeed, in order to bring his doll to life, Oswald Schwerindoch treacherously wrenched out the soul of the sleeping burgomaster and attempted to transplant it into his Homunculus. However, the sense of horror and of the grotesque is missing, because human dimension is not convincing. Therefore no alienating contrast exists between the two simultaneous worlds, that of humans and that of inhuman automata, "false pretenders" to humanity.

The ominous and the sinister, which the German Romantics represented for its own sake, in Kaverin's fiction becomes a puzzle, i.e., an element of suspense contributing to the construction of an absorbing plot. In this respect Kaverin followed E. A. Poe and imitated the genre of detective stories in his *Bol'šaja igra*, *Bočka* and even *Konec Xazy*. He owns to an intense interest for Poe in an autobiographic reference in *Xudožnik neizvesten*:

Юноша, начитавшийся Эдгара По и каждую бочку принимавший за Бочку Амонтильядо, когда-то я старательно изучал унылые кабаки Ленинграда.[47]

The notion of play as discussed above, that of "spoiling the game", the vein of phantasmagoria and the habit of "toying" with the plot – which Kaverin may have derived from the Sternian tradition – blended into a harmonious concordance in Kaverin's very short novel *Xudožnik neizvesten*. This novel appeared in 1931, when the Serapion Brotherhood had long since been past and gone. However, in its spirit the novel is quite "Serapion-like" and one cannot help thinking that by writing the novel Kaverin repaid his debt to Lunc.

One of the implications of Sternianism consists in the fact that the ironical author tends to destroy the artistic organization of conventionally meaningful material. E.g., partition of a novel into chapters or into any other subdivisions helps the writer single out isolated motives in the chain of events and, the reader be aware of differences.[48] Now, a Sternian-minded writer would, e.g., invert or otherwise transpose the normal sequence of chapters in order to "estrange" the material from its

[47]   V. Kaverin, *Xudožnik neizvesten*, vid. footnote 45, p. 99.
[48]   Viktor Šklovskij, *Xudožestvennaja proza. Razmyšlenija i razbory* (Moskva, 1959), p. 298.

conventional meaning and value, to impair the thematic unity of the given work and to make the reader keenly sense how artistic effect is achieved. One critic called this procedure "'okartonivanie' literary".[49] So, in Book Four of *Tristram Shandy* Chapter XXIV is missing altogether. The narrator confesses that he has torn it out saying at the beginning of Chapter XXV:

– No doubt, Sir – there is a whole chapter wanting here – and a chasm of ten pages made in the book by it – but the book-binder is neither a fool, or a knave, or a puppy – nor is the book a jot more imperfect, (at least upon this score) – but, on the contrary, the book is more perfect and complete by wanting the chapter, than by having it, as I shall demonstrate to your reverences in this manner – I question first by the bye, whether the same experiment might not be made as successfully upon sundry other chapters – but there is no end, an' please your reverences, in trying experiments upon chapters – we have enough of it – So there's an end of that matter.[50]

Kaverin quite obviously imitates Sterne when he omits Chapter XI in his early eccentric story *Xronika goroda Lejpciga za 18.. god*:

Целый ряд непредвиденных несчастий обрушился на XI главу, начиная с того, что я позабыл написать ее своевременно, и, написав несвоевременно, неожиданно утерял. [...]

Но она сбежала, говорю я вам, и там, где она была – совсем чистое место и совершенно девственное бумажное поле.

Я не виноват ни в чем и во всем подозреваю студента Бира. Это он, это он утащил главу, коварнейшим образом лишив меня возможности оправдаться в неясности моего рассказа.[51]

This was the chapter in which the author should have revealed the mysteries surrounding the story. So the story remains within the sphere of rampant experimentation, phantasmagoria and eccentricity. Such an accentuated Sternianism appears to be a symptom of transition and instability of the genre, perhaps, a symptom of its growth.

In *Xudožnik neizvesten* all these elements come integrated and organized; nothing remains unexplained. The division into *encounters* (vstreči) instead of chapters communicates to the whole novel a dramatic movement. The narrator "toys" with the plot but not "destructively". He does so in order to enhance its value. For example, toward the end of the story the author introduces the motive of a fantastic night ride that Arximedov, attired in a helmet and armed with a spear and a shield, takes

---

[49]   N. Berkovskij, *Tekuščaja literatura. Stat'i kritičeskie i teoretičeskie* (Moskva, 1930), p. 133.

[50]   Laurence Sterne, *Tristram Shandy* (New York, 1957), p. 246.

[51]   *Serapionovy Brat'ja. Zagraničnyj Al'manax* (Berlin, 1922), pp. 153-155.

on horseback from Teheran to Moscow. But it is only Arximedov's dream that the author takes care to have a third person narrate. The purpose of this motive is clear: the author needs a most poignant contrast between the illusion of Arximedov and the reality of Špektorov. In his own dream Arximedov sees himself as a gallant knight pledging loyalty to his lady, then, still in his dream, he realizes that the attributes of his knighthood turn into a griddle, oven-prongs, a jam pan and a wretched bast-tailed horse on three wheels. Thus Arximedov, a Soviet Don Quixote,[52] foresees his physical defeat.

The attitude of the narrator also looks Sternian but, at the same time, it seems more sophisticated. The typical Sternian attitude aims at "spoiling the game" by violating the "rules of the game", i.e., the author uses a certain device meant to create a certain illusion and simultaneously he reveals to the reader the very function of the device in question. In other words the author discusses his poetic methods while delivering his poetic message. In *Tristram Shandy* this circumstance betrays itself with particular obviousness in Slawkenbergius's hilariously absurd Tale or at the end of Book Six, Chapter XL where the author shows the "design" of his book.

Kaverin also discusses his devices while composing his work. But the purpose is just the opposite: Sternian attitude destroys the illusion, whereas Kaverin's cultivates it even more. Here is an example:

Минуло целых полгода с тех пор, как на Ждановском мосту я выслушал речь о городах, в которых няньки будущего будут укачивать питомцев сказками о дне, который был воскресеньем, – и двадцать шесть воскресений прошло над изучением людей и книг.

Подчас мне случалось, перебирая бумаги, встречать заметки, относящиеся к Шпекторову, Архимедову, Эсфири, а однажды я нашел план и был поражен, убедившись в том, что эта книга представлялась мне хладнокровно изложенным состязанием между "расчетом на романтику" и "романтикой расчета", а о моем участии в этом состязании должна была свидетельствовать лишь фамилия автора на титульном листе.

Дважды я прочитал этот план, а потом положил его в самый дальний угол моего письменного стола, – мне показалось, что сама юность, та самая, полузабытая, легкая, которая когда-то ходила на университетские лекции закутавшись в длинный рыцарский плащ, глядит на меня из беспорядочных строк.

Так в третий раз я простился с мыслью написать эту книгу, – и без сомнения так и не написал бы ее, если бы не прочитал однажды

---

[52] In an article published in the collection *Kak my pišem* (Leningrad, 1930), pp. 59-74, V. Kaverin mentioned that he had been working on a tale tentatively entitled *Don Kixot i Sovety*. This is undoubtedly the original title of *Xudožnik neizvesten*.

на витрине Дома печати о том, что такого-то числа в такой-то группе состоится лекция Жабы под названием "Бюрократизация языка".[53]

The narrator's attitude splits in two. On the one hand, he knows, – i.e., he claims that he knows – the characters of the story personally: Špektorov was the narrator's personal friend and through him the narrator came to meet the other characters of the novel. On the other hand, these same characters emerge, transformed, in a work of fiction. The process of novelistic creation, i.e., something felt by the reader as partaking of the nature of "fiction", is woven into the narrator's intense personal experience, i.e., something claimed by the author to partake of the nature of "reality". This situation bears resemblance to the theme of *Les Faux-Monnayeurs* of André Gide: the "inner fiction" (F_1) fitted inside the "outer fiction" (F_2). Then F_2 tends to become "reality" when viewed against the background of F_1. To be sure, both F_1 and F_2 are equally the products of the author's imagination but, since F_1 is avowedly "fiction", by virtue of sheer contrast F_2 is felt in the reader's mind to be something else, namely, "reality".

Thus, in *Xudožnik neizvesten* the "outer fiction" synthesizes "truth in life" and "truth in art".[54] This situation presents a curious similarity to those concentric "circles of credibility" that I observed while discussing *Pjatyj strannik*:[55] "outer circles" conveying greater sense of reality than "inner circles".

The "outer fiction" refers to the narrator's personal experience with the characters and his factual observations. The "inner fiction" refers to the same characters familiar to the author but as they appear in the story that he is writing about them. This complex interrelation between the narrator and his characters makes the action more credible and the characters, more valid.

This situation also gives the author the possibility to "reconstitute" what his characters would do or say under different circumstances arising throughout the story. And more than once "facts" "belie" the narrator's "expectations". "Encounters" between Špektorov and Arximedov are of this nature. This oscillation between one "expectation" and another "fulfillment" accounts for both the poetry and the sadness of the novel.[56]

[53]   V. Kaverin, *Xudožnik neizvesten* (Leningrad, 1931), p. 119.
[54]   The expressions in the quotation-marks are taken from E. M. Forster, *Aspects of Novel* (New York, 1954), p. 101.
[55]   *Vid.* p. 146 of this study.
[56]   Professor G. Struve thoughtfully discussed this novel in his *Soviet Russian Literature 1917-1950* (Norman, Okla., 1951), pp. 108-111.

CONCLUSION

When we place the Serapion Brotherhood in proper literary perspective we come to the conclusion that their literary achievement is modest. The Serapion Brothers did not found a literary school. In fact – as it appears from the Serapion "Manifesto" and from Fedin's words[1] – the Brotherhood did not even intend to found one. The Serapion Brotherhood was not a formal organization as different proletarian "literary" groups of that time. Professor Struve observes that "Their 'Brotherhood' was not a literary school, held together by any real or fictitious tenets. What united them was their youth, their zest for life, their eager interest in literature, and their firm belief in the autonomy of art and in the freedom of the writer."[2]

For this reason it cannot even be determined when the Brotherhood broke up. Insofar as I know, there was no formal "dissolution" of the Brotherhood. Actually there could not have been any, precisely because the Brotherhood was not an "incorporated" association. It is more appropriate for us to speak of individual authors endowed with unequal talents and different temperaments, who wrote quite dissimilar works insofar as the literary substance of their works is concerned. In 1929 Ležnev said: "After the cessation of the Civil War they were one of the centers of crystallization of the new prose; they [i.e., the Serapion Brothers, H.O.] are gradually losing their importance as a group."[3]

I do not concern myself too much with purely chronological problems.

---

[1]   *Vid.* p. 14 of this study.
[2]   Gleb Struve, *Soviet Russian Literature 1917-1950* (Norman, Okla., 1951), p. 45.
[3]   A. Ležnev and D. Gorbov, *Literatura revoljucionnogo desjatiletija 1917-1927* ("Proletarij", 1929), p. 69.
   Here is an excerpt from a letter dated May 17, 1928 that one of his readers wrote to Zoščenko: "[...] Zimoj mne nado bylo opponirovat' po dokladu 'Serapionovy brat'ja kak obščestvo!' [...]" (Mix. Zoščenko, *Pis'ma k pisatelju*, Leningrad, 1929, p. 9). This would testify to the fact that the common reading public took a certain interest in the Serapion Brotherhood even at this late date.

What really matters is the actual achievement of the Serapions in Russian literature, their over-all impact on its development.

The Symbolists had created a literary "epoch": their "theory" and their "practice" blended to bring about a grand literary and cultural spring-tide. The Acmeists, reacting against Symbolism, had also created a literary "epoch", although upon a more limited scale.

The Serapion Brothers did not create a similar "epoch" in narrative prose whose state of crisis both Lunc, Gruzdev and Kaverin had repeatedly proclaimed.[4] Their "practice" fell short of their "theory", i.e., they did not substantially attain the purposes by which they were inspired when creating their literary works. They borrowed their fundamental principle from the Russian Formalists: they regarded literary performance as *craftsmanship* (masterstvo), literary work as a *thing made* (vešč' sdelannaja) in which *device* (priëm) is the key-stone. Lunc, the Brotherhood's main theoretician, challenged his fellow Serapions to infuse into Russian literature a solid tradition of plot construction.

To take the attitude that a literary work is a thing made is neither good nor bad. Everything depends on what we make of this attitude. Now, in the Serapion Brothers' works this attitude frequently breeds certain pedestrianism. Although the themes appear exotic and the treatment, "estranged", ultimately there persists the prevalent impression that many of the Serapion Brothers' works lack sophistication and vitality. The notion of "device" often developed nothing more than extravagant and unjustifiable mannerism. Some of those "ornamental" prose works desperately faded out. High-flown declamation, stylistic graces and the author's effusion sound hollow to-day. Nikitin's works seem to have suffered particularly in this respect. "Documentary" (protokol'nyj) style *à la* Pil'njak,[5] physiological crudeness of description, over-use of dialectal phraseology, jargon and slang, all this has turned out to be a deadweight ruinously overburdening their prose. These deficiencies show that the Serapion Brothers·lacked, at the time, a substantial stylistic culture. In this "word-conscious" literature Zoščenko in his smaller genre achieved relative success by artistically imitating "non-literary" living speech.

The tradition of plot construction was not enriched and perpetuated in the Serapion Brothers' works to any great extent. In this respect the

---

[4] One of such exchanges of critical comments can be found in the account "Diskussii o sovremennoj literature", *Russkij sovremennik*, 2 (1924), pp. 273-278. The "epoch" that the Serapion Brothers failed to create might have been a new literary Baroque.
[5] *Vid.* p. 63 *et seq.* of this study.

Serapion Brothers had not quite met Lunc's challenge. Kaverin's works stand out most conspicuously. His early works are a mixture of eccentric phantasmagoria parodying E. T. A. Hoffmann and experimentation with plot inspired, no doubt, by Sterne. Later, Kaverin blended successfully all those disparate elements, e.g., in his excellent *Xudožnik neizvesten*. It seems to me that in this work Kaverin achieved the crispness of literary form that is the sign of real literary culture. In my opinion Kaverin and Fedin achieved more in plot construction than the other Serapions. These two authors are also the most interesting to read.

The final balance may appear somewhat disappointing. The achievement falls short of the initial purpose. Except Fedin and Kaverin at their best – *Goroda i gody* and *Xudožnik neizvesten* – the Serapion Brothers did not attain, in their works, the higher form of the "synthesis" toward which Lunc had urged them to strive.[6]

Now, for justice's sake, we must keep in mind the following "extenuating" circumstances. In 1921 when the Brotherhood emerged, the Serapions were in their twenties; Lunc had barely grown out of his teens, whereas Kaverin was only nineteen years old. "La valeur n'attend pas le nombre des années" of course. However, Cid was a soldier. And it takes probably a longer time to mature into a distinguished writer than to distinguish oneself as a brave soldier. A great literature grows from free experimentation, in an atmosphere of – at least relative – creative freedom.

The Serapion Brothers as "Serapion-inspired" had neither time nor opportunity to realize their potentialities and to establish their own vivifying tradition. Under other circumstances the Serapion Brotherhood might have developed in quite another way.

[6]   *Vid.* pp. 47-49 of this study.

BIBLIOGRAPHY*

A. THE WRITINGS OF THE SERAPION BROTHERS

1. *Belles-lettres*

Константин Александрович ФЕДИН:

——, *Светает* (П., Гос. Изд-во, 1921).
——, *Бакунин в Дрездене. Театр в двух актах* (П., Гос. Изд., 1922).
——, "Песьи души", *Серапионовы Братья. Альманах Первый* (Петербург, 1922).
——, "Песьи души", *Серапионовы Братья. Заграничный Альманах* (Берлин, 1922).
——, "Про радость, Сказочка (Наточке Грековой)", *Петербургский Сборник*, 1922.
——, "Анна Тимофеевна, Повесть", *Альманах артели писателей "Круг"*, кн. 2 (1923).
——, *Анна Тимофеевна. Повесть* (Берлин, 1923).
——, "Бакунин в Дрездене, Театр в 2 актах", *Наши Дни*, № 1 (1923).
——, *Пустырь. Сборник* (М.-П., Изд. "Круг", 1923).
——, *Сад* (П., Изд. "Петроград", 1923).
——, "О 1919-м (Из романа *Города и годы*)", *Наши Дни*, № 4 (1924).
——, *Города и годы. Роман* (Ленинград, 1924).
——, *Рассказ об одном утре* (1924, Изд. "Круг").
——, "Тишина, Рассказ", *Русский Современник*, кн. 4 (1924), pp. 59-73.
——, "Наровчатская хроника", *Ковш*, кн. 2 (1925).
——, *Рассказы* (= *Библиотека "Огонек"*, 113) (Москва, 1926).
——, *Собрание сочинений в 4-х томах.*(Л., Изд. "Прибой", 1927).
——, *Собрание сочинений в 4-х томах* (М.-Л., ГИХЛ, 1929-1930)
       т. I. *Пустырь. Повести и рассказы*
       т. II. *Города и годы. Роман*
       т. III. *Трансвааль. Повести и рассказы*
       т. IV. *Братья. Роман.*
——, *Трансвааль. Рассказы* (М.-Л., Гиз, 1927).
——, *Братья. Роман* (Берлин, 1928).
——, "Старик, Рассказ", *Красная Новь*, № 1 (1930), pp. 3-30.
——, *Старик* (Ленинград, 1930).

---

* At the suggestion of the publishers I have expanded the bibliography that I had originally used in my doctoral dissertation.

——, *Повести и рассказы* (Издательство писателей в Ленинграде, 1933).
——, *Города и годы. Роман* (Москва, ГИХЛ, 1934).
——, *Похищение Европы. Роман* (Л., Гослитиздат)
      кн. I (Л., 1934)
      кн. II (Л., 1935).
——, *Повести и рассказы. Изд-ние 2-е* (Москва, 1936).
——, *Я был актером. Повесть* (Ленинград, 1937).
——, *Сочинения* (Москва, ГИХЛ, 1952-54)
      I. *Города и годы*
      II. *Братья*
      III. *Похищение Европы*
      IV. *Санаторий Арктур*
      V. *Необыкновенное лето*
      VI. *Повести и рассказы, очерки, статьи, лит. воспоминания, речи.*
——, *Города и годы* (Москва, ГИХЛ, 1959).
——, *Собрание сочинений (в 9-ти томах)* (Москва, Гослитиздат, 1959-62).
——, *Cities and years. A novel.* Translated by Michael Scammell (New York, 1962).

Всеволод Вячеславович ИВАНОВ:

——, "По Иртышу, Дед Антон (Рассказы)", *Сборник пролетарских писателей*, 1917, pp. 85-107.
——, *Рогульки. Первая книжка рассказов* (Тайга, 1919).
——, "Алтайские сказки", *Красная Новь*, кн. 2 (1921), pp. 3-11.
——, *Огненная душа* (Харбин, 1921).
——, "Партизаны, Рассказ", *Красная Новь*, № 1 (1921), pp. 3-40.
——, *Партизаны. Повесть* (П., Изд. "Космист", 1921).
——, "Смерть, Рассказ", *Грядущее*, №№ 4-6 (1921).
——, *В гражданской войне (из записок омского журналиста)* (Харбин, Изд. "Заря", 1921).
——, "Амулет", *Сибирские огни*, кн. 2 (1922), pp. 3-15.
——, "Бронепоезд 14-69, Повесть", *Красная Новь*, № 1 (5) (1922), pp. 75-124.
——, *Бронепоезд № 14-69. Повесть* (Москва, Гиз, 1922).
——, *Цветные ветра. Повесть* (Петербург, "Эпоха", 1922).
——, *1. Дитё. 2. Лога. Рассказы* (П., И-во "Эпоха", 1922).
——, *Глухой мак* (П.-Б., "Эпоха", 1922).
——, "Голубые пески, Роман", *Красная Новь*, кн. 3, 4, 5, 6 (1922), кн. 1, 2, 3 (1923).
——, *Кургамыш – зеленый бог* (П., Изд. "Космист", 1922).
——, "Лоскутное озеро, Рассказ", *Петербургский сборник*, 1922.
——, "Полая Арапия, Повесть", *Правда*, № 77 (1922).
——, *Седьмой берег. Сборник рассказов* (Москва, Изд. "Круг", 1922).
——, *Седьмой берег. Сборник рассказов. Изд. 2-ое доп.* ("Круг", 1923)
      Содержание: "Глиняная шуба"; "Лога"; "Синий зверюшка"; "Алтайские сказки"; "Рассказы о себе"; "Подкова"; "Полая Арапия"; "Лоскутное озеро"; "Вахада"; "Сара"; "Гу-я-тук"; "Берег жёлтых рыб"; "Шо-Гуанг-Го, амулет великого города"; "История Чжель-Люна, искателя корня женшень"; "Бык времени"; "Жаровня архангела Гавриила"; "Глухие маки".
——, "Синий зверюшка", *Серапионовы Братья. Альманах Первый* (Петербург, 1922).
——, "Синий зверюшка", *Серапионовы Братья. Заграничный Альманах* (Берлин, 1922).

158 BIBLIOGRAPHY

——, *Голубые пески. Дитё. Роман* (М.-П., Изд. "Круг", 1923).

——, *Голубые пески. Роман* (Берлин, 1923).

——, *Сопки. Партизанские повести* (М., ГИ, 1923).

——, "Возвращение Будды, Повесть", *Наши Дни*, № 3 (1923).

——, *Возвращение Будды. Повесть* (Берлин, 1923).

——, "Жаровня Архангела Гавриила", *Завтра*, № 1 (1923), рр. 49-60.

——, "Ферганский хлопок, Рассказ", *Литературно-художественный альманах для всех*, № 1 (1924).

——, "Как создаются курганы, Рассказ", *Красная Новь*, кн. 4 (21) (1924), рр. 3-8.

——, "Из романа *Северосталь* (отрывок)", *Красная Новь*, № 5 (1924).

——, *Сопки. Партизанские повести* т. I. Изд. 2-е ("Мосполиграф", 1924).

——, "Створчатые зеркала, Пять рассказов", *Красная Нива*, № 2 (1924), рр. 34-36.

——, *Возвращение Будды. Рассказы* т. II (Мосполиграф, 1924)
    Содержание: "Возвращение Будды"; "Заповедник"; "Рыбы"; "Створчатые зеркала"; "Очередная задача"; "Долг".

——, *Чудесные похождения портного Фокина. Повесть* (Л., Гиз, 1925).

——, *Экзотические рассказы* (Харьков, ТИ Украины, 1925).

——, *Иприт. Роман* 9 выпусков: В. Иванов-В. Шкловский (Гиз, 1925).

——, "Каменные калачи. Рассказ", *Новый Мир*, № 11 (1925).

——, *По следам битв* (Кинешма, Изд. "Приволжская Правда", 1925)
    Содержание: "Река Соша"; "Даешь Варшаву"; "У Нарвы".

——, *Рассказы.* С предисловием А. Луначарского и вступ. статьей А. Воронского (М., Изд. "Никитинские субботники", 1925)
    Содержание: "Бронепоезд № 14-69"; "Китаец Сень-Вьюн-чу"; "Прапорщик Обаб"; "Рельсы"; "Смерть капитана Незеласова"; "Пена"; "Дитё"; "Лога"; "Долг"; "Партизаны".

——, *Возвращение Будды* (Москва, "Круг", 1925).

——, *Хабу. Повесть* (Москва, "Московский рабочий", 1925).

——, "Бегствующий остров", *Альм. Пролетарий*, 1926.

——, *Бразильская любовь. Рассказы* (М., "Огонек", 1926).

——, "Егор Иваныч", *Молодая Гвардия*, № 8 (1926), рр. 35-39.

——, *Гафир и Мариам. Рассказы и повести* (М., Изд. "Круг", 1926)
    Содержание: "Встреча"; "Путешествие на реку Тун"; "Когда я был факиром"; "Орленое время"; "Гафир и Маркалэ"; "Чудесные похождения портного Фокина"; "Хабу".

——, "Яицкие притчи, Рассказ", *Новый Мир*, № 1 (1926), рр. 10-16.

——, "Кавказские сказы", *Молодая гвардия*, № 9 (1926), рр. 55-58.

——, *Нежинские огурцы. Рассказы* (Л., Изд. "Земля и Фабрика", 1926).

——, *Пустыня Тууб-коя. Рассказы* (М.-Л., 1926)
    Содержание: "Пустыня Тууб-коя"; "Лощина Кары-сор"; "Киргиз Темер-Бей"; "Чудо актера Смирнова"; "Жиры"; "Денежный ящик"; "Обсерватория"; "Рассказы об Октябре"; "Атаман из Семипалатинска"; "Андрейман"; "Случай в Алалайских камнях".

——, "Блаженный Ананий", *Альманах Круг. Кн.* 6-ая (Москва, Артель писателей "Круг", 1927).

——, *Дыхание пустыни. Рассказы* (Ленинград, "Прибой", 1927).

——, *Избранное.* Со вступительной статьей Лежнева, портретом автора и автобиографией (Харьков, Изд. "Пролетарий", 1927).

——, *Тайное тайных. Рассказы* (Москва, 1927).

——, *Собрание сочинений* (Москва, Гос. изд., 1928-31)
    т. I.   ???
    т. II.   *Экзотические рассказы* (1928)
    т. III. *Счастье епископа Валентина и другие рассказы* (1928)

т. IV. *Бегствующий остров и другие повести* (1928)

т. V. *Гибель Железной. Голубые пески*

т. VI. *???*

т. VII. *Путешествие в страну, которой еще нет* (1931).

——, *Бронепоезд 14-69. Партизаны* Изд. 2 (Москва, Гос. изд-во, 1930).

——, *Компромисс Наиб-хана (Сцены пограничной жизни)* (Л., 1931).

——, *Повести бригадира Н. М. Синицына* (Л., 1931).

——, *Партизанские повести* (“Бронепоезд 14-69”, “Партизаны”, “Цветные ветра”) (Л., 1932).

——, *Васька Запус, или Голубые пески* (Ленинград, 1933).

——, *Бронепоезд № 14-69.* Повесть переработанная автором для юношества (Москва, Гос. изд. детской литературы, 1934).

——, *Бронепоезд 1469. (Пьеса) В 4-х действиях* (Москва, Центральное Бюро по распространению драматической продукции [ЦЕДРАМ], 1934).

——, *Дикие люди. Рассказы* (Москва, 1934).

——, *Пархоменко. Бронепоезд 14-69* (= *Библиотека избранных произведений советской литературы 1917-1947*) (Москва, 1948).

——, *Бронепоезд 14-69; пьеса в четырёх действиях.* Новая ред. (Москва, Гос. изд-во культурно-просветительской лит-ры, 1952).

——, *Повести, рассказы, воспоминания* (Москва, 1952).

——, *Партизанские повести* (“Бронепоезд 14-69”, “Партизаны”) (Москва, 1956).

——, *Партизанские повести* (Москва, 1958).

——, *Собрание сочинений (В восьми томах)* (Москва, 1958-60)

    Содержание:

    I. *Партизанские повести*

    II. *Повести*

    III. *Рассказы* 1917-27

    IV. *Рассказы* 1930-55

    V. *Пархоменко*

    VI. *Похождения факира*

    VII. *Мы идем в Индию*

    VIII. *Очерки, статьи, воспоминания.*

——, *Panzerzug Nr. 14-69. Erzählung.* Deutsch von E. Schiemann, 2. Aufl. (Hamburg, 1923).

——, *Le train blindé numéro 1469.* Traduit du russe par Sidersky, 3e éd. (Paris, 1927).

——, “Unfrozen water”, *Bonfire: Stories out of Soviet Russia. An Anthology of Contemporary Russian Literature.* Ed. S. Konovalov (London, 1932).

——, *Armoured train, 14-69.* A play in 8 scenes translated from the Russian by Gibson-Cowan and A. T. K. Grant (London-New York, 1933).

Вениамин Александрович КАВЕРИН:

——, “Хроника города Лейпцига за 18.. год”, *Серапионовы Братья. Альманах Первый* (Петербург, 1922).

——, “Хроника города Лейпцига за 18.. год”, *Серапионовы Братья. Заграничный Альманах* (Берлин, 1922).

——, *Мастера и подмастерья. Рассказы* (М., Изд-во “Круг”, 1923).

——, “Пятый странник, Повесть”, *Альманах Круг*, кн. 1 (1923), pp. 157-198.

——, “Бочка”, *Русский Современник*, кн. 2 (1924), pp. 100-126.

——, “Большая игра”, *Литературная мысль*, № 3 (1925).

——, "Девять десятых судьбы, Повесть", *Ковш* № 3 (1925), pp. 73-120, *Ковш* № 4 (1926), pp. 139-205.

——, "Конец Хазы, Роман (Памяти Льва Лунца)", *Ковш*, № 1 (1925), pp. 161-236.

——, *Конец Хазы. Повесть* (Ленинград, 1925).

——, *Рассказы* ("Столяры", "Щиты и др.") (Москва, Изд. "Круг", 1925).

——, *Девять десятых судьбы. Роман* (М.-Л., Гиз, 1926).

——, *Девять десятых судьбы.* Изд. 3-е (1929).

——, *Ночь на 26-е октября. Рассказ* (Л., "Прибой", 1926).

——, *Осада дворца. Повесть* (для детей и юношества) (М.-Л., 1926).

——, "Ревизор". *Звезда*, № 4 (1926), pp. 5-33.

——, *Впереди всех* (для детей и юношества) (М.-Л., 1926).

——, *Большая игра. Рассказы* (М., 1927).

——, *Бубновая масть. Рассказы* (Л., Изд. "Книжные новинки", 1927).

——, *Ревизор* (Берлин, 1927).

——, *Воробьиная ночь. Рассказы* (Москва, Артель писателей "Круг", 1927)
    Содержание: "Воробьиная ночь"; "Ревизор"; Сегодня утром"; "Большая игра"; "Друг Микадо".

——, "Скандалист, или Вечера на Васильевском острове, Роман", *Звезда*, №№ 2, 3, 4, 5, 6, 7 (1928).

——, *Скандалист, или Вечера на Васильевском острове* (Ленинград, "Прибой", 1929).

——, *Конец Хазы. Повесть* (Ленинград, "Прибой", 1930)
    Added title-page: В. Каверин, Сочинения, I
    Содержание: "Конец Хазы, Повесть"; "Фантастические рассказы: Друг микадо"; "Сегодня утром"; "Голубое солнце"; "Пятый странник"; "Щиты и свечи"; "Бочка"; "Ревизор"; "Воробьиная ночь".

——, *Черновик человека* (Ленинград, 1931).

——, *Скандалист, или Вечера на Васильевском острове. Роман.* Изд. 3-е (Ленинград, 1931).

——, *Художник неизвестен* (Ленинград, 1931).

——, *Укрощение Мистера Робинзона, или Потерянный рай. Комедия в 5-ти действиях* (Москва, Всекдрам, [1933?]).

——, *Укрощение Робинзона, или Потерянный рай. Комедия в пяти актах и шести картинах* (Ленинград, 1934).

——, *Избранные повести и рассказы* (Ленинград, 1935).

——, *Открытая книга. Трилогия* (Москва, 1956)
    т. I: части 1-ая и 2-ая
    т. II: часть 3-ья.

——, *Укрощение Мистера Робинзона*; *Актеры*; *Сказка о Мите и Маше*; *Утро дней*; *пьесы* (Москва, 1959).

——, *The unknown artist*: Olesha I. K., *Envy* (by) Y. Olesha. The unknown artist (by) V. Kaverin. With an introduction by Gleb Struve. Translated by P. Ross (London, 1947).

——, *Open book*. Translated from the Russian by B. Pearce. Ed. by D. Skvirsky (Moscow, 195?).

——, *Open book*. English translation by B. Pearce (L., 1955).

Лев Натанович ЛУНЦ:

——, "Исходящая № 37, Рассказ", *Россия*, № 1 (1922), pp. 21-23.

——, "В пустыне, Рассказ", *Серапионовы Братья. Альманах Первый* (Петербург, 1922).

——, "В пустыне, Рассказ", *Серапионовы Братья. Заграничный Альманах* (Берлин, 1922).

——, "Бертран де Борн, Трагедия в 5 д., послесловие", Сборник *Город*, № 1 (1923), pp. 9-48.

——, "Обезьяны идут!, Пьеса", *Весёлый Альманах* (изд. "Круг", 1923).

——, "Родина, Повесть (В. Каверину)", *Еврейский Альманах*, 1923.

——, "Вне закона, Трагедия в 5 д. и 7 акт", *Беседа*, № 1 (1923), pp. 43-125.

——, *Вне закона. Трагедия в 5 д. и 7 акт* (П., Изд. Гржебина, 1923).

——, "Город правды, Пьеса в 3 д." , *Беседа*, № 5 (1924), pp. 63-101.

Николай Николаевич НИКИТИН:

——, "Мокей, Рассказ: 1. Питер кружевной; 2. О том и о сём", *Дом искусств*, № 2 (1921).

——, "Мокей. Сказка", *Красная Новь*, № 3 (1921), pp. 13-20.

——, *Американское счастье. Рассказы* (П., Изд. "Былое", 1922).

——, "Барка", *Альманах Шиповник*, I (1922), pp. 27-39.

——, "Чаване, Рассказ", *Наши дни*, № 2 (Москва, 1922), pp. 35-54.

——, "Дези", *Серапионовы Братья. Альманах Первый*, 1922.

——, *Камни. Рассказы* (П., "Алконост", 1922).

——, "О лете огненном", *Новая Россия*, № 3 (1922), pp. 3-7.

——, "Пес", *Серапионовы Братья. Заграничный Альманах*, 1922.

——, *Рассказы* (М., "Круг", 1922).
    Содержание: "25-го июля 1918"; "Шесть дней"; "Трава-пышма"; "Ночь"; "Пес"; "Подвал"; "Американское счастье"; "Лес".

——, "Из пов. *Рвотный форт*", *Красная Новь*, IV (1922), pp. 64-86.

——, *Рвотный форт. Рассказы* (М.-Л., 1922).

——, *Рвотный форт. Изд. 2-е* (М.-Л., 1926).

——, "Жизнь гвардии сапера, Рассказ", *Петербургский сборник*, 1922.

——, *Бунт. Рассказы* (М.-П., Изд-во "Круг", 1923)
    Содержание: "25-го июля 1918 года"; "Шесть дней"; "Трава-пышма"; "Ночь"; "Пес"; "Подвал"; "Американское счастье"; "Лес".

——, *Камни. Рассказы* (П., "Былое", 1923).

——, "Ночь, Рассказ", *Альманах артели писателей "Круг"*, кн. 2 (1923).

——, *Русские ночи. Повесть* (Берлин, 1923)
    Содержание:
    Первая Ночь. Ночь
    Вторая Ночь. Кол
    Третья Ночь. Форт.

——, *Ночной пожар. Рассказы* (Берлин, 1924)
    Содержание: "Отступление"; "Трава-Пышма"; "Лес"; "Пелла"; "Чаване"; "Пес"; "Американское счастье"; "Подвал".

——, "Полет", *Звезда*, №№ 1-2 (1924).

——, *Полет. Повесть* (Берлин, 1924).

——, *Сейчас на Западе. Берлин-Рур-Лондон* (Л.-М., "Петроград", 1924).

——, *Суровый день* (М., ГИ, 1924).

——, *Вещи о войне* (Ленгиз, 1924)
    Содержание:
    I. Восток: "25-го июля 1918 года"; "Шесть дней"; "Трава-Пышма"
    II. Запад: "Обыкновенный эпизод"; "Пес"
    III. Север: "Барка"; "Камни"; "Чаване"

IV. Юг: "Ночь".

——, 1. "Белый лес", 2. "Тоска", *Ковш*, кн. 2 (1925).

——, *Могила Панбурлея. Рассказы* (Л., "Прибой", 1925).

——, *Полёт. Рассказы* (Л., Гиз, 1925).

——, "Юбилей" (Из "Обояньских повестей"), *Новый Мир*, кн. 10 (1926), pp. 29-47.

——, *Митька Брень. Рассказ* (Ленинград, 1926).

——, *О бывшем купце Хропове, об Олимпиаде Ивановне и о веселом художнике Мокине. Повесть* (М., ГИ, 1926).

——, *Рассказы* (= Биб-ка ж. "Смехач") (Л., 1926).

——, *Рвотный форт. Рассказы* Изд. 2-ое, испр. и доп. (М., ГИ, 1926).

——, *С карандашом в руке. Очерки и рассказы* (Москва, 1926)
    Содержание: Петербург; "Город 'Пиковой дамы'"; "Зимний порт"; "Зимние дни"; "Темной ночью"; "Утро в Ленинграде"; "Завод"; "В Европу"; "'Жадное дело'"; "Политика Иван Павлыча"; "Монастырь на Череменецком озере"; "Столица Урала"; "Капитал"; "Предание"; "Перед судом"; "Из записок охотника Арсеньева 'О мистическом мужике'".

——, *Екатеринбургские рассказы* (Л., 1927).

——, *Лирическая земля. Рассказы и очерки* (Ленинград, "Мысль", 1927)
    Содержание: "50000 километров"; "По озерам"; "Письма о себе"; "Планида"; "Встречи"; "Английские зеркала".

——, *Могила Панбурлея. Рассказы* (Харьков, "Пролетарий", 1927).

——, "Преступление Кирика Руденко, Повесть", *Красная Новь*, 1927, кн. 9, pp. 3-46; кн. 10, pp. 3-32; кн. 11, pp. 3-56.

——, *Обоянские повести* (Харьков, "Пролетарий", 1928).

——, *Собрание сочинений* (Харьков, Изд. "Пролетарий", 1928-1929)
    т. I: *Рвотный форт*: "Подвал"; "Чавалы"; "Барка"; "Камни"; "Мокей"; "Пелла"; "Дэзи"; "Жизнь гвардии сапера"; "Хлеб"; "Кошка-собака"
    т. II: *Полёт*
    т. VI: *Преступление Кирика Руденко*.

——, *Преступление Кирика Руденко (Сапожник из Парижа). Роман* (Берлин, 1928) (= *Библиотека* "Литературные новинки", т. 5).

——, *Собачий ящик. Повесть* (Ленинград, "Мысль", 1928).

——, *Шпион. Роман* (М., "Земля и Фабрика", 1930).

——, *Линия огня. Пьеса в 4-х действиях и 78 картинах* (Москва," Федерация", 1931).

——, *Шпион. Линия огня. Наивный Вениамин* (Л., Лен ГИХЛ, 1932).

——, *Обоянь. Рассказы о войне* (Ленинград, 1933).

——, *Конкурс хитрецов* (Ленинград, 1934).

——, "Потерянный Рембрандт, *Повесть*", *Новый Мир*, кн. 3 (1935), pp. 9-27.

——, *Избранное (в двух томах)* (Москва, 1959)
    т. I: "Преступление Кирика Руденко"; "Суровый день"; "О бывшем купце Хропове".

——, *Scènes de la révolution russe*, par I. Ehrenburg, N. Nikitine, Boris Pilniak, A. Rémisov; traduit du russe avec l'autorisation des auteurs par S. Lieskov (Paris, 1923). Contents: ... N. Nikitine, "La capitale de L'Oural".

——, *Der Flug* (Berlin, 1926).

Елизавета Григорьевна ПОЛОНСКАЯ:

——, *Знамения (стихи)* (П., Изд. "Эрато", 1921).

——, Стихи: "На память о тяжелом годе..."; "Сухой и гулкий щелкнул бара-

бан…”, *Серапионовы Братья. Заграничный Альманах*, 1922.

——, “Смешалось все. Года войны…”, *Петербургский сборник, 1922.*

——, *Под каменным дождем, 1921-1923. Стихи* (П., Изд. “Полярная звезда”, 1923).

——, *Зайчата. Сказка в стихах* (для детей) (П.-М., Изд. “Радуга”, 1923).

——, *Зайчата. Сказка в стихах.* Изд. 4-е (Ленинград, 1926).

——, *Гости* (Ленинград, Изд. “Книга”, 1924).

——, *Часы* (Ленинград, 1925).

——, *Про пчёл и про мишку-медведя* (Ленинград, 1925).

——, *Про пчёл и про мишку-медведя.* Изд. 2-е (Москва, 1927).

——, Посв. М. Шагинян. В петле (Лирическая фильма), “Плеть свистела Копали ров…”, *Ковш*, кн. 1 (1925).

——, Прощальная ода:

    1. “Другие пускай воспевают работу…”,
    2. “А помнишь, как начинались стихи?…”,
    3. “Дырявы подошвы, а ноги крылаты…”,
    4. “Ямбы, любовь, безделье…”,
    5. “Утреет. Морозный рассвет…”,
       Ковш, кн. 4 (1926).

——, *Город и деревня* (Ленинград, 1927).

——, *Про очаг да ясли и пирог на масле* (М.-Л., 1927).

——, *Упрямый календарь. Стихи и поэмы 1924-1927* (Ленинград, 1929).

——, *Жак и Жанна (Парижская коммуна)* (Ленинград, Изд. “Красная газета”, 1929).

——, *Немного спорта разного сорта* (для детей) (Москва, 1930).

——, *Пеппе Ракони* (М.-Л., Изд. “Молодая гвардия”, 1931).

——, *Закусочная Зиве. Рассказ* (М.-Л., Изд. “Молодая гвардия”, 1931).

——, *Года. Избранные стихи* (Ленинград, 1935).

——, *Новые стихи, 1932-1936* (Ленинград, 1937).

——, *Стихотворения и поэмы* (Ленинград, 1960).

Михаил Леонидович СЛОНИМСКИЙ:

——, “Антихристово причастие”, *Петербургский сборник*, 1922, pp. 95-98.

——, “Дикий”, *Серапионовы Братья. Альманах Первый* (Петербург, 1922).

——, “Дикий”, *Серапионовы Братья. Заграничный Альманах* (Берлин, 1922).

——, *Шестой стрелковый. Рассказы* (Петербург, “Время”, 1922).

——, “Тумба, Пьеса”, *Россия* (1922), III.

——, “Под предлогом сапог, Рассказ”, *Россия* (1922), IV.

——, “Артистка”, Сборник *Молодая Россия* (Берлин, 1923), pp. 7-42.

——, “Четвертая ставка”, *Альманах Петроград*, 1923, pp. 29-39.

——, *Шестой стрелковый. Рассказы* Изд. 2-е (Москва, “Круг”, 1923)
    Содержание: “Варшава”; “Дикий”; “Лопата Еремея”; “Копыто коня”; “Зыря”; “Шестой стрелковый”; “Генерал”; “Чортово колесо”.

——, *Палата смертников. Рассказ* (П., Изд-во “Былое”, 1923).

——, “Поручик Архангельский”, *Завтра*, № 1 (1923), pp. 61-78.

——, *Машина Эмери. Рассказы* (Ленинград, Изд-во “Атеней”, 1924).
    Содержание: “Актриса”; “Машина Эмери”; “Начальник станции”; “Сельская идиллия”.

——, “Штабс-капитан Рапченко. Рассказ”, *Звезда*, IV (1924), pp. 38-44.

——, “Сухопутная жизнь”, *Литературно-художественный журнал для всех*, кн. 1 (1924).

——, *Удар. Рассказы* (Ленгиз, 1924).
——, "Однофамильцы", *Альманах Ковш*, кн. 1 (1925).
——, "Черныш, Рассказ", *Ковш*, кн. 3 (1925).
——, *Воздушный корабль* (Ленинград, Изд-во "Время", 1925).
——, *Рассказы о девятьсот пятом* (Ленинград, "Прибой", 1926).
——, *Лавровы. Роман* (Ленинград, ГИ, 1927).
——, *Лавровы. Роман* Изд. 2-е (Москва, 1927).
——, *Сухопутная жизнь. Рассказы* (Москва, ГИ, 1927).
——, *Сочинения.* С критико-биографическим очерком Зел. Штейнмана. т. 1-4, *Земля и Фабрика* (Москва, 1928-29)
    Содержание:
    т. 1. *Шестой стрелковый*
    т. 2. *Западники*
    т. 3. *Средний проспект*
    т. 4. *Лавровы.*
——, "Пощечина, Рассказ", *Земля и фабрика*, кн. 4 (1929), pp. 301-325.
——, *Пощечина* (Ленинград, 1930).
——, *Фома Клешнев. Роман* (М.-Л., ГИХЛ, 1931).
——, *Германия* (Москва, 1932).
——, *Лавровы. Фома Клешнев* (Москва, 1936).
——, *Повести и рассказы* (Ленинград, 1937)
    Содержание: "Гибель"; "Варшава"; "Чортово колесо"; "Шестой стрелковый"; "Комиссар временного правительства"; "Копыто коня"; "Начальник станции"; "Средний проспект"; "Повесть о Левине".
——, *Фома Клешнев.* Заново перер. изд. (Ленинград, 1938).
——, *Инженеры. Лавровы* (Москва, 1953).
——, *Избранные произведения (в двух томах)* (Москва, 1958).

Николай Семенович ТИХОНОВ:

——, Стихи в альманахе стихов *Островитяне*, № 1 (1921).
——, "Махно. Стихи", *Серапионовы Братья. Заграничный Альманах* (1922).
——, *Орда. Стихи* (1920-1921 гг.) (П., Изд. "Островитяне", 1922).
——, *Брага. Вторая книга стихов 1921-1923* (М.-П., Изд. "Круг", 1922).
——, 1. "Глухие крики, песни непростые…",
    2. "Товарищ милый и безрассудный…" *Петербургский сборник* (1922).
——, "Осень: Костры лугам, костры, как дар…", *Петроград* (1923).
——, Стихи:
    1. "Сапожник" ("Окно и в окне примелькавшийся лед…"),
    2. "Смерть бойца" ("Железо в жилах уже не то…"),
    3. "От шопота уж не встает метель…",
    4. "Судьбы не читал я в летящих глазах…",
    Наши дни, № 3 (1923).
——, "Арены чисты, вымыты решетки…", *Город*, Сборник 1 (1923).
——, "Море (стихи)", *Звезда*, № 2 (1924), pp. 148-150.
——, "Ночь в гостях, Стих", *Русский Современник*, кн. 3-я (1924), pp. 7-8.
——, "Сами (стихи)" (Ленинград, 1924).
——, "Сами", Изд. 2-е и 3-е (1924/25).
——, "Сами", Изд. 5-е (Москва, 1934).
——, *Сами. Стих (инсценировка)* (Харьков, 1924).
——, "Дорога, Поэма. М.К.Н." ("Моим гортанным толмачом…"), *Ковш*, кн. 2 (1925).

——, *Двенадцать баллад* (*стихи*) (Ленинград, 1925).

——, "Красные на Араксе, Поэма" ("Зажми слова и шпоры дай им..."), *Ковш*, кн. 1 (1925).

——, "Поиски героя" ("Прекрасный город – хлипкие каналы..."), *Ковш*, кн. 3 (1925).

——, *Вамбери* (повесть для юношей) (Ленинград, 1925).

——, *Вамбери*, Изд. 3-е (М.-Л., 1930).

——, *Друг народа* (*Сун-Ят-Сен*) (повестъ для детей старшего возраста) (М.-Л., 1926).

——, *Друг народа*, Изд. 3-е (М.-Л., 1930).

——, "Избиение трутней, Стихотворение", *Молодая гвардия*, № 7 (1926), pp. 39-40.

——, "Ночь президента" ("Не грогом горячим, но жиденьким пивом..."), "Гулливер играет в карты" ("В глазах Гулливера азарта нагар..."), *Ковш*, кн. 4 (1926).

——, *От моря до моря* (повесть для юношей) (М.-Л., 1926).

——, *От моря до моря*, Изд. 3-е (1930).

——, "Веселые лошади", *Молодая гвардия*, № 8 (1926), pp. 40-51.

——, "Бетховен, Рассказ", *Молодая гвардия*, № 10 (1926), pp. 21-35.

——, *Красные на Араксе. Дорога. Лицом к лицу* (*стихи*) (М.-Л., 1927).

——, *Поиски героя* (*стихи 1923-1926*) (Ленинград, 1927).

——, "Рискованный человек (повесть)", *Молодая гвардия*, 1927, № 1, pp. 35-57; № 2, pp. 17-46.

——, *Рискованный человек. Рассказы* (Ленинград, 1927)
    Содержание: "Бирюзовый полковник"; "Чайхана у Ляби-Хоуза"; "Рассказ с примечанием"; "Камуфляж"; "Шесть туманов"; "Английские жены"; "Халиф"; "Рискованный человек".

——, *Военные кони. Рассказы* (рассказы для юношей) (М.-Л., 1927).

——, *Военные кони*, Изд. 4-е (Ленинград, Детгиз, 1935).

——, *Избранные стихи* (Москва, 1928).

——, *От моря до моря*. Изд. 2-е (Москва, 1928).

——, *Поэмы* (М.-Л., 1928).

——, *Шесть туманов* (*рассказ*) (М.-Л., 1928).

——, *Бетховен* (для детей) (М.-Л., 1929).

——, *Чорт* (М.-Л., 1929).

——, *Чорт*. Изд. 3-е (М.-Л., Детгиз, 1936).

——, *Анофелес* (*проза*) (Ленинград, 1930).

——, *Фриц* (лдя детей) (М.-Л., 1931).

——, *Собрание стихотворений. В двух томах*
    т. I. *Стихотворения 1917-1926* (Л.-М., ГИХЛ, 1931)
    т. II. *Стихотворения 1924-1930* (Л.-М., ГИХЛ, 1932).

——, *Кочевники* (*очерки. Туркменистан*) (Москва, 1931).

——, *Кочевники*. Изд. 3-е (Ленинград, 1933).

——, *Кочевники* (= *Школьная серия*) (М.-Л., ГИХЛ, 1933).

——, *Туркменские записи* (для детей) (М.-Л., 1931).

——, *Война* (*проза*) (Ленинград, 1931).

——, *Война*, Изд. 3-е (Ленинград, 1933).

——, *Чайхана у Ляби-Хоуза* (*рассказы*) (Москва, 1932).

——, *Дискуссионный рассказ* (Москва, 1932).

——, *Избранные стихи* (Москва, 1932).

——, *Избранные стихи* (Ленинград, Ленгихл, 1932).

——, *Клинки и тачанки* (*проза*) (Ленинград, 1932).

——, *Кочевники*, Изд. 2-е (Ленинград, 1932).

——, *Рискованный человек. Рассказы* 2-е изд. (Ленинград, 1932)

Содержание: "Бирюзовый полковник"; "Чайхана у Ляби-Хоуза"; "Рассказ с примечанием"; "Камуфляж"; "Шесть туманов"; "Английские жены"; "Халиф"; "Рискованный человек".

——, *Война*, 2-е изд. (Ленинград, 1932).

——, *Чтец-декламатор. Избранные произведения революционной поэзии.* Составили: Н. Браун, А. Прокофьев и В. Саянов под редакцией Н. Тихонова (Ленинград, 1933).

——, *Избранные рассказы* (Л.-М., 1933).

——, *Клятва в тумане (проза)* (Ленинград, 1933).

——, *Война* (Ленинград, Огиз, 1933).

——, *Сами. Поэма* (Москва, 1934).

——, *Симон большевик* (М.-Л., 1932).

——, *Симон большевик*, 2-е изд. (Ленинград, Детиздат, 1934).

——, *Вечный транзит (рассказы)* (Ленинград, 1934)

Содержание: "Вечный транзит"; "Клятва в тумане"; "Река и шляпа"; "Шутники"; "Начатые сыры"; "День отдыха"; "Анофелес".

——, *Рассказы* (Ленинград, 1935).

——, *Стихи о Кахетии* (Москва, 1935).

——, *Стихотворения и поэмы в одном томе* (Ленинград, 1935).

——, *Военные кони. Рассказы*, Изд. 4-е (Гос. изд-во детской лит-ры, 1935).

——, *Простые рассказы* (Ленинград, 1936).

——, *Тень друга (стихи)* (Ленинград, 1936).

——, *Друзья. Киноповесть* (в соавторстве с Л. Арнштам) (Москва, 1937).

——, *Стихи и проза* (Москва, 1947).

Содержание: "Две поэмы"; "Огненный вид"; "Палатка под Выборгом"; "Годовщина"; "Осенние прогулки"; "Горы. Чудесная тревога"; "Из трагедии 'Нумансия'"; "Орда"; "Брага"; "Поиски героя"; "Юрга"; "Стихи о Кахетии"; "Ранние стихотворения"; "Тень друга"; "Ленинградские рассказы (Черты советского человека)"; "Рассказы разных лет"; "Маленькие рассказы"; "Из войны с белофиннами".

——, *Повести и рассказы* (= *Библиотека избранных произведений советской литературы 1917-1947*) (Москва, 1948).

——, *Вамбери. Повесть* (Москва, Географгиз, 1957).

——, *Собрание сочинений (в 6 томах)* (Москва, 1958-59)

    I. *Стихотворения*

    II. *Стихотворения, поэмы, переводы*

    III. *Рассказы, очерки*

    IV. *От моря до моря*

    V. *Рассказы. Белое чудо. Из путевых дневников*

    VI. *Ленинград принимает бой, статьи. Выступления.*

Михаил Михаилович ЗОЩЕНКО:

——, "Гришка Жиган", *Петербургский сборник*, 1922.

——, "Лялька Пятьдесят, Рассказ", *Красная Новь*, кн. 5 (1922), pp. 31-35.

——, *Рассказы Назара Ильича господина Синебрюхова* (Петербург-Берлин, "Эпоха", 1922).

——, *Рассказы Назара Ильича господина Синебрюхова* (П., "Эрато", 1922).

——, "Виктория Казимировна", *Серапионовы Братья. Альманах Первый* (Петербург, 1922).

——, "Виктория Казимировна", *Серапионовы Братья. Заграничный Альманах* (Берлин, 1922).

——, "Чёрная магия", *Наши дни*, № 1 (1923).

——, "Коза, Рассказ", Альманах артели писателей *Круг*, кн. 1 (1923).

——, *Разнотык. Рассказы* (П., "Былое", 1923).

——, *Рассказы* (П., 1923).

——, *Аристократка. Рассказы* (Петроград, 1924).

——, *Веселая жизнь. Рассказы* (Л., Гиз, 1924).

——, "Страшная ночь, Рассказ", *Ковш*, кн. 1 (1925).

——, "О чем пел соловей (Вторая сентиментальная повесть)", *Ковш*, кн. 2 (1925).

——, *Десять рассказов* (Л., Изд. "Красная газета", 1926).

——, *Избранные рассказы и повести* (Харьков, 1926).

——, *Рассказы* (= *Библиотека "Огонек"*, № 29) (Москва, 1926)
    Содержание: "Искусство Мельпомены"; "Баня"; "Случай в больнице"; "Аристократка"; "Жених"; "Исторический рассказ"; "Ошибочка"; "На живца"; "Крестьянский самородок".

——, *Собачий нюх. Юмористические рассказы* (= *Библиотека "Огонек"*, 61) (Москва, 1926).

——, *Уважаемые граждане* (Москва, Изд. "Земля и Фабрика", 1926).

——, *Уважаемые граждане*, Изд. 3-е (Москва, 1927).

——, *Бледнолицые братья. Юмористические рассказы* (= *Библиотека "Огонек"*, № 267) (Москва, 1927).

——, *Царские сапоги. Юмористические рассказы.* С предисловием В. Гадалина (Рига, 1927).

——, *Мелочи жизни. Сборник фельетонов* (Л., 1927).

——, *Нервные люди* (Харьков, Изд. "Пролетарий", 1927) ("Рассказы Назара Ильича господина Синебрюхова", pp. 151-208).

——, *Нервные люди* (Париж, 1927).

——, *О чем пел соловей. Сентиментальные повести* (Л., Гиз, 1927).

——, *О чем пел соловей*, Изд. 3-е (Л., "Прибой", 1929)
    Содержание: "Коза"; "Аполлон и Тамара"; "Страшная ночь"; "О чем пел соловей"; "Веселое приключение"; "Мудрость"; "Люди".

——, *О чем пел соловей. Повести* (Рига, 1927).

——, *Уважаемые граждане. Юмористические рассказы* (Париж, 1927).

——, *Веселые рассказы* (= *Библиотека новейших писателей*, № 2) (Париж, 1927)
    Содержание: "Точная идеология"; "Бочка"; "Режим экономии"; "Театральный механизм"; "Ошибочка"; "Часы"; "Американская реклама"; "Бывает"; "Рачис"; "Пауки и мухи"; "Хозрасчет"; "Фома неверный"; "Именинница"; "Паразит".

——, *Над кем смеетесь?* (= *Библиотека новейшей литературы*, т. 29) (Рига, 1928).

——, *Над кем смеетесь?!* (= *Библиотека сатиры и юмора*), Изд. 3-е (М., 1928).

——, *Нервные люди* (Рига, 1928)
    Содержание: "Нервные люди"; "Четыре дня"; "На посту"; "Бочка"; "Прискорбный случай"; "Кино-драма"; "Телефон"; "Режим экономии"; "Кузница здоровья"; "Гипноз"; "Театральный механизм"; "Ошибочка"; "Случай в больнице"; "Паутина"; "Гибель человека"; "Часы"; "Американская реклама"; "Туман"; "Бывает"; "Рачис"; "Человеческое достоинство"; "Старая крыса"; "Хозрасчёт"; "Точная идеология"; "Пауки и мухи"; "Сильное средство"; "Фома неверный"; "Именинница"; "Крестьянский самородок"; "Паразит"; "Барон Некс"; "Монастырь"; "Веселая жизнь"; "Последний барин".

——, *О том, что было и чего не было. Новые рассказы* (Рига, 1928).

——, *Скупой рыцарь. Рассказы* (Рига, 1928).

——, *Дни нашей жизни. Рассказы* (Рига, 1929).

——, *Избранные рассказы и повести*, Изд. 2-е (Харьков, 1930).

——, "М. П. Синягин, Воспоминания о Мишеле Синягине", *Новый Мир*, кн. 12 (1930), pp. 112-140.

——, *Рассказы о Ленине* (Москва, 1930).

——, *Приятная встреча. Новые повести и рассказы* (Рига, 1930).

——, *Собрание сочинений (в пяти томах)* ("Прибой", 1930-3)

    т. 1-2. *Рассказы*

    т. 4.   *Сентиментальные повести*

    т. 5.   *Рассказы*

    т. 6.   *Письма к писателю. Уважаемый товарищ; комедия в 3-х действиях.*

——, *Воспоминания о Мишеле Синягине* (Берлин, 1930).

——, *Избранные рассказы* (Ленинград, 1931).

——, *Избранные рассказы и повести* (Рига, 1931).

——, *М. П. Синягин. Воспоминания о Мишеле Синягине* (Ленинград, 1931).

——, *Счастливые идеи* (М. Зощенко и Н. Радлов) (Ленинград, 1931).

——, *Альманах эстрады. Под общей редакцией Мих. Зощенко* (Ленинград, 1933).

——, *Возвращенная молодость* (Рига, 193?).

——, *История одной жизни* (Ленинград, 1934).

——, *Избранное. Однотомник* (Ленинград, 1934)

    Содержание: "Рассказы 1925-1933"; "Повести 1922-1932"; "Фельетоны 1923-1933".

——, *Личная жизнь* (Ленинград, 1934).

——, *Голубая книга* (Ленинград, 1935).

——, *Избранные рассказы* (Ленинград, 1935).

——, *Возвращенная молодость.* Изд. 3-е (Москва, 1935).

——, *Бедная Лиза. Новые рассказы* (Рига, 1937).

——, *Избранные повести* ("Советский писатель", 1937)

    Содержание: Первые повести: "Мудрость"; "Коза"; "Рассказы Назара Ильича господина Синебрюхова"; "Предисловие"; "Великосветская история"; "Виктория Казимировна"; "Чертовинка"; "Гиблое место".

    Сентиментальные повести: "Предисловие"; "Аполлон и Тамара"; "Страшная ночь"; "О чем пел соловей"; "Веселое приключение"; "Сирень цветет"; "Мишель Синягин: Предисловие"; "М. П. Синягин: История одной жизни".

——, *1935-1937. Рассказы, повести, фельетоны, театр, критика* (Ленинград, 1937).

——, "Шестая повесть И. П. Белкина ('Талисман')", *Звезда*, № 1 (1937), pp. 25-32.

——, *Федот, да не тот* (Рига, 1939).

——, *Повести и рассказы* (Нью Йорк, изд. имени Чехова, 1952).

——, *Избранные рассказы и повести 1923-1956* (Ленинград, 1956).

——, *Сборник малоизвестных рассказов.* Recueil de récits humoristiques. Paris, 1962 (?) (Visages de la Russie).

——, *Four sketches* by Mikhail Zochtchenko. Translated and ed. by Cargill Sprietsma and Georges Nazaroff, "Reprinted from the Bulletin of the American Women's Club, 1929" (Paris, 1929?).

——, "A Hasty Affair"; "The Night of Horror"; "A Damp Business"; S. Konovalov (ed.), *Bonfire: Stories out of Soviet Russia. An Anthology of Contemporary Russian Literature* (London, 1932).

——, *Russia laughs.* Translated from the Russian by Helena Clayton (Boston, 1935).

——, "A miserable day, or Honesty is the best Soviet policy". A comedy in one act, by Mark Schweid. From the Russian of M. Zoschenko. *One-act plays for stage and study*, 9th ser. (New York, 1938), pp. 299-313.

——, "Bad business". A Soviet comedy by Michael Zoschenko. Translated from

the Russian by Morris Spiegel. *One-act play magazine*, New York, February 1939, pp. 691-702.

——, *The wonderful dog, and other tales*. 2nd ed. Translated by E. Fen (L., 1942).

——, *Der redliche Zeitgenosse*. Sowjetrussische Satiren. Übersetzung aus dem Russischen von Grete Willinsky (Kassel, [1950 c. 1947]).

——, *Before Sunrise*. English translation by John Richardson, in *Partisan Review*, 3-4 (1961), pp. 451-474.

——, *Scenes from the Bathhouse*, and other stories of Communist Russia (Ann Arbor, The University of Michigan Press, 1961).

——, *Nervous people*, and other stories. Edited with an introduction by Hugh McLean. Translated from the Russian by Maria Gordon and Hugh McLean (New York, 1963).

2. *Other writings*

Константин Александрович ФЕДИН:

——, Рецензия о *Доме Искусств*, № 1 (1921) и статье Замятина "Я боюсь", помещенной в этом номере *Дома Искусств*, *Книга и Революция*, № 8-9 (1921), pp. 85-86.

——, "Мелок на шубе", *Жизнь Искусства*, № 2-7 авг., №№ 792-797.

——, "Лев Лунц, *Некролог*", *Жизнь Искусства*, № 22 (1924).

——, "Автобиография", *Писатели: Автобиографии и портреты современных русских прозаиков*, В. Лидин [редактор]), (=*Современные проблемы*) (Москва, 1926).

——, "Об искусстве и критике", *Новый Мир*, кн. 3 (1927), pp. 174-177.

——, "Фельетон о языке и критике", *Звезда*, № 9 (1929).

——, Статья в "Споре о социальном заказе", *Печать и Революция*, кн. 1 (1929), pp. 74-75.

——, "Как я работаю", *Литературная учёба*, № 4 (1930), pp. 111-118.

——, Статья в сборнике *Как мы пишем* (Изд-во Писателей в Ленинграде, 1930), pp. 169-181.

——, "Язык литературы". *Литературная учеба*, №№ 3-4 (1933), pp. 110-115.

——, *Горький среди нас: двадцатые годы* (*Картины литературной жизни*) (Москва, 1943).

——, *Горький среди нас* (*Картины литературной жизни*) (Москва, ГИХЛ, 1943-)
Содержание:
ч. 1. Двадцатые годы (1920-21)
ч. 2. 1921-1928.

——, *Писатель. Искусство. Время* (о Николае Тихонове, pp. 154-158; о Михаиле Зощенко, pp. 171-181) (Москва, 1957).

——, "Автобиография", *Советские Писатели. Автобиографии в двух томах* (Москва, ГИХЛ, 1959), т. II, pp. 565-575.

——, *Писатель. Искусство. Время*. Новое, дополненное изд. (Москва, 1961).

Илья Александрович ГРУЗДЕВ:

——, "О маске как литературном приёме (Гоголь и Достоевский)", *Жизнь Искусства*, №№ 816, 817 (1921).

——, "О книгах Гершензона", *Дом искусств*, отдел Художественная критика, Библиография, № 2 (1921).

——, Рецензия: "Анна Баркова, *Женщина, Стихотворения*", *Литературные Записки*, № 2 (1922).

——, "Лицо и маска, Статья", *Серапионовы Братья. Заграничный Альманах* (Берлин, 1922), pp. 205-237.

——, "О приемах художественного повествования", *Записки Передвижного Театра*, №№ 40, 41, 42 (1922).

——, "Вечера Серапионовых Братьев", *Книга и Революция*, № 2 (1922), pp. 110-111.

——, "Всеволод Иванов", *Книга и Революция*, № 6 (18) (1922), pp. 24-26.

——, "Утилитарность и самоцель", *Петроград. Литературный альманах* (П., Изд. "Петроград", 1923).
Reprinted in *Современная русская критика 1918-1924. Сборник (Образцы и характеристики)*. Под ред. Иннокентия Оксенова (Ленинград, 1925), pp. 245-250.

——, "Мих. Слонимский, *Удар, Рассказы 1924* (рецензия)", *Русский Современник*, кн. 3-я (1924), pp. 256-257.

——, "Молодой Горький", *Молодая Гвардия*, №№ 1, 2, 3, 4 (1927).

Всеволод Вячеславович ИВАНОВ:

——, "О себе как об искусстве", *Писатели об искусстве и о себе. Сборник статей*, № 1 (1924), pp. 55-63.

——, Автобиографические сведения, *Писатели. Автобиографии и портреты современных русских прозаиков*. Под ред. В. Лидина (Москва, 1926).

——, *Встречи с Максимом Горьким* (Москва, 1947).

——, "Страницы автобиографии", *Советские писатели. Автобиографии в двух томах* (Москва, ГИХЛ, 1956), т. I, pp. 431-455.

Вениамин Александрович КАВЕРИН:

——, Доклад о путях современной прозы в очерке "Дискуссии о современной литературе", *Русский Современник*, № 2 (1924), pp. 273-278.

——, Автобиография в сборнике *Писатели. Автобиографии и портреты современных русских прозаиков*. Под ред. В. Лидина (Москва, 1926), pp. 133-134.

——, (В. Зильберг) "Сенковский (Барон Брамбеус)", *Русская проза. Сборник статей* под ред. Б. Эйхенбаума и Ю. Тынянова (= *Вопросы поэтики*) (Л., Изд. "Academia", 1926).

——, Писатели о себе. *На Литературном Посту*, №№ 17-18 (1927).

——, *Барон Брамбеус. История Осипа Сенковского, журналиста, редактора "Библиотеки для чтения"* (Ленинград, 1929).

——, "Против работы наугад (В лаборатории писателя)", *Резец*, № 26 (1929), p. 8.

——, Статья в сборнике *Как мы пишем* (Ленинград, 1930), pp. 59-74.

——, *Пролог. Путевые рассказы* (М.-Л., 1931)
Содержание: "Степь"; "Грязь"; "Бой-страх"; "Чечевица"; "Табор"; "Суховей"; "Дорога"; "Нигрол"; "Последняя ночь"; "Возвращение".

——, Автобиография. *Советские Писатели. Автобиографии в двух томах* (Москва, 1959), т. I, pp. 496-510.

——, "Неизвестный друг (воспоминания в форме серии рассказов)", кн. 10, *Октябрь* (1959).

——, *Неизвестный друг*. Повесть (Москва, 1960)
Содержание: "Ночные страхи"; "Дважды два"; "Первая любовь";

"День рождения"; "На даче"; "Похвальный лист"; "Трус"; "Актеры"; "Спиритический сеанс"; "Гимназисты"; "Тенор"; "Скрипка Амати"; "Доктор Парве"; "Бойкот"; "В летнем саду"; "План обороны"; "Марина"; "Волчий билет"; "Немая клавиатура", "Дуэль"; "Пауки и мухи"; "Вурдалак"; "Как я не стал поэтом"; "Баллада"; "Измена"; "Испанка"; "Два вечера в 'Стойле Пегаса'"; "Вильямс"; "Неизвестный друг"; "Первый урок".

——, *Автобиографические рассказы* (Москва, Изд-во "Правда", 1961).

Лев Натанович ЛУНЦ:

——, Рецензия: "Цех поэтов, Альманахи Цеха поэтов №№ 1 и 2, Георгий Иванов: 'Сады', Н. Гумилев: 'Огненный столп'", *Книжный угол*, № 8, 1922, pp. 48-54.
——, "Почему мы Серапионовы Братья", *Литературные Записки*, № 3, pp. 30-31.
——, Рецензия: "Илья Эренбург: 'Необычайные похождения Хулио Хуренито и его учеников'", *Город*, Сборник 1, 1923.
——, "На Запад", *Беседа* (Журнал под ред. Горького), № 3, 1923, pp. 259-274.
——, "Об идеологии и публицистике", *Новости*, № 3, октябрь 23, 1922. Reprinted in *Современная русская критика 1918-1924. Сборник (Образцы и характеристики)*. Под ред. Иннокентия Оксенова (Ленинград, 1925), pp. 240-244.
——, "Автобиография". В сборнике *Писатели. Автобиографии и портреты современных русских прозаиков* (Москва, 1926), pp. 169-171.

Николай Николаевич НИКИТИН:

——, "Вредные мысли", *Писатели об искусстве и о себе* (Москва, 1924), pp. 111-124.
——, Автобиографические сведения в сборнике *Писатели. Автобиографии и портреты современных русских прозаиков* (Москва, 1926), pp. 201-202.
——, Статья в сборнике *Как мы пишем* (Ленинград, 1930).

Елизавета Григорьевна ПОЛОНСКАЯ:

——, *Поездка на Урал (брошюра)* (Ленинград, 1927).
——, *Люди советских будней* (Ленинград, 1934).

Vladimir POZNER:

——, *Littérature russe* (Paris, 1929).

Михаил Леонидович СЛОНИМСКИЙ:

——, Статья в серии авторских заметок "Серапионовы Братья о себе", *Литературные Записки*, № 3 (1922), p. 25.
——, Автобиографические сведения в сборнике *Писатели. Автобиографии и портреты современных русских прозаиков* (Москва, 1926), pp. 285-286.
——, "Писатели о себе", *На Литературном Посту*, IX (1927), p. 78.
——, Статья в сборнике *Как мы пишем* (Ленинград, 1930), pp. 130-133.

——, *Как я работаю над своими произведениями. Переработанная стенограмма беседы, проведенной в Ленинградском Кабинете рабочего автора Профиздата* (Москва, 1934).

Николай Семенович ТИХОНОВ:

——, "Весло и лопата", *Резец*, № 29 (1929), pp. 11-13.
——, "Как я работаю", *Литературная Учеба*, № 5 (1930), pp. 92-106.
——, Статья в сборнике *Как мы пишем* (Ленинград, 1930), pp. 134-142.
——, *Моя работа над стихами и прозой. Переработанная стенограмма беседы, проведенной в Ленинградском Кабинете рабочего-автора Профиздата* (Москва, 1934).
——, *О ленинградских поэтах. Доклад на 1-м Всесоюзном съезде советских писателей* (Москва, 1934).
——, "Автобиография", *Советские Писатели. Автобиографии в двух томах* (Москва, 1959), т. II, pp. 426-433.

Михаил Михаилович ЗОЩЕНКО:

——, "Дружеские пародии (Пародии о Серапионовых Братьях)", *Литературные Записки*, № 2 (1922), pp. 8-9.
——, "О себе, об идеологии и ещё кое о чем", *Литературные Записки*, № 3 (1922), pp. 28-29.
——, Автобиография в сборнике *Писатели. Автобиографии и портреты современных русских прозаиков* (Москва, 1926).
——, "О себе, о критиках и о своей работе", *Михаил Зощенко. Статьи и материалы* (Ленинград, 1928).
——, *Письма к писателю* (Ленинград, 1929).
——, Статья в сборнике *Как мы пишем* (Ленинград, 1930), pp. 48-58.
——, Статья в журнале *Литературная Учеба*, № 3 (1930), pp. 107-113.

B. WRITINGS ABOUT THE SERAPION BROTHERS AND THEIR WORKS

Борис АРВАТОВ, "Серапионовцы и утилитаризм", *Новости*, № 5 (20) (1922). Reprinted in *Современная русская критика 1918-1924*, под ред. Иннокентия Оксенова (Ленинград, 1925), pp. 166-171.
Н. АСЕЕВ, "Рвотный форт", *Печать и Революция*, кн. 2 (1923), pp. 226.
——, "Ключ сюжета", *Печать и Революция*, кн. 7 (1925), pp. 67-68 *et seq.* (short references to Vsevolod Ivanov).
В. БАКИНСКИЙ, рецензия на книгу В. Каверина *Художник неизвестен 1931*, *Октябрь*, № 2 (1932), pp. 186-189.
А. Г. БАРМИН, "Пути Зощенки", *Михаил Зощенко. Статьи и материалы* (Ленинград, 1928).
М. БЕККЕР, рецензия о сборнике *С| карандашом в руке* Ник. Никитина, *Октябрь*, III (1927).
А. И. БЕЛЕЦКИЙ, Н. Л. БРОДСКИЙ, Л. П. ГРОССМАН, И. Н. КУБИКОВ, В. Л. ЛЬВОВ-РОГАЧЕВСКИЙ, *Новейшая русская литература. Критика-Театр-Методология. Темы. Библиография* (Иваново-Вознесенск, "Основа", 1927)

Содержание: "Творческие приёмы у Ремизова и Замятина", p. 194 (библиография); "Зощенко и сказ Лескова", p. 196 (библиография); "Сюжет в поэзии Н. Тихонова", p. 196; "Всеволод Иванов", p. 198 (библиография).

БЕЛЕНЬКИЙ, рецензия о книге В. Каверина *Девять десятых судьбы*, *Красная Новь*, № 2 (1926).

Г. БЕРЕЗКО, рецензия о сборнике *Двенадцать баллад* Н. Тихонова, *Печать и Революция*, VII (1925).

П. БЕРЕЗОВ, рецензия на книгу В. Каверина *Художник неизвестен 1931*, *Пролетарский авангард*, № 2 (1932), p. 178.

Н. БЕРКОВСКИЙ, "О прозаиках (о Н. Тихонове)", *Звезда*, № 12 (1929), pp. 147-149.

П. М. БИЦИЛЛИ, "Зощенко и Гоголь", *Числа* (Париж), кн. 6 (1932), pp. 211-215.

Я. БРАУН, "Десять странников в 'осязаемое нечто'", *Сибирские огни*, кн. I (1924), p. 214.

В. БРЮСОВ, рецензия о сборнике Н. Тихонова *Орда*, *Печать и Революция*, VI (1922).

П. БУГАЕНКО, *Мастерство Константина Федина* (Саратов, 1959).

А. С. БУШМИН, "О ранней советской прозе", *Вопросы советской литературы*, I, под ред. В. А. Десницкого и А. С. Бушмина (Москва-Ленинград, АН СССР, 1953).

М. ЧУМАНДРИН, "Чей писатель – Михаил Зощенко?", *Звезда*, № 3 (1930), pp. 206-219.

Д.В., рецензия о книге Ник. Никитина *Американское счастье Россия*, III (1922).

Ю. ДОБРАНОВ, "Путь противоречий и исканий (о Н. Тихонове)", *На Литературном Посту*, № 23 (1929), pp. 74-82.

В. ДРУЗИН, "О поэзии Николая Тихонова", *Звезда*, № 10 (1928), pp. 153-170.

Валентина ДЫННИК, "Переставленные главы (о *Городах и годах* Федина)", *Красная Новь*, № 9 (1925), pp. 270-276.

William EDGERTON, "The Serapion Brothers: an Early Soviet Controversy", *The American Slavic and East European Review*, vol. VIII, 1 (February 1949), pp. 47-64.

А. ЕФРЕМИН, "Евг. Замятин", *Красная Новь*, № 1 (1930).

Ж. ЭЛЬСБЕРГ, рецензия о сборнике *Лирическая земля* Ник. Никитина, *На Литературном Посту*, XV-XVI (1927).

——, "Творчество Вс. Иванова", *На Литературном Посту*, кн. XIX (1927), pp. 39-51.

А. ФИЛИППОВ, "Евг. Замятин, *Островитяне, 1922* (рецензия)", *Новости литературы*, кн. 1 (1922), pp. 51-53.

М. ГЕЛЬФАНД, "От *Партизан* к *Особняку* (к характеристике одной писательской эволюции: о Всеволоде Иванове)", *Революция и культура*, кн. XXII (1928), pp. 70-76.

——, Статья о Всеволоде Иванове, *Литературная Энциклопедия*, т. IV, pp. 400-404.

Г.Л., Статья о В. Каверине, *Литературная Энциклопедия*, т. V, pp. 12-13.

А. ГЛАГОЛЕВ, рецензия об *Обоянских повестях* Н. Никитина, *Печать и Революция*, I (1929), p. 139.

В. ГОФФЕНШЕФЕР, рецензия на книгу Каверина *Скандалист...* (*Звезда* [1928]), *Молодая Гвардия*, № 12 (1928), pp. 203-204.

В. ГОЛЬЦЕВ, рецензия о книге В. Каверина *Девять десятых судьбы*, *Печать и Революция*, № 8 (1926).

——, рецензия о книге Н. Никитина *С карандашом в руке*, *Печать и Революция*, I (1927), pp. 203-204.

В. ГОЛЬЦЕВ, рецензия о *Рвотном форте* Н. Никитина, *Молодая гвардия*, II (1927), p. 206-207.

Георгий ГОРБАЧЕВ, *Очерки современной русской литературы* (Ленинград, Гос. Издат., 1924)
    Глава IV, pp. 76-88: "Серапионовы Братья";
    Глава V, pp. 89-96: "Н. Тихонов".

——, "Серапионовы братья", *Современная русская критика 1918-1924*, под ред. Иннокентия Оксенова (Ленинград, 1925), pp. 63-83.

——, "Н. Тихонов", *Печать и Революция*, кн. 6 (1927), pp. 77-87 (рецензии о следующих произведениях: "Красные на Араксе", "Дорога", "Лицом к лицу", "Поиски героя").

——, *Современная русская литература. Обзор литературно-идеологических течений современности и критические портреты современных писателей* (Ленинград, 1928)
    Содержание: Зощенко (глава "Мелкобуржуазная литература", pp. 112-115); Всеволод Иванов (глава "Левое крыло мелкобуржуазной литературы", pp. 220-237); Каверин (глава "Мелко-буржуазная литература", pp. 120-121); Ник. Никитин (глава "Мелкобуржуазная литература", pp. 112-118); М. Слонимский, Н. Тихонов (глава "Левое крыло мелкобуржуазной литературы", pp. 264-280); К. Федин (глава "Мелкобуржуазная литература", pp. 154-163).

Д. ГОРБОВ, "Итоги литературного года", *Новый Мир*, № 12, pp. 129-148 (о Вс. Иванове и К. Федине, pp. 139-140 и 'попутчиках').

Анатолий Ефимович ГОРЕЛОВ, *Путь современника. О творчестве Мих. Слонимского* (Ленинград, 1933).

——, *Испытание временем. Сборник критических статей* (Ленинград, 1935)
    Содержание:
    1. "Маяковский"
    2. "Шолохов"
    3. "Федин"
    4. "Зощенко"
    5. "Слонимский".

М. ГОРЬКИЙ, "Памяти Лунца", *Беседа*, № 5 (1924), pp. 61-62.

С. ГОРОДЕЦКИЙ, "Зелень под плесенью (о Серапионовых Братьях)", *Известия ВЦИК*, № 42 (1922).

М. ГРИГОРЬЕВ, "Литературный гомункулюс (о Каверине)", *На Литературном Посту*, №№ 23-24 (1930), pp. 35-45.

——, "Под знаком формализма (О творчестве В. Каверина)", *Литературная Газета*, № 4 (1931).

Б. ГРОССМАН, статья о Ник. Никитине, *Литературная Энциклопедия*, т. VIII, pp. 73-76.

И. С. ГРОССМАН-РОЩИН, статья о Всев. Иванове, "Без мотивов и без цели", *На Литературном Посту*, кн. XX-XXI (1928), pp. 43-48.

Б. ГУБЕР, рецензия о *Полёте* Ник. Никитина, *Новый Мир*, VI (1926).

Борис ГУСМАН, *100 поэтов. Литературные портреты. С приложением библиографического указателя русской поэзии за последнее десятилетие* (Тверь, 1923)
    Содержание: "Е. Полонская", pp. 215-216; "Н. Тихонов", pp. 249-250.

Л.(?) КАГАН(?), Статья о М. М. Зощенке, *Литературная Энциклопедия*, т. IV, pp. 376-378.

Рецензия о книге Каверина *Конец Хазы 1930*, *Книга строителям социализма*, № 1 (1931), p. 80.

Рецензия на книгу Каверина *Художник неизвестен 1931, Книга строителям социализма*, № 35 (1931), pp. 84-85.

В. К-н, рецензия на произведение М. Слонимского, *Шестой стрелковый, Книга и Революция*, IX-X (1922).

П. С. КОГАН, "О манифесте Серапионовых братьев", *Красная Газета*, 215 (1368), сентябрь 23, 1922.

——, "Об искусстве и публицистике", *Красная Газета*, № 274 (1425), 2-го декабря, 1922.
Reprinted in *Современная русская критика 1918-1924* (под ред. Иннокентия Оксенова) (Ленинград, 1925), pp. 84-87
(ответ на статью Лунца, "Об идеологии и публицистике").

П. С. КОГАН, *Литература этих лет, 1917-1923* (Иваново-Вознесенск, 1924)
(глава седьмая: "О жизни и платформе Серапионовых братьев, о триумфе беллетристики и поражении лирики, о глазах, которыми смотрит Пильняк, о Всеволоде Иванове и о 'Перегное' Сейфуллиной").

——, *Литература великого десятилетия* (Москва-Ленинград, 1927)
(глава "Попутчики, о Серапионовых братьях и Вс. Иванове").

А. КОЛЕСНИКОВ, "Города и годы", *На Посту*, кн. I [6] (1925), pp. 207-214.

Н. КОВАРСКИЙ, *Н. С. Тихонов. Критический очерк* (Ленинград, 1935).

В. КРАСИЛЬНИКОВ, "О Михаиле Слонимском", *Книга и Революция*, № 11 (1929), pp. 13-16.

А. КРУЧЕНЫХ, *Заумныйязык у: Сейфуллиной, Вс. Иванова, Л. Леонова, И. Бабеля, И. Сельвинского, А. Веселого и др.* (Москва, Изд. Всерос. Союза Поэтов, 1925).

——, *Новое в писательской технике* (Вс. Иванов, pp. 18-25) (Москва, Изд. Всерос. Союза Поэтов, 1927).

Павел Иванович ЛЕБЕДЕВ (Валерьян Полянский), *Вопросы современной критики* (Москва, 1927)
Содержание: "Писатели об искусстве и о себе", pp. 143-155; "Серапионовы Братья", pp. 156-162.

Г. ЛЕЛЕВИЧ, "По журнальным окопам (о Каверине)", *Молодая гвардия*, VII-VIII (1924).

Н. ЛЕОНОВ, "Сибирь в новой литературе (о Вс. Иванове)", *Северная Азия*, кн. I (1927), pp. 101-117.

Мих. ЛЕВИДОВ, "Судьба эклектика, К. Федин, *Братья*", *Молодая гвардия*, № 11 (1928), pp. 205-206.

А. ЛЕЖНЕВ, *Современники. Литературно-критические очерки* (Москва, Изд. Артель писателей "Круг", 1927)
(в главе "Три книги. Диалоги о критике и писателе" упоминается Вс. Иванов).

Абрам Захарович ЛЕЖНЕВ, *Литература революционного десятилетия,1917-1927*. Со-автор: Д. Горбов (Харьков, 1929)
(А. Лежнев, "Русская литература за 10 лет":
  VIII. "Возрождение прозы; Бор. Пильняк и его школа; Динамизм; Многоплановность; Разорванность композиции; 'Метельное' восприятие революции; Вкус к сказу и этнографии; Всев. Иванов".
  XI.   "Бабель; Леонов; Федин; Пант. Романов; Огнев".
  XII.   "Самоизживание 'динамической' прозы; Психологизм; Последние произведения Всев. Иванова".
  XIII. "Серапионы; Зощенко; Каверин; Ник. Никитин".
  XV.   "'Правый фланг'; Е. Замятин".
  XVIII. "Дальнейшее развитие поэзии (1921-1927 гг.); Тихонов и его романтика").

Абрам Захарович ЛЕЖНЕВ, (Горелик, А. З.), *Литературные будни* (о Всеволоде Иванове, pp. 270-274) (Москва, Изд. "Федерация", 1929).

——, *Об искусстве* (В главе "Мысли вслух", о Зощенко, p. 236; Шкловском)
(Москва, 1936).

К. ЛОКС, "Современная проза", *Печать и Революция*, кн. V (1923), pp. 82-86
("Цветные ветра" и "Голубые пески", Вс. Иванова).

——, "Современная проза", *Печать и Революция*, кн. VII (1923), pp. 75-81
(Вс. Иванов, *"Голубые пески"*; Ник. Никитин, *"Бунт"*; Слонимский,
"Шестой стрелковый"; Каверин, *"Мастера и подмастерья"*).

Э. ЛУНИН, статья о Евг. Замятине, *Литературная Энциклопедия*, т. IV, pp.
302-310.

М. МАЙЗЕЛЬ. "Лев Натанович Лунц", *Литературная Энциклопедия*, т. VI,
pp. 635-637.

——, *Краткий очерк современной русской литературы* (Москва, 1931)
(brief references to Замятин, Зощенко, Иванов Вс., Каверин, Лунц,
Никитин Н., Полонская Ел., Слонимский, Федин).

А. МАЛИНКИН, "Тихонов Николай Семенович", *Литературная Энциклопедия*,
т. XI, pp. 276-279.

Р. С. МАНДЕЛЬШТАМ, *Художественная литература в оценке русской
марксистской критики* (о Всев. Иванове, Замятине). Изд. 4-е (Москва, 1928).

Николай МАСЛИН, "Вениамин Каверин", *Новый Мир*, № 4 (1948), pp. 272-290
(в отделе 'Литературные портреты').

Р. МЕССЕР, "О творчестве М. Л. Слонимского", *Звезда*, № 6 (1932), pp. 159-172.

Р. МИЛЛЕР-БУДНИЦКАЯ, "Эпигон формализма (о Каверине)", *Звезда*, № 2
(1932), pp. 151-160.

Не Критик, "Роман лишнего человека, К. Федин, *Города и годы*", *Звезда*, кн. 1
(1925).

С. НЕЛЬДИХЕН, "Л. Лунц (некролог)", *Россия*, № 2 (1924), pp. 207-208.

Книга – строителям социализма, № 17 (1931), о романе *Шпион* Ник. Никитина.

Е. Ф. НИКИТИНА, *Русская литература от символизма до наших дней.
Литературно-социологический семинарий*. С предисловием Н. К. Пиксанова, "Никитинские субботники" (Москва, 1926)
    I. 1. "Темы"; 2. "Вопросы поэтики", p. 217; 3. "Литературные приемы
        Вс. Иванова"; 4. "Беллетристы", p. 197; "Замятин", p. 205; "Литера-
        турная группа 'Серапионовы братья'", pp. 218-223; "Зощенко,
        Вс. Иванов, Никитин Н., Слонимский, Федин".
    II. Био-библиографический словарь: "Замятин, Иванов Вс., Лунц,
        Никитин Н., Полонская Е., Слонимский, Тихонов, Федин".
    III. Синхронические таблицы 1890-1925.

Николай ОЦУП, *Современники* (Париж, 1961)
(часть I: Петербургские воспоминания 1926, в частности статья "Пролет-
культовцы и Серапионы").

И. ОКСЕНОВ, о Е. Г. Полонской, *Книга и Революция*, № 13 (1922).

——, рецензия на книгу Ник. Никитина *Рвотный форт*, *Книга и Революция*, I (1923).

И. ОКСЕНОВ, рецензия на книгу Ник. Никитина *Преступление Кирика Руденко*,
Красная Новь, X (1928), p. 250.

——, "Н. Тихонов – прозаик", *Звезда*, № 1 (1928), pp. 84-88.

Абрам Рувимович ПАЛЕЙ, *Литературные портреты* (Москва, 1928)
(Вс. Иванов, p. 12; Конст. Федин, p. 39).

——, рецензия на книгу Ник. Никитина *Преступление Кирика Руденко*, *Новый
Мир*, VII (1928), p. 219.

——, рецензия на книгу Ник. Никитина *Обояньские повести*, *Новый Мир*, VIII
(1928), pp. 219-221.

Абрам Рувимович ПАЛЕЙ, рецензия на книгу В. Каверина *Воробьиная ночь, 1927, Правда*, 8 февр., 1928.

Мих. ПАВЛОВ, рецензия на сборник стихов *Знамения* Е. Г. Полонской, *Летопись Дома литераторов*, № 8 (1922).

——, рецензия о книге стихов *Орда* Н. Тихонова, *Литературные Записки*, № 3 (1922), pp. 16-17.

В. ПЕРЦОВ, *Этюды о советской литературе* (Москва, 1937)
(references to Šklovskij and to Fedin's *Goroda i gody* and *Brat'ja* from the point of view of personality and Socialist society, chapt. II, part II).

В. ПЕРЕВЕРЗЕВ, "На фронтах текущей беллетристики", *Печать и Революция*, кн. 4 (1923), pp. 127-133
(о Вс. Иванове, Зощенко, Ник. Никитине, Федине, Каверине).

——, "Вс. Иванов. Седьмой берег", *Печать и Революция*, кн. I (1923), pp. 220-221.

Л. ПОЛЯК, статья о Константине А. Федине, *Литературная Энциклопедия*, т. XI, pp. 674-677.

Валерьян ПОЛЯНСКИЙ, "Серапионовы Братья", *Московский Понедельник*, № 11 (28 авг. 1922). Reprinted in Павел Иванович Лебедев (В. Полянский), *Вопросы современной критики* (Москва, 1927).

——, "Об идеологии в литературе", *Современная русская критика, 1918-1924*, под ред. Иннокентия Оксенова (Ленинград, 1925), pp. 98-107.

Вячеслав ПОЛОНСКИЙ, *Очерки литературного движения революционной эпохи* (заметки о Серапионовых Братьях), 2-е изд. (Москва-Ленинград, 1929).

——, *О современной литературе*. Изд. 2-е (Москва-Ленинград, 1929)
(глава о Вс. Иванове, pp. 5-44).

В. ПРАВДУХИН, *Литературная современность 1920-1924* (Москва, 1924)
(глава III: "Пафос современности и молодые писатели, Вс. Иванов, Н. Никитин, Замятин, Н. Тихонов", pp. 57-88).

——, *Творец. Общество. Искусство. Статьи о современной литературе* (Новониколаевск, Изд. "Сибирские огни", 1923)
(гл. III. Вс. Иванов, Н. Никитин).

Н. ПРЕСМАН, статья о Е. Г. Полонской, *Литературная Энциклопедия*, т. IX, pp. 62-63.

А. РАШКОВСКАЯ, "Восходящие силы литературы: 1. Борис Пильняк; 2. Ник. Никитин" (Петроград, 1923).

Василий Львович РОГАЧЕВСКИЙ, *Новейшая русская литература* 2-е изд. испр. и доп. (Москва, 1924).
At head of title: В. Львов-Рогачевский (о Вс. Иванове).

——, *Новейшая русская литература* 3-е изд. исправленное (Москва, 192–?)
(глава XVI: "Беллетристика революционной эпохи". Some brief references to Vs. Ivanov, N. Nikitin, Nik. Tixonov, Zoščenko, Fedin, Slonimskij, Kaverin, Zamjatin).

——, *Новейшая русская литература* 6-е изд., переработанное автором (Москва, 1927)
(глава о Вс. Иванове, pp. 397-410).

——, (В. Львов-Рогачевский), *1917-1927. Художественная литература революционного десятилетия* (Москва, "Мир", 1927)
(short references to the Serapion Brothers in section 1: "Есть ли у нас в РСФСР новая художественная литература?").

Н. РОСТОВ, "Конст. Федин, *Трансвааль, Рассказы* (рецензия)", *Молодая Гвардия*, № 3 (1927), p. 226.

К. РЫЖИКОВ, "Оптимизм и пессимизм Вс. Иванова", *На Литературном Посту*, № 16 (1929), pp. 49-60.

М. ШАГИНЯН, "Письмо из Петербурга", *Россия*, I (1922), pp. 29-30 (о Ник. Тихонове).

——, *Литературный дневник. Статьи 1921-1923* Изд. 2-е (Москва-Петербург, "Круг", 1923)
  Содержание: "Формальная эстетика" (по поводу статьи К. Державина, дек. 1921 в газете *Жизнь Искусства*); "Условность и быт" (Л. Лунцу); "Серапионовы братья", pp. 128-133.

——, рецензия на произведение *Анна Тимофеевна* К. Федина, *Россия*, № 2 (1924).

А. СЕЛИВАНОВСКИЙ, рецензия на сборник *Упрямый календарь* Е. Г. Полонской, *Молодая гвардия*, № 5 (1929), p. 91.

——, "Островитяне искусства (О *Скандалисте* Каверина)", Сборник *В литературных боях* (Ленинград, 1930).

——, "Поиски новаторства (о творчестве Н. Тихонова)", *Красная Новь*, № 9 (1932), pp. 185-200.

——, рецензия на книгу Каверина *Художник неизвестен*, *Литературная газета*, № 1 (1932).

——, *Очерки по истории русской советской поэзии* (Москва, 1936) (глава VII: "Николай Тихонов").

Е. СЕВЕРИН, "Вениамин Каверин", *Печать и Революция*, № 1 (1929), pp. 83-91.

Ernest J. SIMMONS, *Russian Fiction and Soviet Ideology. Introduction to Fedin, Leonov and Sholokhov* (New York, 1958).

В. ШКЛОВСКИЙ, "Серапионовы братья", *Книжный угол*, № 7 (1921), pp. 18-21.

——, *Сентиментальное путешествие. Воспоминания, 1917-1922. Петербург, Галиция, Саратов, Киев* (Москва-Берлин, 1923)
  (pp. 377-381 о Серапионовых Братьях).

В. ШКЛОВСКИЙ, "Современники и синхронисты (о Л. Лунце)", *Русский современник*, № 3 (1924), pp. 232-237.

——, *Сентиментальное путешествие. Воспоминания 1918-1923 гг.* (Ленинград, Изд. "Атеней", 1924)
  (pp. 129-131: "о существе формального метода и об отдельных приемах литературного построения").

Victor CHKLOVSKI, *Voyage sentimental*. Traduction de Vladimir Pozner. 4e ed. (Paris, 1926).

——, "О Зощенке и большой литературе", *Михаил Зощенко. Статьи и материалы* (Ленинград, 1928).

Марк СЛОНИМ, "Серапионовы Братья", *Воля России*, 8 1 (29), 15 сент., 1922 pp. 46-54.

——, *Портреты советских писателей* (Париж, 1933)
  (Евгений Замятин, Всеволод Иванов, Михаил Зощенко, Константин Федин).

Юрий СОБОЛЕВ, рецензии на *Рвотный форт*, *Американское счастье* Ник. Никитина, *Красная Новь*, № 1 (1923), pp. 326-329.

——, "Сейчас на Западе (рецензия на произведение Ник. Никитина)", *Красная Новь*, кн. 4, pp. 339-341.

Зелик Яковлевич ШТЕЙНМАН, "О Мих. Слонимском", *Звезда*, VII (1927), pp. 132-140.

——, "Замятины, их алгебра и наши выводы", Альманах *Удар*, кн. 1 (1927).

——, "Почему победил Тихонов и потерпел неудачу Михаил Козаков", *Резец*, № 25 (1931), pp. 13-16.

Н. ТЕРЕЩЕНКО, "Философия эротизма и диалектика живого опыта (*Любовь Жанны Ней* Эренбурга и *Города и годы* Федина)", *Звезда*, кн. 3-я (1925), pp. 277-290.

Лев ТРОЦКИЙ, "Серапионовы Братья, Всеволод Иванов", *Правда*, № 224 (5-го октября 1922).

——, *Литература и Революция* (*Литературные попутчики революции. Серапионовы Братья*) (Москва, Изд. "Красная Новь", 1923).

Leon TROTSKY, *Literature and Revolution* (New York, 1957).

В. ТУКАЛЕВСКИЙ, "Литературные рисовальщики (Вс. Иванов и Серапионовы Братья)", *Новая Русская Книга*, № 4 (1922), p. 2.

Юрий ТЫНЯНОВ, рецензия о сборнике *Серапионовы Братья. Альманах Первый*, *Книга и Революция*, № 6 (1922), pp. 62-64.

——, "Литературное сегодня (Замятин, Никитин Н., М. Слонимский, Зощенко, Федин, Шкловский)", *Русский современник*, кн. 1 (1924), pp. 291-306.

——, "Промежуток (О поэзии, о Ник. Тихонове)", *Русский современник*, IV (1924), pp. 209-221.

Ипполит УДУШЬЕВ, "Взгляд и нечто (отрывок, о Ник. Никитине)", Сборник *Современная литература* (Ленинград, Изд. "Мысль", 1925), pp. 154-182.

В. ВЕШНЕВ, "К. Федин: литературный портрет", *Новый Мир*, № 9 (1925), pp. 113-127.

В. В. ВИНОГРАДОВ, "Язык Зощенки (Библиографическая справка)", *Михаил Зощенко. Статьи и материалы* (Ленинград, 1928).

——, "Изучение русского литературного языка за последнее десятилетие в СССР, Библиография и общая характеристика состояния изучения языка советских писателей"
(доклады советской делегации на международном совещании славяноведов в Белграде) (Москва, АН СССР, 1955), pp. 35-41 (p. 38, brief reference to Fedin).

Б. ВОЛИН, "Клеветники (Эренбург; Н. Никитин, *Рвотный форт*; Брик)", *На Посту*, кн. 1 (1923), pp. 9-23.

Александр Константинович ВОРОНСКИЙ, "Литературные силуэты, Вс. Иванов", *Красная Новь*, № 5 (1922), pp. 254-275.

——, рецензия о сборнике *Серапионовы Братья. Альманах Первый*, *Красная Новь*, № 3 (1922), pp. 265-268.

——, "Литературные отклики", *Красная Новь*, № 2 (1923)
(рецензии: *На куличках* Замятина"; "*Анна Тимофеевна* Федина"; "*Пятый странник* Каверина"; "Никитин *Ночь*"; "Зощенко 'Коза'").

——, "На перевале (о Ник. Никитине)", *Красная Новь*, VI (1923).

——, *На стыке. Сборник статей* (*Литературные силуэты, публицистика*) (Москва, 1923)
 1. Литературные отклики: "Вс. Иванов, Ник. Никитин, Конст. Федин, Мих. Зощенко"
 2. Из современных литературных настроений: "Никитин, Зощенко, Вс. Иванов"
 3. Литературные силуэты: "Евг. Замятин, Вс. Иванов"
 4. Литературная хроника: "Зощенко, Слонимский".

——, *Искусство и жизнь. Сборник статей* (о Ник. Никитине; статья "В вечных боях" о Ник. Тихонове) (Москва-Ленинград, Изд. "Круг", 1924).

——, *Литературные Записи* (Москва, "Круг", 1926)
(главы "О том, чего у нас нет" и "Докука писательского быта: Вс. Иванов, Федин, Тихонов").

——, *Литературные типы* (*Евг. Замятин, Всеволод Иванов*), изд. 2-е (Москва, "Круг", 1927).

——, "Один оглушительный аплодисмент", Альманах *Круг*, кн. 6-я, Артель писателей "Круг", 1927
(статья, p. 183: Федин, Каверин).

Александр Константинович ВОРОНСКИЙ, *Литературные портреты*, 2 тома
  (Москва, "Федерация", 1928-1929)
    т. I: *о Вс. Иванове*
    т. II: *о Н. Тихонове.*
Д. ВЫГОДСКИЙ, рецензия на сборник *Брага* Тихонова, *Россия*, VI (1923).
——, рецензия на сборник *Под каменным дождем* Е. Г. Полонской, *Книга и
  Революция*, № 3 [27] (1923).
Евгений ЗАМЯТИН, "Серапионовы Братья", *Литературные Записки*, № 1 (1922),
  pp. 7-8.
——, "Новая русская проза (о Серапионовых Братьях)", *Русское искусство*,
  № 2-3 (1923), pp. 57-67.
——, "Ник. Никитин, *Сейчас на западе* (рецензия)", *Русский Современник*, кн. 2-я
  (1924), pp. 287-288.
——, "Новая русская проза (О прозе Серапионовых Братьев)", статья в сборнике
  Лица Замятина (Нью Йорк, Изд. имени Чехова, 1955), pp. 191-210.
А. ЖДАНОВ, *Доклад о журналах 'Звезда' и 'Ленинград'* (*о Серапионовых Братьях*)
  (Госполитиздат, 1952).
Современные Записки, "Михаил Зощенко", т. 34 (1928), pp. 442-451.
Зощенко, М., *Михаил Зощенко. Статьи и материалы* (Ленинград,
    "Academia", 1928), "О себе, о критиках и о своей работе";
  Шкловский, В., "О Зощенке и большой литературе";
  Бармин, А. Г., "Пути Зощенки";
  Виноградов, В. В., "Язык Зощенки (Библиографическая справка)".

C. SELECTED BACKGROUND READINGS

Miriam ALLOTT, *Novelists on the Novel* (New York, 1959).
ARISTOTLE's *Theory of Poetry and Fine Art*. Translated and with critical notes by
  S. H. Butcher (New York, 1951).
И. БАБЕЛЬ, *Рассказы* (Москва, 1935)
    (из рассказов "Конармия"; "Одесские рассказы ("Король" и др.);
    "Рассказы").
Андрей БЕЛЫЙ, *Петербург* (*в двух томах*) (Берлин, 1922).
Н. БЕРКОВСКИЙ, *Текущая литература. Статьи критические и теоретические*
  (Москва, 1930).
Dmitri ČIŽEVSKY, "Comenius' *Labyrinth of the World*: its themes and their sources",
  Harvard Slavic Studies, vol. I (Cambridge, Mass., 1953), pp. 83-135.
Constant COQUELIN, *L'Art du Comédien* (Paris, 1894).
Ch.-M. DES GRANGES, *Histoire Illustrée de la Littérature Française des Origines
  à 1930* (Paris, 1933).
Emile DURKHEIM, *The Rules of Sociological Method* (Glencoe, Ill., 1950).
Leon EDEL, *The Modern Psychological Novel* (New York, 1955).
Б. ЭЙХЕНБАУМ, *Сквозь литературу. Сборник статей* (Ленинград, "Academia",
    1924)
    "(статья Иллюзия сказа", pp. 102-117).
——, *Idem*, Photomechanic reprint (The Hague, Mouton & Co., 1962).
——, *Литература. Теория, критика, полемика* (Ленинград, "Прибой", 1927)
    (Статьи: "Предисловие"; "Путь Пушкина к прозе"; "Лев Толстой";
    "Некрасов"; "Теория 'формального метода'"; "Как сделана 'Шинель'
    Гоголя"; "О. Генри и теория новеллы"; "Лесков и современная проза";
    "О камерной декламации"; "Ораторский стиль Ленина"; "В ожидании
    литературы"; "В поисках жанра"; "Литература и кино").

Victor ERLICH, *Russian Formalism. History — Doctrine* (The Hague, Mouton & Co., 1955).

А. Ф. ЕРШОВ, *Советская сатирическая проза 20-х годов* (Москва-Ленинград, 1960).

Henri FLUCHÈRE, *Laurence Sterne. De l'homme à l'œuvre. Biographie critique et essai d'interprétation* (Paris, 1961).

E. M. FORSTER, *Aspects of the Novel* (New York, [copyright renewed], 1954).

Дмитрий ФУРМАНОВ, *Чапаев* (Москва, 1947).

Викт. ГОФМАН, "Место Пильняка", *Мастера современной литературы. Бор. Пильняк* (Ленинград, 1928), pp. 7-44.

А. Н. ГВОЗДЕВ, *Современный русский литературный язык* (Москва, 1958)
  I: *Фонетика и морфология* II: *Синтаксис*.

J. HUIZINGA, *Homo ludens. A study of the play-element in culture* (London, 1949).

Roman INGARDEN, *Das literarische Kunstwerk. Eine Untersuchung aus dem Grenzgebiet der Ontologie, Logik und Literaturwissenschaft* (Halle, 1931).

Роман ЯКОБСОН, *Новейшая русская поэзия* (*Набросок первый*). *Виктор Хлебников* (Прага, 1921).

Roman JAKOBSON and Morris HALLE, *Fundamentals of Language* (the chapter "The Metaphoric and Metonymic Poles" by R. Jakobson, pp. 76-82 (The Hague, 1956).

——, *Shifters, Verbal Categories and the Russian Verb* (Cambridge, Mass., Harvard University, 1957).

Henry JAMES, "The Art of Fiction", *The Portable Henry James* (New York, 1956), pp. 391-418.

Otto JESPERSEN, *Essentials of English Grammar* (London, 1959).

Wolfgang KAYSER, *The Grotesque in Art and Literature*. Transl. by U. Weisstein (Bloomington, 1963).

Павел Иванович ЛЕБЕДЕВ (Валерьян Полянский), *На литературном фронте. Сборник статей* (Москва, "Новая Москва", 1924)
  (статья "Об идеологии в литературе, о Серапионовых Братьях").

Леонид ЛЕОНОВ, *Вор* (Москва, 1934).

Percy LUBBOCK, *The Craft of Fiction* (New York, 1958).

Horace G. LUNT, *Fundamentals of Russian* (The Hague-New York, 1958).

Владимир МАЯКОВСКИЙ, "Как делать стихи" (1927), *Полное собрание сочинений в 13-ти томах* (Москва, 1959), т. XII, pp. 81-117.

Rufus W. MATHEWSON, Jr., *The Positive Hero in Russian Literature* (New York, 1958).

François MAURIAC, *Le Romancier et ses personnages* (Paris, 1933).

D. S. MIRSKY, *A History of Russian Literature* (New York, 1955).

Walter L. MYERS, *The Later Realism. A Study of Characterization in the British Novel* (Chicago, 1927).

Б. ПАСТЕРНАК, *Доктор Живаго* (Ann Arbor, 1959).

Henri PEYERE, *The Contemporary French Novel* (New York, 1955).

Борис ПИЛЬНЯК (Вогау), *Голый год* (= *Собрание сочинений*, I). Введение А. Пинкевича (Москва-Ленинград, 1929).

Александр А. РЕФОРМАЦКИЙ, *Опыт анализа новеллистической композиции* (Москва, 1922).

Мариетта Сергеевна ШАГИНЯН, *Дневники 1917-1931* (Ленинград, 1932)
  (the year 1921: short references to *Dom iskusstv* and *Dom literatorov*).

V. SETSCHKAREFF, *N. V. Gogol, Leben und Schaffen* (Berlin, 1953).

——, *N. S. Leskov, Sein Leben und Sein Werk* (Wiesbaden, 1959).

А. СКАФТЫМОВ, "О психологизме в творчестве Стендаля и Л. Толстого", *Статьи о русской литературе* (Саратов, 1958), pp. 282-294.

В. Б. ШКЛОВСКИЙ, *Эпилог* (Петербург, 1922).
    At head of title: Виктор Шкловский, Лазарь Зервандов.
——, *Ход коня. Сборник статей* (Москва-Берлин, 1923).
——, *Зоо, или письма не о любви* (Берлин, 1923).
    (Cover title: Zoo, письма не о любви или третья Элоиза).
——, *Матерьял и стиль в романе Льва Толстого 'Война и Мир'* (Москва, "Федерация, 1928).
——, *О теории прозы* (Москва, 1929).
——, статья в сборнике *Как мы пишем* (1930), pp. 211-216.
——, *Заметки о прозе русских классиков.* Изд. 2-е исправ. и допол. (Москва, 1955).
——, *Художественная проза. Размышления и разборы* (Москва, 1959).
Laurence STERNE, *The Life and Opinions of Tristram Shandy, Gentleman* (New York, 1957).
Gleb STRUVE, *Soviet Russian Literature 1917-1950* (Norman, Okla., 1951).
А. ТОЛСТОЙ, "Литературные заметки, Задачи литературы", *Писатели об искусстве и о себе.* Сборник статей, № 1 (Москва-Ленинград, 1924), pp. 113-123.
Л. Н. ТОЛСТОЙ, *Война и мир* (*Правда*, 1948).
Б. ТОМАШЕВСКИЙ, *Теория литературы: Поэтика* (Ленинград, 1925).
——, *Стилистика и стихосложение. Курс лекций* (Ленинград, 1959).
P. VALERY, *Introduction à la poétique* (Paris, 1938).
A. M. VAN DER ENG-LIEDMEIER, *Soviet Literary Characters. An Investigation into the Portrayal of Soviet Men in Russian Prose 1917-1953* (The Hague, Mouton & Co., 1959).
В. В. ВИНОГРАДОВ, *Современный русский язык: Морфология* (Изд. Московского Университета, 1952).
——, (редактор), *Грамматика русского языка* (АН СССР, 1954)
    I: *Фонетика и морфология*
    II: *Синтаксис* (в двух частях).
——, *О языке художественной литературы* (Москва, 1959).
René WELLEK and Austin WARREN, *Theory of Literature* (New York, 1956).
Владислав ХОДАСЕВИЧ, *Литературные статьи и воспоминания* (Нью Йорк, Изд. имени Чехова, 1954).
Евг. ЗАМЯТИН, *Островитяне. Повести и рассказы* (Берлин-Петербург-Москва, 1923)
    ("Островитяне"; "Ловец человеков"; "Север"; "Землемер"; "Дракон"; "Мамай"; "Пещера"; "Глаза").
——, "The Cave" (translated by D. S. Mirsky), *The Slavonic Review*, vol. II, 4 (June 1923).
——, *Автобиография. Писатели. Автобиографии и портреты современных русских прозаиков*, под. ред. В. Лидина (Москва, 1926).
——, *Островитяне. Повести, рассказы, театр* (Москва, 1929)
    ("Островитяне"; "Ловец человеков"; "Землемер"; "Детская"; "Мамай"; "Пещера"; "Глаза"; "Рассказ о самом главном"; "Огни святого Доминика").
——, Статья в сборнике *Как мы пишем* (1930), pp. 29-47.
——, "The Cave", *Bonfire: Stories out of Soviet Russia.* Ed. by S. Konovalov (London, 1932).
Vyacheslav ZAVALISHIN, *Early Soviet Writers* (New York, 1958)
    (pp. 224-229: "The Serapion Brothers").

D. PERIODICALS, LITERARY ALMANACS,
COLLECTIONS OF CRITICAL AND (AUTO)BIOGRAPHIC ARTICLES,
DICTIONARIES

Альманах артели писателей "Круг" (Москва, "Круг", 1923-1927), 6 томов.

Беседа. Журнал литературы и науки. Издатель: М. Горький (Берлин, 1923-1925). Кн. 1-7.

Числа. Сборники (Париж). Под ред. И. В. де Манциарли и Н. А. Оцупа. Кн. первая (1930-).

Дом Искусств. (*Сборник*)
   № 1 (Пб., 1921),
   № 2 (Пб., 1921).

Эпопея. Литературный ежемесячник (Москва-Берлин, 1922-1923). Под ред. А. Белого.

Город. Литература, искусство. (Петербург, 1923), Сборник 1.

Грядущее. Пролетарский художественно-литературный журнал (Петербург, изд. Пролеткульта), № 2-4 (1919).

Как мы пишем (изд-во Писателей в Ленинграде, 1930), Андрей Белый; М. Горький; Евг. Замятин; Мих. Зощенко; В. Каверин; Борис Лавренев; Ю. Либединский; Ник. Никитин; Борис Пильняк; М. Слонимский; Ник. Тихонов; А. Толстой; Ю. Тынянов; Конст. Федин; Ольга Форш; А. Чапыгин; Вяч. Шишков; В. Шкловский.

Книга и Революция. Ежемесячный критико-библиографический журнал (Петербург, July 20 1923).
   Continued as *Книга и пролетарская революция* (Moscow, 1935).

Книга строителям социализма. Бюллетень библиографического института (Москва, ОГИЗ, 1931-).

Книжный угол. Критика, Библиография, Хроника (Петроград, издат. "Очарованный странник", 1918-1922).

Ковш. Литературно-художественные альманахи (Ленинград, Госиздат, 1925-1926).
   Кн. 1-4.

Красная Нива. Литературный сборник (Москва, Всерос. союз крестьянских писателей, 1922). Под ред. Павла Логинова и Г. Деева-Хомяковского.

Красная Новь. Литературно-художественный и научно-публицистический журнал (Москва, 1921-1942).

Леф. Журнал левого фронта искусств, (Москва, 1923-1925) № 1-7. Под ред. В. Маяковского.
   Superseded by: *Новый Леф* (1927).

Летопись Дома литераторов. Литературно-исследовательский и критико-библиографический журнал (Петербург, 1921-1922), № 1-9 (ноябрь 1, 1921-Февраль 25, 1922). Под ред. Б. И. Харитона.
   Superseded by *Литературные Записки* (1922).

Литературная Россия. Сборник современной русской прозы. Под ред. Вл. Лидина (Москва, "Новые вехи", 1924)
   Содержание: Е. И. Замятин, "Автобиография, библиография", "Пещера"; Зощенко, "Автобиография, библиография", "Аристократка", "Молитва"; Всеволод Иванов, "Автобиография, библиография", "Дитё"; Ник. Никитин, "Автобиография, библиография", "Камни"; К. А. Федин, "Автобиография, библиография", "Из романа *Города и годы*".

Литературная Энциклопедия (Москва, Изд. Коммунистической Академии, 1930-1939). Том 1-9, 11. Ответственный редактор В. М. Фриче.

Литературная Мысль. Альманах (Петроград, Центральное кооперативное изд-тво "Мысль"). Вып. 1-3 (1922-1925).

Литературная учёба. 1930, 36, М. Горький.

Литературно-художественный альманах для всех (Ленинград, "Прибой", 1924). Кн. 1.

Литературные Записки. Литературно-общественный и критико-библиографический журнал (Петербург, 1922)
    № 1 (25-е мая 1922),
    № 2 (23-е июня 1922),
    № 3 (1-е авг. 1922).

Молодая гвардия. Ежемесячный литературно-художественный общественно-политический научно-популярный журнал ЦК ВКП(б) и ЦК ВЛКСМ (Москва, 1922-).

На Посту (Июнь 1923-).

На Литературном Посту. Двухнедельный журнал марксистской критики (Москва, 1927-1932).

Наши дни. Художественные альманахи (Москва)
    № 1 (1923-),
    № 5 (1925). Под ред. В. В. Вересаева.

Новый Леф. Журнал левого фронта искусств
    № 1 (1927),
    № 12 (1928).

Новый Мир. Литературно-художественный и общественно-политический журнал (Москва, 1924-).

Октябрь. Литературно-художественный и общественно-политический журнал Всероссийской и Московской ассоциации пролетписателей.
    Кн. 1 (1931-).

Островитяне (альманах стихов, Стихи Вагинова, Колбасьева и Тихонова) (Петербург, дек. 1921), № 1.

Печать и Революция. Журнал критики и библиографии (Москва, 1921-1930). Superseded by *Литература и искусство*.

Перевал. Литературно-художественный альманах. Сборник (Москва, 1923-). Под ред. Артема Веселого, А. Воронского, Мих. Голодного и В. Казина.

Петербургский альманах (Петербург-Берлин, З. И. Гржебин, 1922).
    Кн. 1 (1922).

Петербургский сборник. Поэты и беллетристы (Петербург, "Летопись Дома литераторов", 1922).

Петроград. Литературный альманах I (Петроград-Москва, "Петроград", 1923).

Писатели. Автобиографии и портреты современных русских прозаиков (Москва, Кн-во "Современные проблемы", Н. А. Столляр, 1926). Редактор: В. Лидин.

——, Изд. 2-е, расширенное (Москва, 1928).

Писатели об искусстве и о себе (Москва-Ленинград, "Круг", 1924). Сборник статей № 1.

Революция и культура (Москва, Изд. газеты *Правда*).

Русский современник. Литературно-художественный журнал, издаваемый при ближайшем участии: М. Горького, Евг. Замятина, А. Н. Тихонова, К. Чуковского, Абр. Эфроса (Ленинград, 1924).
    Кн. 1-4.

Русское искусство (художественный журнал) (Москва, 1923), №№ 1, 2/3.

Сборник пролетарских писателей (Петроград, Изд. "Парус", 1917). Под ред. М. Горького, А. Сереброва и А. Чапыгина
    (Участники: Герасимов, Одинцов, Черноков, Ширяевец, Артамонов,

Всев. Иванов, М. Дозоров, Ив. Морозов, Кон, Худяков, Рыбацкий,
Хохлов, Дракин, Яковлев, Бунаков, Логинов, Радлов).

Серапионовы Братья. Альманах Первый (Посвящается Марии Сергевне Алонкиной)
(Петербург, "Альконост", 1922).

Серапионовы Братья. Заграничный альманах (Берлин, Изд. "Русское творчество",
1922).

"Серапионовы Братья о себе", *Литературные Записки,* № 3 (1922).

Северная Азия. Общественно-научный журнал (Москва, 1925-).
  Кн. 1.
  Superseded by *Советская Азия* (1930-1931).

*Сибирские огни. Литературно-художественный и общественно-политический
журнал* (Новосибирск [Новониколаевск], Новосибгиз, март 1922), № 1.

Шиповник. Сборники литературы и искусства (Москва, "Шиповник", 1922),
№ 1. Под ред. Ф. Степуна.

Скифы (С.-Петербург, "Скифы", 1917-1918). Сборник 1-2.

Советские писатели. Автобиографии в двух томах (Москва, ГИХЛ, 1959).

*Советский театр. Общественно-политический журнал по вопросам театра и
марксистского театроведения* (Москва, 1930-1933).

Современная русская критика 1918-1924. Сборник (Образцы и характеристики)
(Ленинград, Гиз, 1925). Под ред. Иннокентия Оксенова. Предисловие
В. Лебедева-Полянского.

Современные Записки. Общественно-политический и литературный журнал
(Париж, 1920-1940), №№ 1-70.

Удар за ударом... Литературный альманах (Москва 1927-1930), №№ 1/2. Ред.:
А. Безыменский.
  Title of v. 1: *Альманах Удар.*

Толковый словарь русского языка (Москва, 1935), в 4-х томах. Под ред. Д. Н.
Ушакова.

Веселый альманах (Москва, Артель писателей "Круг", 1923).

Воля России. Журнал политики и культуры (Прага, 1922-).

Записки мечтателей (Петербург, "Алконост", 1919-1922), №№ 1-6.

*Завтра. Литературно-критический сборник под ред. Евг. Замятина, М. Кузмина
и М. Лозинского* (Берлин, Петрополис, 1923), I.

Земля и Фабрика. Литературно-художественный альманах (Москва, 1928-).
  Кн. 1.

Жизнь искусства (Ленинград, 1924).

Звезда. Литературно-общественный и научно-популярный журнал (Петроград,
1924-).

E. WORKS OF BIBLIOGRAPHY

С. БАЛУХАТЫЙ, *Теория литературы. Аннотированная библиография*
  I: *Общие вопросы* (Ленинград, "Прибой", 1929).

В. ГОЛУБКОВ (редактор), *Писатели современники. Пособие для лабораторных
занятий в школе и для самообразования*, 2-е изд. перераб. (Москва-
Ленинград, ГИЗ, 1927).

Борис Павлович КОЗЬМИН (редактор), *Писатели современной эпохи. Био-
библиографический словарь русских писателей XX века*, т. I (= *Государст-
венная Академия художественных наук, Социологическое отделение*, Труды,
Вып. I) (Москва, 1928).

*Литературно-художественные альманахи и сборники. Библиографический указа-
тель* (Изд-во Всесоюзной книжной палаты)

I. *1900-1911 годы.* Под ред. О. Д. Голубева (Москва, 1957)

II. *1912-1917 годы.* Под ред. Н. П. Рогожина (Москва, 1958)

III. *1918-1927 годы.* Под ред. Н. П. Рогожина (Москва, 1960)

IV. *1928-1937 годы.* Под ред. О. Д. Голубева (Москва, 1959).

ЛЬВОВ-РОГАЧЕВСКИЙ и Р. С. МАНДЕЛЬШТАМ, *Рабоче-крестьянские писатели. Библиографический указатель* (= *Российская Академия Художественных Наук, Комитет выставки революционной литературы*) (Московское Акционерное Издат. Общество, 1926).

Николай Иванович МАЦУЕВ, *Художественная литература и критика, русская и переводная 1926-1928 гг. Библиографический указатель. Статьи и рецензии о книгах, теория и история литературы, критика, иконография писателей.* С предисловием Н. К. Пиксанова (Москва, 1929).

——, *Художественная литература, русская и переводная 1928-1932 гг. Указатель статей, рецензий и аннотаций* (Москва, ГИХЛ, 1936).

——, *Три года советской литературы 1931-1933* (Москва, 1934).

Новая русская книга. Критико-библиографический журнал 1921-1923 (Берлин, "Москва").

Новости литературы. Критико-библиографический журнал (Берлин, 1922), №№ 1-2. Под ред. М. Слонима.

Периодическая печать СССР 1917-1947. Библиографический указатель. Журналы, труды и бюллетени по языкознанию, литературоведению, художественной литературе и искусству (Москва, Изд-во Всесоюзной Книжной Палаты, 1958).

Ив. Н. РОЗАНОВ, *Путеводитель по современной русской литературе* (Москва, "Работник просвещения", 1929).

Мария Александровна РЫБНИКОВА, А. М. ВИТМАН, *Восемь лет русской художественной литературы (1917-1927). Библиографический справочник под редакцией и со статьей М. А. Рыбниковой* (Москва, Госиздат, 1926). At head of title: А. М. Витман, Н. Д. Покровская (Хаимович), М. Е. Эттингер.

В. ТАРСИС, *Современные русские писатели, Под ред. и с дополнениями Иннокентия Оксенова* (Ленинград, 1930).

И. В. ВЛАДИСЛАВЛЕВ (Гульбинский), *Русские писатели. Опыт библиографического пособия по русской литературе XIX-XX в.*, 4-е изд. с приложением обзоров:

    1. "Литература революционного периода (1918-1923)"

    2 "О пролетарском творчестве"

    3 "Вопросы поэтики" (Москва, ГИЗ, 1924).

——, *Литература великого десятилетия (1917-1927). Художественная литература – Критика – История литературы – Литературная теория и методология*, том I (Москва-Ленинград, Гос. Изд., 1928).

SLAVISTIC PRINTINGS AND REPRINTINGS

Edited by C. H. van Schooneveld

4. VICTOR ERLICH: Russian Formalism. History — Doctrine. Second, revised edition. 1965. 311 pp. Cloth. Glds. 24.—

13. J. VAN DER ENG: Dostoevskij romancier. Rapports entre sa vision du monde et ses procédés littéraires. 1957. 115 pp. Cloth. Glds. 10.—

14. LAWRENCE LEO STAHLBERGER: The Symbolic System of Majakovskij. 1964. 151 pp. Cloth. Glds. 20.—

15. ROBERT L. JACKSON: Dostoevsky's Underground Man in Russian Literature. 1958. 223 pp. Cloth. Glds. 20.—

19. GEORGETTE DONCHIN: The Influence of French Symbolism on Russian Poetry. 1958. 242 pp., 7 ills. Cloth. Glds. 24.—

23. PETER K. CHRISTOFF: An Introduction to Nineteenth-Century Russian Slavophilism. Volume I: A. S. Xomjakov. 1961. 301 pp., 2 plates. Cloth. Glds. 33.—

33. ROBIN KEMBALL: Alexander Blok. A Study in Rhythm and Metre. 1965. 539 pp., portrait. Cloth. Glds. 80.—

35. CHARLES E. PASSAGE: The Russian Hoffmannists. 1963. 261 pp. Cloth. Glds. 30.—

36. VSEVOLOD SETCHKAREV: Studies in the Life and Works of Innokentij Annenskij. 1963. 270 pp. Cloth. Glds. 32.—

42. CHARLES A. MOSER: Antinihilism in the Russian Novel of the 1860's. 1964. 215 pp. Cloth. Glds. 22.—

52. WACŁAW LEDNICKI: Tolstoj between War and Peace. 1965. 169 pp., 4 plates. Cloth. Glds. 25.—

56. N. S. TRUBETZKOY: Dostoevskij als Künstler. 1965. 178 pp. Cloth. Glds. 28.—

57. F. C. DRIESSEN: Gogol as a Short-Story Writer. A Study of his Technique of Composition. Translated from the Dutch by Ian F. Finlay. 1965. 243 pp. Cloth. Glds. 36.—

MOUTON & CO · PUBLISHERS · THE HAGUE